Democracy and Deterrence
Foundations for an
Enduring World Peace

DR. WALTER GARY SHARP SR.

Maxwell Air Force Base, Alabama

May 2008

Published by Books Express Publishing
Copyright © Books Express, 2010
ISBN 978-1-907521-53-9
To purchase copies at discounted prices please contact
info@books-express.com

*Dedicated to my loving wife Anne Marie Sharp
from whom all good in my life flows*

Contents

CONTENTS

Illustrations

Tables

CONTENTS

Foreword

The causes of armed conflict have historically been viewed in primarily sociological terms, with political, religious, economic, and military factors sharing primacy. Few have examined the causes of warfare in the context of a deterrence model or, specifically, the deterrence factors inherent in the checks and balances of a democratic state and the absence of such factors in the nondemocratic state. More significantly, none before Prof. John Norton Moore has argued the value of democratic principles in deterrence and conflict avoidance.

In this important book, Dr. Gary Sharp analyzes the concepts in Moore's seminal work *The War Puzzle* (2005), which describes Moore's incentive theory of war avoidance. Sharp carefully dissects Moore's deterrence model and examines those incentives that discourage nondemocratic governments from pursuing violent conflicts. Arguing that existing democracies must make an active effort to foster the political environment in which new democracies can develop, Sharp discusses the elements critical to promoting democratization and thus strengthening systemwide deterrence at the state and international levels.

Sharp also examines the incentives for conflict avoidance (internal checks and balances) inherent in the democratic state and their relationship to war avoidance. In examining current democracies and comparing them statistically to nondemocratic states, Sharp calculates an aggregated index value of democracy based upon respected databases that rank the jurisdictions of the world on political rights, civil liberties, media independence, religious freedom, economic freedom, and human development. Demonstrating through his analysis that democracies are inherently more peaceful because of the internal checks and balances on the aggressive use of force, Sharp similarly demonstrates how nondemocracies require external checks and balances to preclude aggression.

Sharp's analysis and validation of Moore's incentive theory of war avoidance is critical to an understanding of those foreign policy strategies that the United States and other democratic nations must embrace as they attempt to reverse a course of history in which 38.5 million war deaths were recorded in the twentieth century alone. By demonstrating how democracy,

economic freedom, and the rule of law provide essential mechanisms to deter leaders from precipitous decisions concerning
the use of force, Sharp has provided an invaluable service to
the statesman and international lawyer alike.

JAMES P. TERRY*
Colonel, USMC, Retired
December 2007

---

*Col James P. Terry, USMC, retired, is chairman of the Board of Veterans' Appeals
in the Department of Veterans Affairs. He previously served as the principal deputy
assistant secretary for legislative affairs in the Department of State and as legal counsel
to the chairman of the Joint Chiefs of Staff.

About the Author

Dr. Walter Gary Sharp Sr.

Walter Gary Sharp Sr. serves as a senior associate deputy general counsel for intelligence at the US Department of Defense, where he advises on legal issues related to intelligence, covert action, intelligence and counterintelligence policy, intelligence oversight, information security, information sharing, security classification policy, information operations, and computer network operations.

Prior to his appointment, Dr. Sharp served as an associate deputy general counsel for international affairs at the Department of Defense; the director of legal research for international, comparative, and foreign law at the Law Library of Congress; the director of global and functional affairs within the Bureau of Legislative Affairs at the State Department; and a principal information security engineer at The MITRE Corporation. A veteran with 25 years of service, Dr. Sharp retired as a decorated US Marine Corps lieutenant colonel with prior enlisted service. His military assignments include commanding officer of a field artillery battery, senior prosecutor, deputy legal counsel to the chairman of the Joint Chiefs of Staff, and international law adviser for the commanding general of the Unified Task Force in Somalia during Operation Restore Hope. Dr. Sharp's military decorations include the Defense Superior Service Medal, and his many awards for writing excellence and academic achievement include the Judge Advocate General's School Alumni Association Annual Professional Writing Award and an American Bar Association Award for Professional Merit.

Dr. Sharp is the author of numerous articles and three books: *UN Peace Operations* (1995), *CyberSpace and the Use of Force* (1999), and *Jus Paciarii* (1999). He serves as an adjunct professor of law at Georgetown University Law Center where he currently teaches a counterterrorism course, The Law of 24. He has also taught graduate-level seminars on United Nations peace operations and international peace and security. He lectures internationally in universities and other diverse public forums on wide-ranging topics of international law and national security law, such as international peace and security, conflict management, and peacekeeping operations. Born in Corpus Christi, Texas, Dr. Sharp graduated from the US Naval Academy with a bachelor of science in aerospace engineering. He also holds a doctor of jurisprudence from Texas Tech University School of Law, a master of laws in international and comparative law from Georgetown University Law Center, a master of laws in military law from The US Army Judge Advocate General's School, and a doctor of juridical science from the University of Virginia School of Law. He has been married for 30 years and is the proud father of Gary and Amanda.

Preface

War is a pernicious plague with a ubiquitous presence throughout human history. Many popular theories contribute to our understanding of the causes of war, but none have demonstrated any powerful correlation with the occurrence or non-occurrence of war. However, philosophers and political scientists have reasoned for centuries and used large-scale statistical analyses to prove that democracies are a method of nonviolence. Historians have concluded that war is caused during a competition for power by a failure of states to take appropriate actions to preserve the peace, that is, a failure of deterrence.

After studying war and the causes of war for decades, the distinguished jurist Prof. John Norton Moore has now postulated that the cause of major international armed conflict is the deadly synergy between the existence of a potentially aggressive nondemocratic regime and the absence of effective system-wide deterrence. This postulate on the cause of war is the foundation for Moore's incentive theory of war avoidance—that war is caused by a decision of human leadership and can be prevented by the totality of positive and negative incentives that effectively discourage leaders of nation-states at the individual, state, and international levels from committing aggression. Deterrence is Moore's predominant theme. Democracies are deterred from aggressive action by internal checks and balances. Nondemocracies without internal checks and balances must be deterred from aggressive action by external deterrence incentives that target and affect the leaders of nation-states because they make the decision to commit aggression.

This study validates both Moore's postulate on the cause of war and his incentive theory of war avoidance through a detailed examination of the democratic peace principle and deterrence and the creation of a mathematical formula that can be used to determine the probability of peace as well as to index or quantify deterrence factors. This study concludes that wars and their attendant human misery begin in the minds of national leaders whose power is unchecked by incentives and deterrence mechanisms at the individual, state, and international levels—mechanisms that are inherent in democracies where human freedom, economic freedom, and the rule of law provide a check on the power of national leaders.

Many great minds have affirmed the very unpretentious concept that promoting democracy, human freedom, economic freedom, and the rule of law are the significant contributing factors to world peace and human development. The absence of any meaningful argument to the contrary is remarkable. In validating both Moore's postulate on the cause of war and his incentive theory of war avoidance, this book unequivocally demonstrates how a simple idea such as promoting democracy can reduce the occurrence of war and foster human development. This book demonstrates the power of democracy, deterrence, and the rule of law to create lasting world peace.

WALTER GARY SHARP, SR.
Senior Associate Deputy General
Counsel for Intelligence
Department of Defense
December 2007

Acknowledgments

This book is an edited version of my dissertation submitted in partial fulfillment of the requirements for the degree of doctor of juridical science (SJD) at the University of Virginia School of Law, Charlottesville, Virginia. While credit is conscientiously provided throughout this book for every thought not my own, it is nevertheless important to acknowledge the example and broad framework of thought provided by Prof. John Norton Moore in his incentive theory of war avoidance. His informal conversations, lectures at the University of Virginia School of Law and Georgetown University Law Center, and the volumes of work he has written on this and related issues have been immeasurably important in my developing a meaningful study. When any student embarks upon a course of study on an issue of extraordinary import such as the maintenance of international peace and security, there is always a mentor like Professor Moore who inspires and helps shape the study through his or her own thinking.

I would also like to thank the supervisory committee for my dissertation—Prof. Michael P. Dooley, Professor Moore, and then-principal deputy assistant secretary of state for legislative affairs Dr. James P. Terry—for their willingness to supervise and mentor me as well as their patience during the years it took me to complete my study.

Professor Moore has served as my mentor and role model for more than 20 years, and I shall always be indebted to him for endorsing my study in democracy, deterrence, and the rule of law at the University of Virginia School of Law, as well as agreeing to supervise my research and writing. His inspiration and example made this study possible, and I hope that in return this study makes at least some small contribution to the discussion on the relationship of democracy, deterrence, law, and world peace.

Finally, I must express my deepest gratitude to the entire Air University Press team that worked on this book: Demorah Hayes, Lula Barnes, Steve Garst, Mary Moore, Mary Ferguson, Joan Hickey, and Diane Clark. In particular, I take great pleasure in saying a special thanks to the chief editor, Demorah

ACKNOWLEDGMENTS

Hayes, who has demonstrated an extraordinary and wonderful talent for making my dissertation more readable.

It is important to emphasize that the opinions, conclusions, and recommendations expressed or implied herein are solely those of the author and do not necessarily represent the views of the Department of Defense or any other governmental agency or civilian institution.

Chapter 1

Liberal Democracy and
Its Global Influence

*Democracy is less a system of government than it is a
system to keep government limited, unintrusive; a system of constraints on power to keep politics and government secondary to the important things in life, the true
sources of value found only in family and faith.*

—Pres. Ronald Reagan
Speech at Moscow State University, 1988

Since World War II, the United States has been committed
to a foreign policy that seeks either to contain the spread of
tyranny or, more recently, to actively promote the spread of democracy abroad. Every presidential administration since 1945
has articulated a link between US national interests and its active engagement in international affairs.[1] It is the explicit guiding principle of the current administration to shape "a balance
of power that favors human freedom . . . [and] extend the peace
by encouraging free and open societies on every continent."[2]
The causal relationship between free, open, democratic societies and peace is the subject of this study, which validates the
democratic peace principle—the simple principle that nondemocracies are more prone to war than democracies.

War has had a devastating effect on humankind, and the methods of warfare have grown progressively more destructive. The
most extraordinary cost of war is the loss of and injury to human
life, both combatant and civilian. There is also a corresponding
economic cost in the loss of future wages of those killed and
medical care for those injured. Additionally, there are the direct
economic costs of waging war; the destruction of physical capi-
tal such as buildings, transportation infrastructure, and power-
distribution systems; and the economic burden of postwar reconstruction.[3] Consider also the cost to humanity as described by
Pres. Dwight Eisenhower: "Every gun that is made, every warship

launched, every rocket fired signifies, in the final sense, a theft from those who hunger and are not fed, those who are cold and are not clothed."[4] As of 3 September 2007, the cost of the war in Iraq to the United States had exceeded $448 billion—enough to provide health care for over 268 million children for one year, hire an additional 7.7 million school teachers for one year, pay for over 21.7 million students to attend public universities for four years, or build almost 4 million additional housing units for the poor or homeless.[5] The question of how to prevent war is an urgent one, made increasingly so by the lethality of modern warfare and the threat of weapons of mass destruction.

This study concludes that wars and the human misery that accompanies them begin in the minds of national leaders whose power is unchecked by the incentives and deterrents inherent in democracy. The global spread of democracy is thus essential for creating lasting world peace. Where democracy does not yet exist, the presence of effective systemwide deterrents targeted at non-democratic leaders can increase international security and peace.

Features of a Liberal Democracy

Before we consider the correlation between peace and demo-cratic governance, we must carefully define the term *democracy*, which has been appropriated by some of the modern world's most closed and tyrannical governments. (North Korea, for ex-ample, calls itself the Democratic People's Republic of Korea, and the former Communist East Germany named itself the German Democratic Republic.) The term *democracy* itself is derived from the Greek word *dēmokratia; demos* means "people," and *kratia* means "government" or "rule." Thus *democracy* refers to a form of government in which the right to make political decisions is exer-cised either directly by the people or through elected representa-tives. In a modern liberal democracy, the people exercise political power through chosen representatives within the framework of a constitutional distribution of power and a system of laws in-tended to hold those representatives accountable to the citizens and guarantee all citizens the enjoyment of certain individual or collective rights. Liberal democracy has also been defined as "a government of limited powers, operating under the rule of law in some meaningful system of checks and balances, which protects fundamental political, economic, and religious freedoms and in which minority rights are protected even from a majority."[6]

Robert Dahl has described the modern democratic government as *polyarchal*, a term he uses to denote a "representative democracy with universal suffrage."[7] The polyarchal democracy has six distinguishing institutions, all of which a country must possess to be considered democratic: elected officials; free, fair, and frequent elections; freedom of expression; alternative sources of information; associational autonomy; and inclusive citizenship.[8] John Norton Moore identifies four features as elemental to the modern liberal democracy, emphasizing restraints on government power and protections for individual liberty:

1. The government's powers are limited.

2. The government operates under the rule of law in some meaningful system of checks and balances.

3. Fundamental political, economic, and religious freedoms are protected.

4. Minority rights are protected from the majority.[9]

These contemporary definitions of democracy echo the essential principles of the US government enumerated by Thomas Jefferson in his first inaugural address (1801):

1. Equal and exact justice to all men

2. Peace, commerce, and honest friendship with all nations

3. The support of the state governments in all their rights

4. The preservation of the general government in its whole constitutional vigor

5. A jealous care of the right of election by the people

6. Absolute acquiescence in the decisions of the majority

7. A well-disciplined militia

8. The supremacy of the civil over the military authority

9. Economy in the public expense

10. The honest payment of our debts and sacred preservation of the public faith

11. Encouragement of agriculture, and of commerce as its handmaid

12. The diffusion of information and arraignment of all abuses at the bar of the public reason

13. Freedom of religion

14. Freedom of the press

15. Freedom of person under the protection of the habeas corpus

16. Trial by juries impartially selected[10]

More recently, the Clinton administration's 1999 document *A National Security Strategy for a New Century* reaffirmed and expanded Jefferson's principles. In its discussion of promoting democracy and human rights, it asserts that a genuine, lasting democracy requires "respect for human rights, including the right to political dissent; freedom of religion and belief; an independent media capable of engaging an informed citizenry; a robust civil society; the rule of law and an independent judiciary; open and competitive economic structures; mechanisms to safeguard minorities from oppressive rule by the majority; full respect for women's and workers' rights; and civilian control of the military."[11] In a similar vein, Larry Diamond, co-director of the International Forum for Democratic Studies of the National Endowment for Democracy, defines a liberal democracy as a form of government that "encompasses not only a civilian, constitutional, multiparty regime, with regular, free, and fair elections and universal suffrage, but organizational and informational pluralism; extensive civil liberties (freedom of expression, freedom of the press, freedom to form and join organizations); effective power for elected officials; and functional autonomy for legislative, executive, and judicial organs of government."[12]

Merging these various descriptions of democracy, we can define the features of a model liberal democracy (one that is fully democratic in all its institutions and laws) to include the political rights, civil liberties, and limited governmental powers summarized in table 1.

Table 1. Features of a model liberal democracy

A model liberal democracy . . .	
Political rights	• consists of a robust civil society that exercises its political powers through representatives who are held accountable by the rule of law and who are chosen through regular, free, fair, and multiparty elections that allow universal suffrage
Civil liberties	• guarantees all citizens equal civil liberties that include freedom of expression, freedom of the press, the right to form and join organizations, the right to political dissent, freedom of religion and belief, freedom of the person (habeas corpus), and the right to a fair trial • respects human rights, to include women's and workers' rights • permits an independent media capable of engaging an informed citizenry • safeguards minorities from oppressive rule by the majority • allows open and competitive economic structures
Limited governmental powers	• consists of a civilian, multiparty government of limited powers • consists of a constitutional framework for the distribution of power that yields functional autonomy for legislative, executive, and judicial organs of government • operates under the rule of law in some meaningful system of checks and balances • creates effective power for elected officials • maintains civilian control of the military

Compiled from contemporary and historical descriptions of democracy discussed in this chapter.

To be a liberal democracy, however, it is not enough to simply have a constitution and legal system that contain some or even all the features of a model liberal democracy summarized in table 1. These features must be institutionalized and implemented in practice. Consider, for example, the 1990 Interim Constitution of Saddam Hussein's Iraq, a constitution which contained many of the elements of a model liberal democracy.[13] That constitution declared that the Iraqi people were the source of the government's authority and legitimacy and acknowledged the national rights of the Kurdish people and the legitimate rights of all minorities. It also guaranteed the rights and liberties of all Iraqi citizens in full: private ownership and economic liberty; equality of all citizens before the law, without discrimination because of sex, blood, language, social origin, or religion; equal opportunity to all citizens;

presumption of innocence for the accused until proven guilty at a legal trial; freedom of religion; freedom of opinion and publication; freedom to meet, demonstrate, and form political parties; the right of political asylum for all militants persecuted in their countries for defending liberal principles; and an independent judiciary subject to no other authority than the law. In practice, however, Hussein's Iraq did not remotely resemble a liberal democracy. The Interim Constitution embraced a socialist system and provided full immunity for the president, vice-president, and members of the Revolutionary Command Council. In its report *Freedom in the World 2003*, Freedom House named Iraq as one of the nine worst nations in the world for political rights and civil liberties.[14] To be a liberal democracy, a nation's constitution and legal system must contain fundamental elements of all the features of a model liberal democracy summarized in table 1 above, including the full protection of constitutionally enumerated political rights and civil liberties guaranteed through a constitutional distribution of power to prevent abuse or corruption. Hussein's constitution certainly appeared to embrace the fundamental elements of a liberal democracy, but they were not institutionalized and implemented throughout the government in practice.

In contrast to a full liberal democracy, Freedom House defines an *electoral democracy* as a country that has met certain basic criteria for elections but fails to fully protect political rights and civil liberties. In an electoral democracy, "voters can choose their authoritative leaders freely from among competing groups and individuals not designated by the government; voters have access to information about candidates and their platforms; voters can vote without undue pressure from the authorities; and candidates can campaign free from intimidation."[15] Irregularities during the electoral process do not automatically disqualify a country from being an electoral democracy. A liberal democracy is, by definition, also an electoral democracy; however, an electoral democracy is not necessarily a liberal democracy.[16]

A liberal democracy magnifies human freedom and limits government power. It is a form of government wherein the people exercise their political powers through civilian representatives who are chosen by regular, free, fair, and multiparty elections that allow universal suffrage. Representatives are held ac-

6

countable by a constitutional distribution of effective, yet limited governmental power that ensures meaningful checks and balances for multiple autonomous governmental organs. Other defining characteristics of a liberal democracy include civilian control over the military, an independent media, a free-market economy, and a system of laws that guarantees all citizens, including minorities, the enjoyment of equal and extensive individual and collective human rights and civil liberties. Because of its system of checks and balances, the liberal democracy inclines toward peace.

Global Political Trends

The "ideologicalisms" which challenged us for the last 50 years have all died away—fascism, Nazism, Communism—leaving only the dregs of abused and misused power in their wake. Yes, dictators remain, but they are relics of the past, and the "-isms" they practice can't destroy us, can't overthrow us, can't end our way of life.

—Secretary of State Colin Powell
Senate Confirmation Hearing, 17 January 2001

Ours has not only been a century of bloody struggle between peoples and ideologies, but . . . it also has been a century of struggle for national sovereignty and for the individual's democratic sovereignty within the state.

—Freedom House
Democracy's Century: A Survey of Global Political Change in the Twentieth Century

We are in the midst of a remarkable global political trend toward democratic forms of government. At the turn of the twentieth century, approximately 1 percent of the world's population was under the governance of a multiparty democracy, and 19 percent was under a limited democracy (a government in transition toward democracy but falling short of being a full democracy by, for example, disenfranchising a substantial percentage of the adult population such as women).[17] At the same time, approximately 50 percent of the world's population was under the rule of an absolute monarchy or autocracy (the rule by a single person with unlimited and absolute power), and approximately 30 percent had no self-government (that is, they lived under a government that does not derive its power from the people).[18] This study focuses on the time period extending from the entry into force of the Charter of the United Nations (hereinafter UN Charter) in 1945 through 2000. Table 2 shows the approximate percentage of the world's population living under nine major forms of government from 1942 through 1997.

Table 2. Approximate percentage of world's population under selected forms of government (1942–97)

Form of government	1942	1947	1952	1957	1962	1967	1972	1977	1982	1987	1992	1997
Multiparty democracy	10	25	50	45	40	35	35	35	35	45	55	60
Limited democracy		20			5				5	5	5	5
Communist	10	10	35	35	35	35	35	35	35	30	25	25
One party		5		5	5	5	5	5	5	5	5	5
Autocracy	10		5	5	5	5	5	5				
Military junta					5	15	15	20	20	15	10	5
Absolute monarchy	5	5	5	5	5	5	5					
No self-government	40	10	5	5								
Anarchy	25	25										

Adapted from Matthew White, *Historical Atlas of the Twentieth Century,* http://users.erols.com/mwhite28/20century.htm.

Note: This data provides a rough order of magnitude for trend analysis; it does not necessarily mean, for example, that there were no limited democracies in 1942 or no autocracies in 1997.

Figure 1 groups this data and plots the distribution by percent of the world's population living under three broad categories of government: democratic, nondemocratic, and not self-governing or anarchic.

Figure 1 shows a significant decline from 1942 to 1947 in the percentage of the world's population living in countries and territories that were not self-governing or anarchic and a significant increase in the percentage living under democratic forms of government. However, from 1947 to 1952, the rapid transition to democratic forms of government dramatically slowed, while a number of the remaining countries and territories that

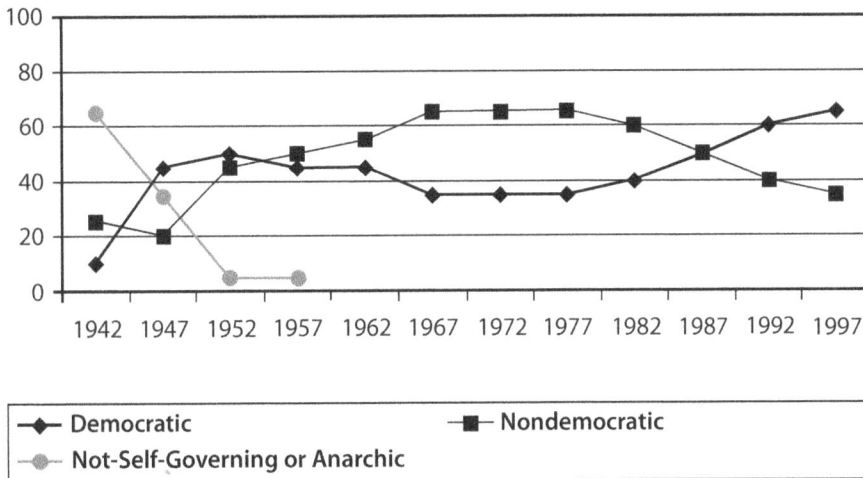

Figure 1. Changes in the percentage of the world's population under democratic, nondemocratic, and not-self-governing or anarchic governments (1942–
97). (*Adapted from* Matthew White, *Historical Atlas of the Twentieth Century*, http://
users.erols.com/mwhite28/20centry.htm.)

were not self-governing or anarchic began to transition to nondemocratic forms of government, principally Communism. By
the mid-1950s, approximately half the world's population was
under democratic governance and approximately half was under nondemocratic rule. The percentage of the world's population under nondemocratic forms of government continued to
increase and peaked in 1967 through 1977, when a majority of
the world's population lived under nondemocratic governments.
After 1977, this trend began to reverse. By 1987, approximately
half of the world's population was once again under democratic
governance, with the other half remaining under nondemocratic
rule. Since 1987, the percentage of the population living under
democratic governments has continued to grow, while the influence of nondemocratic governments has continued to decline.

Not surprisingly, the growth in nondemocratic governance reflects the forceful efforts of the Soviet Union to spread Communism worldwide during the Cold War, and the eventual decline
of nondemocratic governance corresponds to the waning global
influence and ultimate collapse of the Soviet Union in the late

1980s. We can also see a possible correlation between the American foreign policies of internationalism, containment, and engagement during the same time period and the likely success of these policies in increasing the percentage of the world's population under democratic governance.[19] Figure 2 below compares American foreign policy (see appendix B for a brief overview) to the data presented in figure 1. This comparison presents some evidence that the American policies of internationalism and containment fostered, or at the very minimum coincided with, a remarkable growth in the percentage of the world's population under democratic governance. The American Cold-War policy of containment helped eventually to stem the spread of Communism and contributed to the collapse of the Soviet Union. The figure also suggests that the American policy of engagement is continuing to foster growth in the percentage of the world's population under democratic governance.

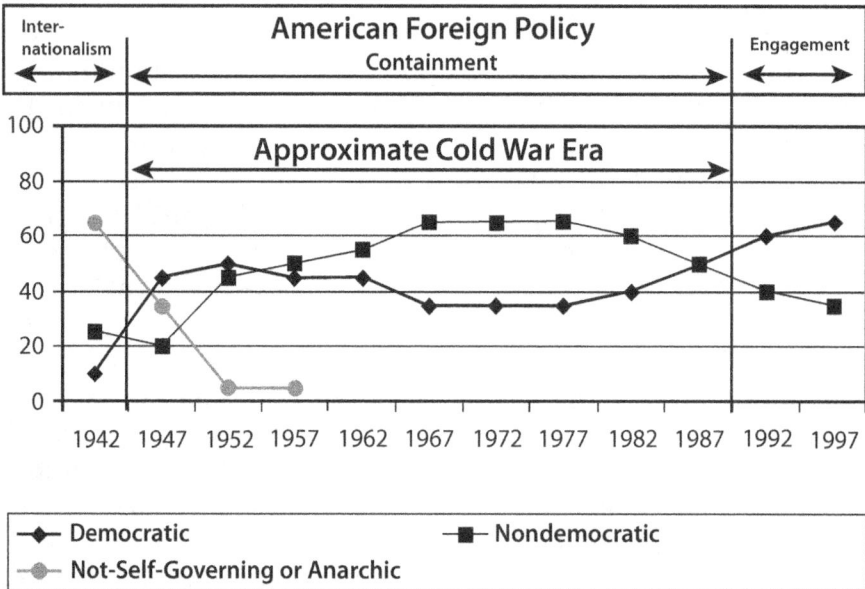

Figure 2. American foreign policy and changes in the percentage of the world's population under democratic, nondemocratic, and not-self-governing or anarchic governments (1942–97). (*Adapted from* Matthew White, *Historical Atlas of the Twentieth Century*, http://users.erols.com/mwhite28/20centry.htm.)

The Center for International Development and Conflict Management (CIDCM) documents in its February 2003 report that global trends toward greater peace and democracy continue. This report notes five very positive global trends:

1. The decline in the global magnitude of armed conflict, which began in the early 1990s, has continued, and few of the many societal wars that were contained since 1995 have resumed.

2. Most democratic regimes established during the 1980s and 1990s have endured and a number of others continue to experiment with and expand democratic reforms, though the wave of democratization has leveled off.

3. Ethnonational wars for independence, which were the main threat to civil peace and regional security in the first post-Cold War decade, have declined to their lowest level since 1960. More armed conflicts over this issue were contained in 2001–02 than in any previous two-year period, often when rebels agreed to begin or resume negotiations.

4. Paralleling the shift toward democracy, there has been long-term improvement in respect for human rights.

5. International crises declined in number and intensity throughout the 1990s, many of them contained by diplomatic means.[20]

The 2003 CIDCM report concludes that the "trend in the total magnitude of global warfare . . . is likely to continue downward over the short-term," but will likely "level off at some lower level."[21] However, while the CIDCM 2008 *Peace and Conflict* report notes a continued decline in the magnitude of armed conflicts when measured by their death toll, it also reports that the number of states involved in armed conflicts is on the increase and the movement toward democratic forms of government has stalled.[22]

The Stockholm International Peace Research Institute (SIPRI) reports in its 2004 *Yearbook* that both the number and intensity of conflicts are on the decline:[23]

In 2003 there were 19 major armed conflicts in 18 locations worldwide, the lowest number for the post-cold war period with the exception

11

of 1997, when 18 such conflicts were registered. Only two of the 19 conflicts were fought between states: the conflict between Iraq and the multinational coalition led by the United States and the United Kingdom and the long-standing conflict between India and Pakistan over Kashmir. Four of the 19 conflicts were in Africa and eight in Asia.

The principal source of major armed conflict in contemporary politics remains intra-state. The persistence of intra-state wars, and their resistance to quick solutions, was amply reflected in 2003. Longstanding conflicts in Colombia and Israel continued, despite the introduction of more offensive military strategies by the government parties in each country. While a more aggressive military stance thwarted opposition attacks and may have contributed to the reduction in fatalities in Colombia and Israel in 2003, it severely hampered efforts to facilitate progress toward peace in both.[24]

SIPRI counts wars that have produced 1,000 or more battle-related deaths in any single year. In 2003, SIPRI counted 19 such conflicts in Afghanistan, Algeria, Burundi, Colombia, India (Kashmir), India-Pakistan, Indonesia, Iraq, Israel, Liberia, Myanmar, Nepal, Peru, Philippines (two conflicts), Russia, Sri Lanka, Sudan, and Turkey.[25]

Freedom House has declared the twentieth century the "democratic century," reporting a "dramatic expansion of democratic governance" with a corresponding significant expansion of market economies.[26] In 1900, not a single state could be judged an electoral democracy by the standard of universal suffrage with competitive multiparty elections, and states with restricted democratic practices such as the United States and the United Kingdom numbered only 25 and accounted for only 12.4 percent of the world's population. However, by the 1950s, there were 22 democracies and 21 states with restricted democratic practices, accounting for 42.9 percent of the world's population. By 2000, liberal and electoral democracies clearly predominated, with 119 such states governing 58.2 percent of the world's population. Of the remaining governments in 2000, 16 had restricted democratic practices, 10 were traditional monarchies, 40 were authoritarian regimes, five were totalitarian regimes, and two were protectorates.[27]

Freedom House concludes from this data that "humankind, in fits and starts, is rejecting oppression and opting for greater openness and freedom," even though this move toward democracy and freedom has "frequently met with brutal repression."[28] Consider, for example, the case of the Democratic Republic of Timor-Leste (East Timor). In August 1999, the vote of the East Timorese people to seek independence from Indonesia was met with violence, looting, and arson, during which many East Timorese were killed and over 500,000 were displaced from their homes. In response, the UN Security Council established the UN Transitional Administration in East Timor in October 1999 to oversee the transition to an independent state.[29] The international community recognized East Timor on 20 May 2002 as an independent state and the world's newest democracy.[30] Timor-Leste became the 191st member state of the UN on 27 September 2002.[31] Despite violence such as that in East Timor, the move toward democracy and human freedom has made the world more peaceful since "history indicates that stable and established democracies rarely war with one another."[32]

Democratically elected governments can now be found "in all parts of the globe and in all major civilizations, although . . . no significant progress toward democracy has been made in China, where over 20 percent of the globe's population lives."[33] Of the 88 countries graded as free in the Freedom House 2004 annual report, 24 are in Western Europe, 23 in the Americas, 17 in the Asia Pacific region, 12 in Central and Eastern Europe and the former Soviet Union, one in the Middle East and North Africa, and 11 in sub-Saharan Africa.[34] The eight worst countries in the world, according to Freedom House, for the protection of political rights and civil liberties are Myanmar (Burma), Cuba, Libya, North Korea, Saudi Arabia, Sudan, Syria, and Turkmenistan.[35]

Freedom House also concludes that "once countries attain freedom, rarely do they regress, reinforcing the idea that democracy and its attendant institutions are the best insurance against tyranny."[36] It warns, however, that the rapid expansion of democracy since the mid-1970s makes many new democracies fragile during transition and that the gains in democratic governance could well be reversed.[37] Newly democratic states have "weak civic cultures and undeveloped rule of law."[38] In 2004 Freedom House reported the "second consecutive year of a global decline in freedom for news media." Their study *Freedom of the Press 2004: A Global Survey of Media Independence* reports "some of the most serious setbacks . . . in countries where democracy is backsliding, such as in Bolivia and Russia, and in older, established democracies, most notably Italy."[39] Freedom of the press improved, however, in Iraq, Sierra Leone, and Kenya.[40]

It has been reported that Russia is "backsliding in key areas of democratic governance and rule of law."[41] Pres. Vladimir Putin's policies are calling into question Russia's ability to protect private property and are seeking to "centralize power, leaving little room for a vibrant civil society, independent media, or political opposition."[42] In a 2004 assessment, Freedom House reports that Russia remains one of the most corrupt countries in the world, and it is headed in an increasingly authoritarian direction.[43]

Notwithstanding the backsliding in a number of extremely important countries such as Russia and the complete lack of progress toward democratization in China, the overall progress during the twentieth century from zero to 119 electoral democracies with universal suffrage was dramatic and extraordinarily promising, and democracy is still on the move.

Other important trends toward democratic institutions transcend national borders. European Commission president Romano Prodi announced in 2002 his desire to create a more powerful European Union (EU), calling for the creation of the "first supranational democracy in the world" and "greater centralization of power" through a federalist constitution for the EU.[44] On 18 June 2004, the EU agreed to a draft constitution that "brings together for the first time the many treaties and agreements on which the EU is based."[45] It also defines the powers of the EU and reserves a right of veto for member states.[46] All 25 member states must ratify this draft constitution before it enters into force. However, several EU member states have had problems ratifying the draft constitution (two countries—France and the Netherlands—have rejected it), and the ratification process has failed. In June 2005, the European Council decided to launch a "period of reflection" on the future of Europe and, in June 2007, agreed to consider a "reform treaty" for the EU.[47]

As this study will show, the global spread of democracy is a significant development for the advancement of international peace and security. The democratic peace principle, which this study will validate, explains why: democracies are conducive to nonviolence, as political scientists have proven through large-scale statistical analyses.[48]

Historians have also concluded that war is caused during a competition for power by a failure of states to take appropriate actions to preserve the peace, that is, an absence or failure of deterrence.[49] Both the presence or absence of democracy and the presence or absence of deterrence are strong correlates of the occurrence and nonoccurrence of war, but neither, when taken alone, fully defines the cause of war. After years of study, Moore has noted the powerful relationship between both factors and the occurrence of war.[50] He postulates that the cause of major international armed conflict is the deadly synergy between the existence of a potentially aggressive nondemocratic regime and the absence of effective systemwide deterrence.[51] Moore broadly defines effective systemwide deterrence as the totality of incentives external to the nondemocratic regime, that is, incentives created by other nations and the international system that prevent aggressive action.[52]

Moore's postulate on the cause of war is the foundation for his incentive theory of war avoidance: war is caused by the decisions of human leadership and can be prevented by the totality of positive and negative incentives that effectively discourage leaders of nation-states at the individual, state, and international levels from committing aggression. Deterrence is Moore's predominant theme: democracies are deterred from aggressive action by internal checks and balances, but nondemocracies without internal checks and balances must be deterred from aggressive action by external deterrence incentives that target and affect the leaders of nation-states because they make the decision to commit aggression.

This study validates both Moore's postulate on the cause of war and his incentive theory of war avoidance through a detailed examination of the democratic peace principle and deterrence. It proposes a mathematical formula that can be used to determine the probability of peace and to index deterrence. To establish a framework for analysis, chapter 2 discusses conventional thinking on the causes of war and conventional approaches to war avoidance, introduces the concept of deterrence and the law of conflict management, and considers the possible nature of future conflicts. Chapter 3 examines the democratic peace principle, including the early debate, contemporary studies, conclusions derived from the principle, challenges to the principle, and its significance.

A thorough analysis of Moore's postulate on the cause of war and incentive theory of war avoidance follows in chapter 4, which discusses how to create peace even in a world that includes non-democratic governments. A mathematical formula describes Moore's incentive theory and establishes a methodology for analysis and for predicting the probability of peace for a given nation. That formula is then applied in chapter 5 to a specific historical context, the 1991 Persian Gulf War.

The analysis of the Gulf War validates Moore's theory of war avoidance.While democracy is important as a means for establishing peace in the world, its true value extends far beyond the prevention of war. Chapter 6 discusses the correlative values of democracy, which promotes human freedom and development wherever it gains influence. This chapter introduces several important indexes that rate the nations of the world according to their levels of freedom and development. Finally, chapter 7 reflects on the meaning and value of Moore's incentive theory of war avoidance in the context of the foreign policy of nations and the purposes of regional and international organizations.

Building on Moore's foundation, this study concludes that wars and human misery begin in the minds of national leaders whose power is unchecked by the deterrence features that occur naturally in democracies. However, people do not always live in a political environment where they can choose their form of governance or where democracies are able to develop naturally. Sometimes those environments must be shaped through the affirmative effort of other democracies; that is, democratic governments must encourage and assist in creating democratic institutions that will help other governments move toward liberal democracy—fully democratic in all their institutions and laws. To do so, nations as well as regional and international organizations should look to Moore's incentive theory of war avoidance as guidance for national-security deterrence policy and charter principles because the spread of democracy and the rule of law worldwide strengthens world peace.

Notes

(All notes appear in shortened form. Complete citations are in the bibliography.)

1. In its infancy, the United States adopted an isolationist stance, electing not to involve itself in foreign disputes and international affairs. See appendix B for an overview of the development of US foreign policy from isolationism, to a limited internationalism, to Cold War–era containment, and finally to an active engagement in the spread of freedom.

2. President Bush, *National Security Strategy*, iv.

3. *Encyclopædia Britannica Online*, s.v. "defense economics," http://www.britannica.com/eb/article?eu=118852.

4. President Eisenhower, "Chance for Peace" speech.

5. National Priorities Project, "Cost of War." See also Kaysen et al., *War with Iraq*.

6. Moore, *Solving the War Puzzle*, xxii.

7. Dahl, *On Democracy*, 90.

8. Ibid., 84–91.

9. Moore, *Solving the War Puzzle*, xxii.

10. President Jefferson, inaugural address.

11. President Clinton, *National Security Strategy*, 25.

12. Diamond, *Promoting Democracy*, 10.

13. Iraq, Interim Constitution, articles 5, 10, 16, 19, 20, 25, 26, 34, and 60.

14. Freedom House, *Freedom in the World 2003*. Freedom House is a nonpartisan voice for democracy and freedom around the world founded nearly 60 years ago by Eleanor Roosevelt and other Americans concerned with the mounting threats to peace and democracy. It has been a vigorous proponent of democratic values and a steadfast opponent of dictatorships of the far left and the far right. See the Freedom House mission statement and history at http://www.freedomhouse.org/aboutfh/index.htm.

15. See chapter 6 for a discussion of the Freedom House annual assessment of political rights and civil liberties. Freedom House defines electoral democracy in its report *Freedom in the World 2003*, "Methodology."

16. Ibid.

17. White, *Historical Atlas*.

18. Ibid.

19. See discussion of American foreign policy in appendix B.

20. Marshall and Gurr, *Peace and Conflict 2003*, 1–2. The CIDCM at the University of Maryland conducts interdisciplinary research, policy analysis, and training on human rights issues, international development, and conflict resolution.

21. Ibid., 47.

22. Hewitt, Wilkenfeld, and Gurr, *Peace and Conflict 2008: Executive Summary*, 12–13.

23. SIPRI conducts research on international conflicts, global security, and conflict prevention and resolution (http://www.sipri.org).

24. SIPRI, "Press Release," 10. This data is discussed in chapter 3, "Major Armed Conflicts," of the *SIPRI Yearbook 2004*.

25. Ibid.

26. Freedom House, *Democracy's Century*.

27. Ibid.

28. Ibid.

29. UN, "East Timor."

30. Central Intelligence Agency (CIA), "East Timor," *World Factbook 2003*.

31. UN, "Member States."

32. Freedom House, *Democracy's Century*.

33. Ibid., "End of Century Survey."

34. Ibid., "Global Freedom Gains."

35. Ibid.

36. Ibid.

37. Ibid., *Democracy's Century*.

38. Ibid., "End of Century Survey."

39. Ibid., "Global Press Freedom Deteriorates."

40. Ibid.

41. Ibid., *Nations in Transit 2004*.

42. Ibid.

43. Ibid.

44. Deutsche Welle, "Prodi Unveils Vision."

45. British Broadcasting Corporation (BBC) News, "What the EU Constitution Says." A provisional consolidated version of the draft treaty that establishes a constitution of Europe is available at http://news.bbc.co.uk/nol/shared/bsp/hi/pdfs/21_07_04cg00086.en04.pdf.

46. BBC News, "What the EU Constitution Says." For a debate over whether this draft constitution is democratic, see BBC News, "Head-to-Head: Is EU Blueprint Democratic?" 20 June 2003, http://news.bbc.co.uk/1/hi/world/europe/3006156.stm.

47. Europa, "A Constitution for Europe."

48. See, for example, Rummel, *Power Kills*, 25–84.

49. See, for example, Kagan, *On the Origins of War*, 6, 68–74, 205–14, 269–74, 413–17, 546–48, 566–73.

50. Moore is viewed by many as the founder of the discipline of national security law.

51. Moore, "Toward a New Paradigm," 811, 840; and Moore, *Solving the War Puzzle*, xx, 39.

52. Moore, "Toward a New Paradigm," 811, 841; and Moore, *Solving the War Puzzle*, xx, 27.

Chapter 2

Conventional Theories of War and War Avoidance

To avoid this State of War . . . is one great reason of Mens putting themselves into Society.

—John Locke
Two Treatises of Government

War is defined under modern international law as an armed conflict or hostilities between two or more governments or states,[1] but it has been an ever-present feature of human history, long before the rise of the state. War has no doubt existed since the origins of humankind; we can document its existence from Sumerian writings that originate from about 3100 BC.[2] Indeed the "written history of the world is largely a written history of warfare."[3] Historian Donald Kagan calculated in 1968 "that there had been only 268 years free of war in the previous 3,421."[4]

War has always been considered the "prerogative right" of sovereign states.[5] Many theorists have viewed it as simply another political instrument at the state's or the ruler's disposal. This view of war can be found in cultures as diverse as Imperial China and Enlightenment Europe. During the Ch'in (Qin) Dynasty (221–206 BC), Chinese philosophers, influenced by Sun Tzu's *The Art of War* (c. 490 BC), wrote that it "is impossible to gain profit without making efforts and to extend one's territory by sitting idly. . . . The only way to attain that goal is to continue doing it *through war*" (emphasis added).[6] Frederick the Great, king of Prussia (1740–86), also believed that a "successful king must understand the use—and abuse—of military force as an *instrument of policy*" (emphasis added).[7] Similarly, the Prussian philosopher and general Carl von Clausewitz (1780–1831) wrote that "war is not merely a political act, but also a real political instrument, a continuation of political commerce, a carrying out of the same by other means."[8] General Clausewitz viewed war as a "rational instrument of national policy" and a "part of the intercourse of the human race" that "can never be separated from political intercourse."[9] Clausewitz also developed a doctrine of total war or complete annihilation.[10] He believed that a country at war must use all of its resources to ensure that an enemy's military power is completely destroyed; the enemy's will and capability to re-create military power must also be completely destroyed. Clausewitz believed that a "political animal is a warmaking animal."[11] According to his views, war is a natural, even inevitable, expression of political power.

Immanuel Kant, the Prussian philosopher, political theorist, and cynic about human nature, observed that the "state of peace among men living side by side is not the natural state," but rather the "natural state is one of war."[12] However, Kant believed that peace could be established and maintained by institutionalizing certain principles that guide international relations and the internal structure of governments.[13]

The concept of total war—one that involves all of a nation's resources and results in the destruction of all an enemy's resources—continued to evolve after Clausewitz. Most new theories no longer regard war as a rational instrument of state policy, and their proponents believe that total war "should be undertaken only if the most vital interests of the state, touching upon its very survival, are concerned."[14] Other theorists believe war is "a calamity and a social disaster" and deny war any rational character.[15] In a sweeping history of warfare from 490 BC to 1950 AD, Lynn Montross concludes that "the heart of man has never been changed by any weapon his mind has conceived" and "war is a disease of the body politic."[16]

The future prevalence of warfare in society is a matter of debate. The noted jurist Eugene Rostow concludes that war is "probably a more pervasive factor in social and political life today [1993] than at any time since the seventeenth century," and that "trend shows no sign of abating."[17] In sharp contrast, historian John Keegan has concluded after a lifetime of study that war "may well be ceasing to commend itself to human beings as a desirable or productive, let alone rational, means of reconciling their discontents," and that humankind "does have the capacity, over time, to correlate the costs and benefits of large and universal undertakings."[18] Given the sheer horror of weapons of mass destruction, one can only hope that Keegan's conclusion is correct. However, while Keegan believes that politics must continue and that war cannot, he unfortunately does not see an end to war in the near future.[19]

Conventional Thinking on the Cause of War

There are several conventional explanations for the cause of war. Many Western philosophers from Aristotle to Clausewitz have believed in the primacy of politics rather than culture as the cause of war. Clausewitz, for example, believed that a "political motive" existed as the "precipitating and controlling factor in warmaking" for all the wars of his time.[20] John Jay acknowledges in *The Federalist Papers* No. 4 the role of *nations* in making war, but also argues that individual leaders will often go to war when it does not benefit the nation. According to Jay, the personal motives of the leader often override the political motives of the nation:

> It is too true, however disgraceful it may be to human nature, that nations in general will make war whenever they have a prospect of getting anything by it; nay, that absolute monarchs will often make war when their nations are to get nothing by it, but for purposes and objects merely personal, such as a thirst for military glory, revenge for personal affronts, ambition, or private compacts to aggrandize or support their particular families or partisans. These and a variety of other motives, which affect only the mind of the sovereign, often lead him to engage in wars not sanctified by justice or the voice and interests of his people.[21]

Alexander Hamilton also attributes many wars to the abusive actions of leaders in *The Federalist Papers* No. 6: "Men . . . have in too many instances abused the confidence they possessed; and assuming the pretext of some public motive, have not scrupled to sacrifice the national tranquility to personal advantage or personal gratification."[22] Hamilton also observes that "territorial disputes have at all times been found one of the most fertile sources of hostility among nations" and concludes that "perhaps the greatest proportion of wars that have desolated the earth have sprung from this origin."[23]

Montross concludes at the end of his study on war that the one constant factor in the cause and nature of war throughout history is the "minds of men," that is, the decisions and motives of individuals. He believes that the history of tomorrow will be governed by the hearts and minds of people, not policy or technology.[24] Similarly, the preamble to the constitution of the UN Educational, Scientific, and Cultural Organization (UNESCO) makes three significant declarations about the cause of war:

1. Wars begin in the minds of men.

2. Ignorance of each other's ways and lives has been a common cause, throughout the history of mankind, of that suspicion and mistrust between the peoples of the world through which their differences have all too often broken into war.

3. World War II was made possible by the denial of the democratic principles of the dignity, equality and mutual respect of men, and by the propagation, in their place, through ignorance and prejudice, of the doctrine of the inequality of men and races.[25]

Most theories about the cause of war fall into one of two major conventional schools of thought: the first attributes war to "innate biological and psychological factors or drives" and the second to "social relations and institutions."[26] The first school of thought was developed by ethologists, who draw analogies from animal behavior, as well as psychologists and psychoanalysts. By studying monkeys and apes in captivity, ethologists have observed that aggressive behavior usually arises in the context of rivalry for possession, the intrusion of a stranger, or the frustration of an activity, but the applicability of these observations to humans is questioned by some ethologists and social scientists.[27] Psychologist Sigmund Freud, in his correspondence with Albert Einstein later published as *Why War?*, asserts that "man has within himself a lust for hatred and destruction," and the only way to offset this lust is a "well-founded dread of the form future wars will take."[28] Most psychologists believe that social adjustments designed to increase transparency and trust within relationships would reduce the likelihood of war by decreasing frustration, insecurity, and fear.[29]

A minority of social and behavioral scientists believe that man is naturally violent, but a majority "regard violent behaviour either as an aberrant activity in flawed individuals or as a response to particular sorts of provocation or stimulation, the inference being that if such triggers to violence can be identified and palliated or eliminated, violence can be banished from human intercourse." Medical scientists have established that "aggression is a function of the lower brain, amenable to control by the higher brain," but they are not sure how those two areas of the brain communicate. They suspect, however, those chemical imbalances or the presence of certain hormones in the brain heightens aggressive behavior.[30]

The second school of thought takes into account how humans behave differently in different social contexts and structures, such as the internal organization of a state or the international system of states. These analyses have been developed by two very different groups of political theorists: classical liberals of the eighteenth and nineteenth centuries and socialists. Some classical liberals believed that political structures were of primary importance in determining the propensity of states to engage in war; they believed that the existence of a basic harmony of interests and economic cooperation among nations would minimize the incidence of wars. A major tenet of classical liberals was universal suffrage because they believed that people could vote any belligerently inclined government out of office.[31]

While classical liberals focused on political structures, socialists analyzed the socioeconomic system of states as the primary factor in determining the propensity of states to engage in war. Socialists such as Karl Marx attributed war to the class structure of society; Marx believed that war resulted from a clash of social forces created by a capitalist mode of production that develops two antagonistic classes, rather than being an instrument of state policy. Thus capitalist states would engage in war because of their growing needs for raw materials, markets, and cheap labor. Socialists believed replacing capitalism with socialism could prevent war, but world events have proven socialists wrong as well.[32]

These two schools of thought—war is caused by innate biological drives or social institutions—do not demonstrate any meaningful correlation with the occurrence or nonoccurrence of war. There are many variables not considered by these two schools: for example, the influence of national special interest groups such as the military or defense contractors that may seek glory through victory, greater resources, greater domestic political power, or justification for their existence.

Legal scholar Quincy Wright has conducted one of the "most thorough studies of the nature of war"[33] and concludes that there "is no single cause of war."[34] In *A Study of War*, he concludes that peace is an equilibrium of four complex factors: military and industrial technology, international law governing the resort to war, social and political organization at the domestic and international level, and the distribution of attitudes and opinions concerning basic values. War is likely when controls on any one level are disturbed or changed.[35] Similarly, the 1997 US *National Military Strategy* identifies the root causes of conflict as political, economic, social, and legal conditions.[36]

Moore has compiled the following list of conventional explanations for war: specific disputes; absence of dispute settlement mechanisms; ideological disputes; ethnic and religious differences; communication failures; proliferation of weapons and arms races; social and economic injustice; imbalance of power; competition for resources; incidents, accidents, and miscalculation; violence in the nature of man; aggressive national leaders; and economic determination. He has concluded, however, that these causes or motives for war explain specific conflicts but fail to serve as a central paradigm for explaining the cause of war.[37]

In the final analysis, Wright is unequivocally correct—there is no single cause or explanation for war. However, there is one clear consistency in all wars: wars always begin through the calculated decisions of men or women, regardless of any cause, motive, or explanation. As the UNESCO constitution asserts, "wars begin in the minds of men."[38] People—national leaders—are always at the core of any decision to wage war, and any strategy for preventing war must address these individuals.

Conventional Approaches to War Avoidance

Since there are multiple theories on the causes of war, there are also multiple philosophies and approaches to war avoidance and conflict prevention. The 1997 US *National Military Strategy*, for example, defines conflict prevention as the "reduction, mitigation, or neutralization of the causes of conflict," but it acknowledges that the military can do little by itself to address the political, economic, social, and legal conditions that are the root causes of conflict. It states that the US effort to prevent conflict includes international arms control measures, transparency and confidence-building measures, international nonproliferation standards, and export controls on fissionable materiel. It also heavily emphasizes deterrence as the military's most important contribution to conflict prevention and US national security. This strategy defines deterrence as "our demonstrated ability and willingness to defeat potential adversaries and deny them their strategic objectives." Our deterrence capability provides the necessary environment "for normal political discourse and peaceful resolution of differences."[39] To organize the discussion, the various approaches to conflict prevention, including those articulated in the *National Military Strategy*, will be explored in the context of five constructs or frameworks for war avoidance.

In the first construct, there are five major tools for war avoidance: diplomacy, regional integration, international law, the UN, and international government.[40] Diplomacy reduces the likelihood of conflict by seeking cooperation among states with competing interests, improving the rationality of the decision-making process and the effectiveness of cost-benefit analysis, eliminating misperceptions and irrational fears, and pursuing a balance of power. Since conflicts usually occur between neighbors, regional integration reduces the likelihood of conflict by increasing cooperation in economic, social, political, and security affairs, as in, for example, the EU and the North Atlantic Treaty Organization (NATO). International law reduces the likelihood of conflict by prohibiting the use of force between states under most circumstances other than self-defense and mitigates the harshness of conflict by regulating the conduct of war. The UN is responsible for maintaining international peace and security, and the UN Charter incorporates the three approaches of pacific settlement of disputes, collective security, and disarmament. However, these three approaches to international peace have not been very successful. Thus the UN secretary-general has also utilized diplomatic initiatives and peacekeeping forces, and the UN General Assembly has attempted to exert its influence by condemning undesirable state activities. Since the UN approaches have shortcomings and limited practicability in war avoidance, some have advocated eliminating war by completely reforming the international system and creating a world government with full legislative powers and an overwhelming military force that can overcome the relative anarchy of independent sovereign states. These approaches, however, are either far-fetched or have not been completely successful and appear highly unlikely to serve as the basis for an effective theory of war avoidance.

In the second construct, there are four theoretical approaches to conflict management through the establishment of world order: balance of power, collective security, world federalism, and functionalism.[41] Balance of power is historically the most significant approach to world order. An international system of sovereign states tends toward a natural equilibrium when rival states strive toward an equal division of power, but this system does not provide an acceptable degree of security in the twenty-first century, in which we find an unequal division of power.

Collective security is predicated upon the primacy of world order and depends upon an institutional arrangement in which member states agree to defend against an attack on any of the other members. In contrast to the balance of power approach where states act independently and in concert, collective security envisions the organization of the entire community. Collective security was the most prominent approach of the twentieth century. Some states, however, are uncomfortable with the fundamental requirement of collective security: any act of aggression against a member state must be treated as a threat to all member states regardless of the strategic implications of geography or the identity of the aggressor.

World federalism is "a radical rejection of the multistate system" that seeks to eliminate states as obstacles to world order.[42] World federalists seek a world government that would approximate a Western liberal state such as the United States, but these federalists ignore the political impracticality of changing the existing state system and creating an enforcement mechanism independent of the states while maintaining the ability of states to discipline individuals. Functionalism relies upon a "network of international organizations of varying size and shape, each tailored to the requirements for effective cooperative action" to deal with important social, economic, and technical problems that transcend national boundaries.[43]

Functionalism does not purport to eliminate states, but to make them more effective in working together and developing a more "complex pluralism." However, this is a very slow process that relegates its relevance to the distant future.[44] While these four theoretical approaches to establishing world order offer insights into conflict management, none offers a simple solution.

The third construct of war avoidance focuses on institutional modes of conflict management.[45] Even though philosophers have advocated theories and practices of conflict management since the beginning of recorded history, war avoidance through institutional modes of conflict management did not emerge until the nineteenth century, when a sufficient number of sovereign states recognized the problems arising from their coexistence and the need for regulating interstate relations. The first major institutional development, albeit unsuccessful, was the Council of Europe, established in the early 1800s to provide a forum for multilateral diplomacy. The next major developments were the Hague Peace Conferences of 1899 and 1907, which involved representatives from a large number of states who were all given diplomatic equality with the great powers. However, "the greatest achievement of the statesmen at the Hague was establishing the precedent that collective diplomacy should be oriented toward the further development and codification of international law, the formulation of procedures for the peaceful settlement of disputes, and the promotion of the principle that a pacific solution might be urged and facilitated by disinterested states in international disputes."[46]

The international community attempted to create a system of collective security in the League of Nations after World War I, and although the League of Nations failed, it laid the groundwork for the UN. The UN "established a modified form of collective security by allowing disputants a variety of methods for solving their disputes, by giving the Security Council flexibility with respect to UN action in response to threats and breaches of the peace, and by allowing the development of regional security arrangements."[47] The UN also created mechanisms for the peaceful settlement of disputes, such as the International Court of Justice.[48] However, the UN's greatest contribution to international conflict management is its charter, which "outlaws the aggressive use of force while recognizing a state's inherent right of individual and collective self-defense in Article 51 and the Security Council's obligation under Article 39 to maintain or restore international peace and security."[49] The UN Charter also authorizes the Security Council to use armed force to maintain international peace and security.[50] Despite its weaknesses, the UN was the vehicle for transforming the international community "from a system of independent states allowed by international law to wage war and to slaughter their own citizens with impunity to a system of interdependent sovereign states that now attempts to govern itself, protect human rights, and enforce global peace."[51]

The fourth construct includes nine approaches to regulating the initiation and conduct of war by establishing international norms that form the basis for the contemporary law of conflict management:

1. Norms and procedures (such as the just war theory) for assessing permissibility of recourse to war

2. Norms that govern the conduct of war

3. Obligations to negotiate an end to ongoing war

4. Dispute resolution procedures

5. Deterrence by establishing criminal responsibility for the violations of certain norms

6. Institutional modes of controlling war through collective actions

7. Arms control and disarmament

8. Deterrence through alliances

9. National measures[52]

However, three conditions of overriding significance must be considered when applying these nine approaches as conflict-management tools. First is the tension created by the bipolar East-West division between Socialist states and Western democracies during the Cold War and the recognition of substantial evidence that totalitarian regimes are "more prone to resort to violence than democracies as a class."[53] Second is the additional emphasis on the maintenance of strategic stability and deterrence caused by the destructive power of nuclear weapons.[54] Third, international law has not adapted well or quickly to the evolving shift in warfare from major armies on the march to low-intensity conflict, terrorism, and civil wars.[55] While all of these nine approaches play a role in war avoidance, the principal focus during the Cold War was on nuclear arms control because of the devastating consequences of nuclear weapons.[56]

The fifth construct, developed by Moore, includes nine conventional approaches to war avoidance: (1) balance of power; (2) third-party dispute settlement mechanism; (3) global mechanism for collective security; (4) pacifism and passive resistance; (5) arms control; (6) functionalism; (7) world federalism; (8) diplomacy, negotiation, and getting to yes; and (9) public and third-track diplomacy.[57] Each approach is based upon a principal assumption about the nature and cause of war. Each approach has strengths and weaknesses, summarized in table 3. While Moore has concluded that these nine approaches to war avoidance individually and collectively make important contributions toward international peace and security, they have not eliminated war. He believes these tools for war avoidance should be placed in a broader framework that serves as a central paradigm for explaining the cause of war, which will make these tools more effective.[58]

Table 3. Principal assumptions, strengths, and weaknesses of selected approaches to war avoidance

Approach to war avoidance	Principal assumption (PA), strength (S), and weakness (W)
Balance of power	PA: equilibrium of power equals security and world peace
	S: power is a component of deterrence; may predict state behavior
	W: fails to focus on importance of government structures and fails to focus on all elements of deterrence
Third-party dispute settlement mechanism	PA: war is primarily a problem of disputes among nations which can be resolved by contract analysis
	S: encourages third-party resolution and the rule of law
	W: erroneous assumption on the cause of war; fails to focus on importance of government structures; fails to focus on all elements of deterrence
Global mechanism for collective security	PA: aggression can be prevented by institutional collective self-defense
	S: systemwide deterrence
	W: free-rider problem (states who do not participate benefit); difficulties in collective community judgment regarding what is aggression; largely dependent on major powers; highly contingent and after-the-fact since existing UN system is weak

Table 3 (*continued*)

Approach to war avoidance	Principal assumption (PA), strength (S), and weakness (W)
Pacifism	PA: war or violence is not a means of settling disputes; pacifism will end war
	S: moral principle to be respected; strong humanitarian and religious basis
	W: only effective if universally accepted
Passive resistance	PA: resistance that does not amount to violence can prevent war
	S: may be effective in limited settings
	W: will not stop aggressive totalitarian regime that does not share values
Arms control	PA: arms races cause war; arms control prevents war
	S: enhances stability; very important for nuclear weapons
	W: erroneous premise; fails to focus on government structures and systemwide deterrence; problems with verification, compliance, excessive reduction of forces, misperception of signals; overreliance may actually reduce deterrence
Functionalism	PA: network of international organizations and other interactions between states will yield cooperation
	S: networks do enhance deterrence; approach enhances understanding between states
	W: fails to focus on government structures and systemwide deterrence; can be exploited by aggressive regime
World federalism	PA: war is a function of the state system; therefore, war is eliminated if the state system is eliminated
	S: theory could possibly eliminate international war (does not address civil wars)
	W: erroneous premise; changing the state system simply redefines wars as civil wars; concentration of power may result in greater abuse; impossible to implement
Diplomacy, negotiation, and getting to yes	PA: diplomacy and negotiations can resolve all disputes without war
	S: promotes diplomacy and rule of law; flexible tool that can resolve some disputes
	W: erroneous assumption that wars result from disputes; creates a pattern of appeasement; fails to focus on government structures and systemwide deterrence
Public and third-track diplomacy	PA: nongovernmental actors can play a role in preventing and resolving conflict
	S: unofficial and people-to-people; enhances understanding and confidence; may have access or opportunities not available to governments
	W: may interfere with government-to-government relations

Adapted from John Norton Moore, seminars, University of Virginia School of Law, Charlottesville, VA, 22 January and 26 February 1997.

It is important to recognize that all of these conventional approaches are valuable tools in war avoidance. Given a particular set of circumstances, one of these approaches may avoid or mitigate war. Nevertheless, these approaches, either independently or collectively, cannot avoid war reliably and predictably enough to be considered a viable, comprehensive theory of war avoidance.

Deterrence as a Tool of War Avoidance

A recurring theme in the various approaches to war avoidance is deterrence. Kagan concludes in his comparative history *On the Origins of War and the Preservation of Peace* that war is caused during a competition for power by a failure of states to take appropriate actions to preserve the peace, that is, an absence or failure of deterrence.[59] Kagan examines five historical examples: the Peloponnesian War (431–404 BC), the Second Punic War (218–201 BC), the First World War (1914–18), the Second World War (1939–45), and the Cuban missile crisis (1962).

The Peloponnesian War was caused by a Corinthian passion for vengeance, Spartan jealousy and fear, and the Athenian miscalculations that failed to account for this passion and fear. The Peloponnesian War was a failure of deterrence measures by all parties, which were either too weak or too strong or failed to account for irrational thought.[60] The Second Punic War was a war of revenge by the Carthaginians, primarily in response to the harsh peace imposed on them by the Romans after the First Punic War. The Carthaginians resented this treatment, and the Romans did nothing to prevent or deter Carthage from becoming too powerful and threatening Roman interests.[61]

The primary cause for the First World War was the confluence of Germany's clear and aggressive aspirations toward "world power" and "a place in the sun" and a failure in deterrence evidenced by the United Kingdom's (UK) refusal to adjust its strategic military capacity.[62] Similar to the Second Punic War, the Second World War was made possible by a failure of the victors to build a strong basis for peace after the First World War. The Allies built a weak League of Nations, the primary mechanism for maintaining peace after the First World War, and then failed to give it the national support it needed. Once again, there was a confluence of an aggressive Germany, which remained largely intact and grew bitter after the First World War, and a failure in deterrence evidenced by the UK's misunderstanding of the causes of the First World War, its naive belief that sin and evil could be overcome by setting a good example, and its emphasis on understanding and patience over military deterrence.[63]

The Cuban missile crisis happened because Soviet premier Nikita Khrushchev was convinced that US president John F. Kennedy "lacked the will to use American military superiority when challenged."[64] Even though Khrushchev believed that the US military was superior to that of the Soviet Union, he persisted in the provocative buildup of nuclear arms in Cuba because Kennedy's previous failure to respond more decisively to the Bay of Pigs, the Berlin Wall, and the flow of Soviet armaments to Cuba created a failure in deterrence.[65]

In short, Kagan concludes that the most fundamental cause of war is the competition for power that is driven by people's wildly subjective sense of "honor, fear, and interest."[66] Deterrence can counter the competition for power, but "to be effective [deterrence] must counterbalance passion with passion, fear with fear."[67] Peace, Kagan concludes, does not keep itself. Nations must take affirmative action to create the right deterrence to war. States must take responsibility and bear the burdens needed to keep the peace, and they must be prepared to defend the peace.[68]

One important component of deterrence is an enforced international legal order. In an earlier analysis of effective deterrence, I concluded that if the international community does "not actively seek to deter aggression and violations of the laws of armed conflict, or if we fail to condemn aggression and prosecute war crimes, then we merely invite future wars and war crimes."[69] Furthermore, "simply having a normative international legal order . . . is insufficient to deter violations of those norms. The existence of proscriptive norms that are not enforced actually undermines the value of the entire legal system."[70] Effective deterrence within the international legal order is comprised of three indispensable elements:

> First, the fundamental cornerstone of deterrence is a set of clear proscriptive norms. . . . Second, these proscriptive norms must be built upon by an established mechanism that facilitates individual and state accountability for violations of those norms. . . . Third, the world com-

munity's demonstrated commitment to condemn all violations of these proscriptive norms consistently and unequivocally is the capstone that completes this deterrence structure. Without this capstone, proscriptive norms and organizations are without effect—that is, "unenforced law is ineffective."[71]

In addition to a legal order, there are a number of other tools for effective deterrence, which Moore defines as "the totality of positive and negative actions influencing expectations and incentives of a potential aggressor":

> [They include] potential military responses and security arrangements, relative power, level and importance of economic relations, effectiveness of diplomatic relations, effective international organizations (or lack thereof), effective international law (or lack thereof), alliances, collective security, effects on allies, and the state of the political or military alliance structure, if any, of the potential aggressor and target state, etc. Most importantly, of course, there is a critical perception and communication component to deterrence since ultimately, it is the perception of the regime elite contemplating aggression that is most critical.[72]

Moore identifies effective military deterrence as "perhaps the most important single feature" of a comprehensive deterrence plan and identifies four key elements of military deterrence:

1. The ability to respond

2. The will to respond

3. Effective communication of ability and will to the aggressive regime

4. Perception by the aggressive regime of deterrence ability and will[73]

The fundamental importance of a potential aggressor's perception cannot be overstated. Robert F. Turner, an expert in national security law, defines deterrence as a "function of two perceptions: *strength* and *will*."[74] The US Department of Defense (DOD) defines deterrence as a "state of mind,"[75] and the US *National Military Strategy* states that deterrence "rests on a potential adversary's perception of our capabilities and commitment."[76] In other words, military deterrence is based on negative incentives, or, as the DOD defines it, "the prevention from action by fear of the consequences . . . brought about by the existence of a credible threat of unacceptable counteraction."[77]

However, US military deterrence theory defines both negative and positive deterrent options, that is, options that discourage undesirable behavior and encourage desirable behavior. A deterrent option is "a course of action, developed on the best economic, diplomatic, political, and military judgment, designed to dissuade an adversary from a current course of action or contemplated operations. (In constructing an operation plan, a range of options should be presented to effect deterrence. Each option requiring deployment of forces should be a separate force module.)"[78]

In a 1998 study, I proposed ways to strengthen systemwide deterrence to war. The study recognizes that international law prohibits an aggressive use of force against other states and imposes individual criminal responsibility on regime elites for waging aggressive war. However, it identifies a lacuna in international law that permits the combatants of an aggressor state to "kill in furtherance of an unlawful use of force . . . [with] absolute and complete immunity so long as they kill enemy combatants [UN military forces] in accordance with the *jus in bello*, i.e., the laws of armed conflict that govern the actual conduct of hostilities."[79] The study concludes that systemwide deterrence can and should be strengthened by imposing individual criminal responsibility on all combatants who engage in armed conflict against military forces serving under the authority of the UN.[80] Regardless of whether one agrees with this specific recommendation, the underlying assumption is absolutely critical in shaping an effective deterrence strategy: to be effective, deterrence must be tailored to the individual circumstances and must focus on all individuals who make major international conflict possible.

Focusing deterrence and incentives on individuals, however, is not a new concept. Kant scholar Lewis Beck describes Kant's argument in *Perpetual Peace* (1795): the first steps toward peace must be "taken by imperfect, warlike, perhaps despotic, rulers of states whose chief glory is self-aggrandizement," and they "must be convinced that war is fatal to them."[81] As discussed earlier, John Jay and Alexander Hamilton also emphasized the role of personal ambition in war, thus underscoring the importance of focusing deterrence on individuals. Jay believed that absolute monarchs often make war "for purposes and objects merely personal,"[82] while Hamilton believed that many leaders would not hesitate to "sacrifice the national tranquility" to secure personal gain.[83]

Contemporary discussions also emphasize the deterrence tool of holding individual leaders accountable for misdeeds in war. Edward Luttwak argues that when "belligerents see that no particular penalty is paid for opening fire first or using any and all means of warfare—even the wholesale destruction of cities by aerial or artillery bombardment—self-imposed restraints on the use of force are everywhere eroded."[84] Similarly, an *Economist* editorial on the extradition of former Chilean dictator Augusto Pinochet argues that "the ease with which dictators have escaped any consequences for their crimes has encouraged more to seize power and to commit further barbarities."[85] A detailed analysis of over 275 pages from contemporary studies and documents on deterrence theory and a thorough study of Moore's and Kagan's conclusions concerning deterrence demands a conclusion of great significance: to maintain international peace and security, states have the responsibility to take affirmative action to create and then clearly and effectively communicate positive and negative, institutional and scenario-specific deterrence incentives that target and personally affect potentially aggressive regime elites. Most importantly, states must clearly and effectively communicate to potentially aggressive regime elites the consistent and demonstrated capability and willingness of other states to respond to unlawful aggression with negative incentives such as military force and criminal prosecution.[86]

The Law of Conflict Management

War has been embraced as a legitimate form of violence throughout human history, at least until the very late nineteenth and early twentieth centuries when the first juristic restrictions on the right of states to resort to war evolved.[87] Until the late nineteenth century, war was judged by many as just or unjust on a moral plane. Others, called realists, believed that war was beyond law and morality—war was simply self-interest, necessity, and survival. Realists believed that *inter arma silent leges*—in time of war the law is silent.[88] In practice, the theory of just war offered no war-preventing effects because either side could argue its use of force was just.[89]

For adherents of a just war theory, the morality of war was judged first with reference to why states fought and second with reference to the means states adopted to fight the war. Medieval writers described these judgments as *jus ad bellum*, an analysis of whether a war itself is just or unjust, and *jus in bello*, an analysis of whether how a war is fought is just or unjust. Any conflict was evaluated on both planes; that is, a just war of self-defense could be fought unjustly, and an unjust war of aggression could be fought justly.[90] All soldiers are morally equal, and within the limitations of *jus in bello*, they all have the right to kill other soldiers even if they are the soldiers of an aggressor clearly engaged in an unjust war.[91] This dichotomy in the just war theory—that all soldiers in a conflict are morally equal under *jus in bello* even if the soldiers of one or more states are engaged in illegal warfare under *jus ad bellum*—is the "most problematic in the moral reality of war."[92] This dichotomy is problematic because it creates a disconnect between the lawfulness of the *initiation* of war and the *conduct* of war. For example, a belligerent who has initiated an illegal war may nevertheless lawfully kill hundreds of thousands of soldiers during the conduct of that war.

Although morality remains important in discussions of war, it is now safe to declare that the theory of just war on a *moral* plane is dead. War can no longer be justified within the international community as morally just and thus permissible. A state's right to resort to war is now defined by contemporary *jus ad bellum* on a *legal* plane. The decline of seeking a moral justification for war and the reliance upon a legal basis for the use of force began in the late 1800s.

A series of efforts began with the Hague Peace Conferences of 1899 and 1907 to create juristic restrictions on a state's right to resort to war. Article 1 of the Hague Convention III of 1907 on the Opening of Hostilities required parties to provide a prior and unambiguous warning before resorting to war; however, this is simply a formalization of a state's right to resort to war. In contrast, Article 1 of the Hague Convention II of 1907 on the Limitation of the Employment of Force for the Recovery of Contract Debts prohibits the recourse to war for the recovery of a contractual debt.[93] From 1913 to 1916, the United States entered into 19 bilateral treaties that required the parties to refer their disputes to a conciliation commission and not to begin hostilities prior to that commission's report. Similarly, after World War I, parties of the Covenant of the League of Nations were prohibited from resorting to war until after they submitted a dispute to judicial settlement, arbitration, or the Council of the League of Nations. Parties were also required to wait for a three-month "cooling-off period" after an arbitral award or council's report and were prohibited from resorting to war against states complying with the arbitral award or council's report. Article 2 of the Geneva Protocol for the Pacific Settlement of International Disputes (1924) obligated states "in no case to resort to war" except in the case of self-defense or collective enforcement measures, but this protocol never became binding law. A number of European states also generally prohibited any attack, invasion, or war in Article 2 of the Locarno Treaty of 1925, but that treaty also had exceptions and lost its binding force in 1935.[94]

The Kellogg-Briand Pact of 1928 was the decisive turning point in the development of juristic restrictions on the resort to war. Almost all states in existence then became a party to this pact that prohibited war except in the case of self-defense. A number of Latin American states did not joint the pact, but they signed the Saavedra Lamas Treaty of 1933 that contained an identical restriction on the resort to war. The provisions of the Kellogg-Briand Pact quickly became customary international law and remain valid today. However, the provisions were not linked to a system of sanctions and did not prohibit the use of force, just the resort to war.[95]

Contemporary *jus ad bellum* is now codified in Articles 2(4), 39, and 51 of the UN Charter.[96] Indeed, contemporary *jus ad bellum* is now a concept of *jus contra bellum*, that is, the law against the aggressive use of force.[97] Elsewhere I have interpreted the restrictions in the UN Charter on the use of force:

> The Charter clearly outlaws the aggressive use of force while recognizing a state's inherent right of individual and collective self-defense in Article 51 and the Security Council's obligation under Article 39 to maintain or restore international peace and security. If a state uses force against another state within the meaning of Article 2(4), it is unlawful unless it is an exercise of that state's inherent right of self-defense or unless

> it is authorized by the Security Council under its coercive Chapter VII authority.
>
> Articles 2(4), 39, and 51 must be read together to determine the scope and content of the Charter's prohibition on the aggressive use of force, the responsibility of the Security Council to enforce this prohibition, and the right of all states to use force in self-defense. . . .
>
> As an exercise of the international community's inherent right of collective self-defense, Article 39 of the Charter imposes an obligation on the Security Council to maintain international peace and security.[98]

Articles 2(4) and 51 are customary international law and binding on all states,[99] and decisions made by the Security Council under Article 39 are binding on all member states.[100] Despite the watershed importance of the UN Charter for war avoidance, there have been significant problems in interpreting the charter's provisions, for example, in determining what is a "threat or use of force," what is the "territorial integrity or political independence" of a state, and what is an "armed attack."[101]

The Future of Armed Conflict

If the last four millennia have any predictive value, then war and armed conflict will certainly plague humankind for many centuries to come. While Keegan has expressed hope that war "may well be ceasing to commend itself to human beings,"[102] Richard Preston and Sydney Wise speak for many historians when they conclude that it "is certain that military force will continue to play a role in the world of the future."[103] Ralph Peters predicts there "will be fewer classic wars but more violence" that will be "shaped by the inabilities of governments to function as effective systems or resource distribution and control, and by the failure of entire cultures to compete in the post-modern age."[104] Some political scientists predict that the multipolar world in a high-technology twenty-first century of ethnic and militant nationalism could be far more dangerous than the bipolar world of the Cold War during the twentieth century.[105]

Future conflict, at least in the coming decades if not centuries, is a certainty, but we can only speculate about how or why future conflict may manifest itself or what dynamics could make long-time allies become enemies and traditional enemies become allies. Conflict in the twenty-first century will be more diverse and less predictable, and the range of potential adversaries will likely be larger than during the Cold War. Alliances may shift or crumble as the leadership of governments changes.[106] Ideological differences and latent economic or geopolitical cleavages may give rise to new enemies, and changes in the economy, communications, and military technology may alter the balance of power.[107] Conflicts could erupt if the EU were to fragment, the Russian economy collapse, the Middle East fall into anarchy, or the United States withdraw from the world stage.[108] In 1998, Europe had seven of the world's 10 largest economies; by 2020, China may have the world's largest economy, and Europe may only have two of the 10 largest economies.[109] Such an extraordinary shift in China's relative economic power could threaten its Asian neighbors, a weakened Russian state, or the European community enough to cause a major conflict in the twenty-first century. There are also environmental, politico-cultural, and techno-scientific "wild cards": those unforeseen events that could cause instability and conflict. Historical wild cards have included the devastation of Europe by the Black Death, the storm that crippled the Spanish Armada, Hitler's rise to power, the Russian revolution of 1917, and the discovery of atomic energy. Potential wild cards could include a highly lethal airborne virus that kills millions, rising global temperatures that cause massive crop failure, a global economic depression, revolutionary collapse of a world power, a new cold war along cultural or religious lines, or new sensor technology that renders the oceans transparent.[110]

Predictive analyses are truly insightful and fascinating to read because they posit trends in economic, social, political, military, and technological evolution, but they nevertheless represent conventional thinking on the cause of war and do not demonstrate any meaningful correlation with the occurrence or nonoccurrence of war. For example, the prediction that the Asia-Pacific region will become the new strategic center of gravity in international politics and the single largest concentration of international economic power outside of Europe or the Americas since the beginning of modernity (circa 1500) is very interesting and quite likely true; however, while analysts admit the implications of this development are "poorly understood," they still conclude that this economic power yields a "capacity to generate conflict."[111] Although not relevant as a tool to predict the occurrence of future war, these predictive analyses are important because they do help suggest the nature of future conflict and the environment in which it may occur.

The nature of conflict in the twenty-first century is evolving and may include local conflicts "dominated by ethnic warfare and humanitarian crises arising from domestic anarchy."[112] A central focus of future conflict may also be along the fault lines between civilizations as between the West and Islam or between the economic haves and have-nots. The nature of warfare may shift from that of major armies to informal nonstate groups of police forces, criminal organizations, gangs, and terrorists; that is, there may be a shift in twenty-first-century conflict from the international to the civil and intranational and a shift from open warfare by states to terrorism and aggression from nonstate forces.[113] Advances in technology mean that major standing armies and huge national budgets are no longer necessary to possess destructive weapons of holocaust dimensions. However, it is difficult to predict what additional conflicts or escalation of conflicts may unintentionally be sparked by the UN taking action intended to maintain international peace and security, by a state taking unilateral action intended to protect its national security interests, or by the UN or a state responding poorly to an unanticipated crisis.

Notes

1. McDougal and Feliciano, *Law and Minimum World Public Order*, 97–98.
2. Keegan, *A History of Warfare*, 115.
3. Ibid., 386.
4. Kagan, *On the Origins of War*, 4.
5. McDougal and Feliciano, *Law and Minimum World Public Order*, 44. See also Rostow, *Toward Managed Peace*, 41.
6. Hanzhang, *Sun Tzu's "Art of War,"* 82–83.
7. Frederick II, *Frederick the Great on the Art of War*, 35.
8. Clausewitz, *On War*, 119.
9. Ibid., 13, 202, 402.
10. Montross, *War through the Ages*, 584.
11. Keegan, *A History of Warfare*, 3.
12. Kant, *Perpetual Peace*, vii–xvi, 10.
13. Ibid., viii.

14. *Encyclopædia Britannica Online*, s.v. "war," http://www.britannica
.com/eb/article-9110187.

15. Ibid.

16. Montross, *War through the Ages*, xiii, 9, 977.

17. Rostow, *Toward Managed Peace*, 25.

18. Keegan, *A History of Warfare*, 59.

19. Ibid., 386–92.

20. Ibid., 46.

21. Hamilton, Madison, and Jay, *Federalist Papers* No. 4, 46.

22. Ibid., *Federalist Papers* No. 6, 54.

23. Ibid., 60.

24. Montross, *War through the Ages*, 1000.

25. UNESCO, *Constitution*, in *Manual of the General Conference*, 7.

26. *Encyclopædia Britannica Online*, s.v. "war," http://www.britannica.com/
eb/article-9110187.

27. Ibid.

28. Freud to Einstein, letter.

29. *Encyclopædia Britannica Online*, s.v. "war," http://www.britannica.com/
eb/article-9110187.

30. Keegan, *A History of Warfare*, 79–82.

31. *Encyclopædia Britannica Online*, s.v. "war," http://www.britannica.com/
eb/article-9110187.

32. Ibid.

33. Moore, "International Law of Conflict Management," *National Security
Law*, 49–50.

34. Wright, *A Study of War*, 1284.

35. Ibid.

36. Joint Chiefs of Staff, *National Military Strategy*, 11.

37. Moore, seminar, 22 January 1997.

38. UNESCO, *Constitution*, in *Manual of the General Conference*, 7.

39. Joint Chiefs of Staff, *National Military Strategy*, 14.

40. *Encyclopædia Britannica Online*, s.v. "war," http://www.britannica.com/
eb/article-9110187.

41. Claude, "Theoretical Approaches," *National Security Law*, 31–45.

42. Ibid., 40.

43. Ibid., 42–43.

44. Ibid., 43–44.

45. Higgins, "Institutional Modes," *National Security Law*, 193–305.

46. Ibid., 193.

47. Ibid., 193–94.

48. Ibid., 269–81.

49. Sharp, *Jus Paciarii*, 280. See also the discussion later in the chapter
of the international law embodied in the UN Charter that outlaws the use of
aggressive force by states.

50. Ibid., 280–82, 290–93.

51. Ibid., 2.

52. The historical evolution of these nine principles and practices is summarized in Moore, "International Law of Conflict Management," *National Security Law*, 52.

53. Moore, "International Law of Conflict Management," 77.

54. Ibid., 78.

55. Ibid., 80.

56. Ibid., 80–81.

57. Moore, seminars, 22 January and 26 February 1997.

58. Ibid.

59. Kagan, *On the Origins of War*, 6, 9, 68–74, 205–14, 269–74, 413–17, 546–48, 566–73.

60. Ibid., 68–73.

61. Ibid., 269–74.

62. Ibid., 205–14.

63. Ibid., 413–17.

64. Ibid., 546–48.

65. Ibid.

66. Ibid., 6–9.

67. Ibid., 74.

68. Ibid., 73, 212–14, 567.

69. Sharp, "Effective Deterrence," 1.

70. Ibid., 4.

71. Ibid., 1, 5. This passage quotes Robert F. Turner, "Don't Let Saddam Escape without Trial," *Atlanta Journal-Constitution*, 31 August 1991. Turner's point is "the real lesson . . . was not that 'law' was ineffective, but rather that unenforced law is ineffective."

72. Moore, "Toward a New Paradigm," 811, 841.

73. Ibid.

74. Turner, "Deception and Deterrence," 23.

75. Joint Publication (JP) 1-02, *DOD Dictionary*, 157.

76. Joint Chiefs of Staff, *National Military Strategy*, 3.

77. JP 1-02, *DOD Dictionary*, 157.

78. Ibid., 158.

79. Sharp, "Revoking an Aggressor's License to Kill," 1, 3.

80. Ibid., 1, 77–79.

81. Beck, introduction to *Perpetual Peace* by Kant, xiii.

82. Hamilton, Madison, and Jay, *Federalist Papers*, No. 4, 46.

83. Ibid., No. 6, 54.

84. Luttwak, "Toward Post-Heroic Warfare," 109.

85. "Ex-Dictators Are Not Immune."

86. The following studies and documents were analyzed: Kaufmann, *The Requirements of Deterrence*, 1–22; Schelling, *Arms and Influence*, 92–125; Huth and Russett, "What Makes Deterrence Work"; Lebow and Stein, "Rational Deterrence Theory"; George and Smoke, "Deterrence and Foreign Policy"; Achen and Snidal, "Rational Deterrence Theory"; Jervis, "Rational Deterrence"; Downs, "Rational Deterrence Debate"; United States, France, United Kingdom, and USSR, The London Charter; UN, *Affirmation of the Principles of International*

Law; International Criminal Tribunal for the Former Yugoslavia, *Rules of Procedure and Evidence*; UN Security Council, resolution for a report on Rwanda; Parks, "Memorandum of Law"; Turner, "Killing Saddam"; Churchill, *The Hinge of Fate*, 682–91; O'Connor, *Diplomacy for Victory*, 48–56; UN, *Charter*, Articles 4–6; Department of the Treasury, Haitian Transaction Regulations; and Executive Order 12872.

87. Sharp, *CyberSpace*, 27, 30–33. See also McDougal and Feliciano, *Law and Minimum World Public Order*, 44, and Rostow, *Toward Managed Peace*, 41.

88. Walzer, *Just and Unjust Wars*, 3.

89. Simma, *UN Charter Commentary*, 109.

90. Walzer, *Just and Unjust Wars*, 21.

91. Ibid., 34–47.

92. Ibid., 21. But see also Sharp, "Revoking an Aggressor's License to Kill" and *Jus Paciarii*; these earlier works detect a shift in the duality of *jus ad bellum* and *jus in bello* and posit that emergent international law is "revoking" an aggressor's right to lawfully kill military forces serving the UN.

93. Simma, *UN Charter Commentary*, 109.

94. Ibid., 109–10.

95. Ibid., 110–11.

96. Ibid., 111. For a more detailed discussion of contemporary *jus ad bellum* and an explanation of the threshold between the lawful and unlawful use of force in UN Charter article 2(4), see discussions in Sharp, *Jus Paciarii*, 279–93, and Sharp, *CyberSpace and the Use of Force*, 27–69. Following are relevant excerpts from the UN Charter:

Article 2. The Organization and its Members, in pursuit of the Purposes stated in Article 1, shall act in accordance with the following Principles:
. . .

(4) All Members shall refrain in their international relations from the threat or use of force against the territorial integrity or political independence of any state, or in any other manner inconsistent with the Purposes of the United Nations.

Article 39. The Security Council shall determine the existence of any threat to the peace, breach of the peace, or act of aggression and shall make recommendations, or decide what measures shall be taken in accordance with Articles 41 and 42, to maintain or restore international peace and security.

Article 51. Nothing in the present Charter shall impair the inherent right of individual or collective self-defence if an armed attack occurs against a Member of the United Nations, until the Security Council has taken the measures necessary to maintain international peace and security. Measures taken by Members in the exercise of this right of self-defense shall be immediately reported to the Security Council and shall not in any way affect the authority and responsibility of the Security Council under the present Charter to take at any time such action as it deems necessary in order to maintain or restore international peace and security.

97. Kotzsch, *Concept of War*, 83, 269–96.

98. Sharp, *Jus Paciarii*, 280–81.

99. Simma, *UN Charter Commentary*, 126–27, 666–67.

100. UN Charter article 25; Simma, *UN Charter Commentary*, 407–18.

101. See, for example, the discussions of interpretive challenges in Moore, "Use of Force," 85–192; Simma, *UN Charter Commentary*, 106–28, 605–16, 661–78; Brownlie, *International Law*, 251–305, 338–423; Sharp, *CyberSpace*, 27; and Sharp, *Jus Paciarii*.

102. Keegan, *A History of Warfare*, 59.

103. Preston and Wise, *Men in Arms*, 1.

104. Peters, "Culture of Future Conflict," 19.

105. Bloomfield and Moulton, *Managing International Conflict*, 34–35.

106. Lesser, "Introduction," *Sources of Conflict*, 1–2.

107. Ibid.

108. Khalilzad and Shlapak, "Future Security Environment," *Sources of Conflict*, 8, 11.

109. Ibid., 12.

110. Ibid., 33–36.

111. Ibid., 43.

112. Bloomfield and Moulton, *Managing International Conflict*, 34.

113. Ibid., 34–37.

Chapter 3

The Democratic Peace Principle

Force [is] the vital principle and immediate parent of despotism.

—Thomas Jefferson
First Inaugural Address, 1801

The principle that nondemocracies are more prone to war and democracies are inherently more peaceful and protective of human liberty has been developed and debated for centuries. The philosophers and political theorists who stirred these contentious political debates, often at great personal sacrifice, not only established the intellectual foundation for the principle that democracies are inherently peaceful but also had a powerful influence on the creation of American liberal democracy. Today the democratic peace principle is widely, though not universally, accepted and can be supported with empirical data.

The Early Debate

In the late 1600s, British philosopher John Locke published his *Two Treatises on Government*, which examine the proper use of political authority and were intended to counter the enemies of reason and freedom.[1] His first treatise is a refutation of the divine right of kings and an argument for the natural rights, freedom, and equality of all human beings.[2] Locke argues in his second treatise that an absolute monarchy has no basis in the consent of the governed and absolutism is not a political society at all but mere violence. His second treatise contends that government is a result of the people themselves agreeing to be governed and the power of the ruler is conditional, based on the security of the common good. Locke concludes that sovereignty rests with the people, and government must protect the property and person of the individual, as well as the individual's freedom of thought, speech, and religion. Locke also strongly favors a separation of powers between an executive and a duly elected legislature. The English government declared Locke a traitor because of his liberal writings; however, his work had an enormous influence on the great political documents of the United States such as the Declaration of Independence and the Constitution.[3]

Locke also recognizes that governmental power is related to peace, and he observes the potential for the abuse of power: "The great Question which in all Ages has disturbed Mankind, and brought on them the greatest part of those Mischiefs which have ruined Cities, depopulated Countries, and disordered the Peace of the World, has been, not whether there be Power in the World, nor whence it came, but who should have it."[4] In his extended discussions of how governments should use law as a tool to protect the people from whom they derive their power, Locke observes that "where-ever Law ends, Tyranny begins."[5] While recognizing the inherently peaceful nature of a government whose only exercise of war power is in self-defense and the protection of the innocent, Locke's monumental work stops short of drawing a direct correlation between peace and democratic forms of government.[6]

In the mid-1700s, Charles de Montesquieu, a French jurist and political philosopher, argued the connection between liberal capitalism, democracy, and peace in his *Spirit of the Laws*, a comparative study of three types of government: republic, monarchy, and despotism.[7] Montesquieu's main theory of government structure is that the functions of governmental power—legislative, executive, and judicial—should be separated and balanced by each other's authority. The *Spirit of the Laws* is of great historical importance and significantly influenced the writing of the US Constitution.[8]

In the late 1700s, Englishman Thomas Paine "forcefully asserted" the incompatibility of democracy and war in his work *The Rights of Man*.[9] Written in response to Edmund Burke's denunciation of the French Revolution, *The Rights of Man* was a powerful influence for freedom in American and British political thought, especially among those who opposed the power of the British monarchy. *The Rights of Man* was banned in England, and Paine was forced to flee England to escape his indictment and eventual conviction for libel.

Paine laments "the wretched condition of man, under the monarchical and hereditary systems of Government" and argues that governments must be founded on the principle that "every citizen is a member of the Sovereignty, and, as such, can acknowledge no personal subjection; and his obedience can be only to the laws." If sovereignty were restored to the nation and its citizens rather than a monarch, "the cause of wars would be taken away." Paine contends that a republican government is a deterrent to war:

> Why are not Republics plunged into war, but because the nature of their Government does not admit of an interest distinct from that of the Nation? Even Holland, though an ill-constructed Republic, and with a commerce extending over the world, existed nearly a century without war: and the instant the form of Government was changed in France, the republican principles of peace and domestic prosperity and economy arose with the new Government; and the same consequences would follow the cause in other Nations.[10]

Kant's 1795 essay *Perpetual Peace* is the "most often cited classical source of the idea that democracy is an important force for peace."[11] In *Perpetual Peace*, Kant formulates his plan for peace: six "preliminary articles" prescribe what states must do to have peace, and three "definitive articles" of political philosophy explain how the constitutions of states should be written and how a league of nations should be structured under international law if peace is to be lasting.[12] Section 1 of *Perpetual Peace* contains the six preliminary articles, which, if followed, will secure a perpetual peace among states:

1. No treaty of peace shall be held valid in which there is tacitly reserved matter for a future war.

2. No independent states, large or small, shall come under the dominion of another state by inheritance, exchange, purchase, or donation.

3. Standing armies (*miles perpetuus*) shall in time be totally abolished.

4. National debts shall not be contracted with a view to the external friction of states.

5. No state shall by force interfere with the constitution or government of another state.

47

6. No state shall, during war, permit such acts of hostility which would make mutual confidence in the subsequent peace impossible: such are the employment of assassins (*percussores*), poisoners (*venefici*), breach of capitulation, and incitement to treason (*perduellio*) in the opposing state.[13]

In his preface to the definitive articles in section 2, Kant argues that war, not peace, is the natural order of relations among neighbors:

> The state of peace among men living side by side is not the natural state (*status naturalis*); the natural state is one of war. This does not always mean open hostilities, but at least an unceasing threat of war. A state of peace, therefore, must be *established*, for in order to be secured against hostility it is not sufficient that hostilities simply be not committed; and, unless this security is pledged to each by his neighbor (a thing that can occur only in a civil state), each may treat his neighbor, from whom he demands this security, as an enemy.[14]

To establish a state of peace, Kant offers the following prescriptions:

First Definitive Article: The civil constitution of every state should be republican.

Second Definitive Article: The law of nations shall be founded on a federation of free states.

Third Definitive Article: The law of world citizenship shall be limited to conditions of universal hospitality.[15]

Kant observes in his closing addendum, "Perpetual Peace as a Moral and Political Ideal," that the "establishment of universal and enduring peace constitutes not just a part but rather the entire final end of jurisprudence within the limits of mere reason" and that the "best constitution is one in which laws, not men, are sovereign."[16]

The powerful influence of Locke, Montesquieu, Paine, and Kant on the views of the US founding fathers can be seen in *The Federalist Papers*. For example, Hamilton observes in *Federalist Paper* No. 6, "The genius of republics (say they) is pacific; the spirit of commerce has a tendency to soften the manners of men, and to extinguish those inflammable humors which have so often kindled into wars. Commercial republics, like ours, will never be disposed to waste themselves in ruinous contentions with each other."[17] However, in asking the question "have republics in practice been less addicted to war than monarchies?" Hamilton observes that even if peace is in the true interest of republics, practice has been to the contrary because "momentary passions, and immediate interests, have a more active and imperious control over human conduct than general or remote considerations of policy, utility, or justice."[18]

Contemporary Studies and Methodologies

This absence of war between democracies comes as close as anything we have to an empirical law in international relations.

—Jack Levy
"The Causes of War"

The early debate surrounding the democratic peace principle in the writings of Locke, Montesquieu, Paine, and Kant was based upon intuition, philosophy, reason, and observation driven by a metaphysical desire to understand and champion human liberty and freedom. When Kant wrote *Perpetual Peace* in 1795, "there was no democracy on earth and none had ever existed," yet he imagined this abstract notion of a peaceful union of liberal republics more clearly than anyone else.[19] Now peace researchers have proven with "scientific analysis, in thousands of tables and tens of thousands of basic examples and testimonies" what liberals have intuitively "imagined or felt" for two centuries: democracies do not fight democracies.[20]

A wide range of empirical research was begun in the twentieth century utilizing large-scale statistical methods and comparative case studies to correlate political systems with the occurrence and nonoccurrence of war. Now it is almost universally accepted that democracies are more peaceful in many respects than nondemocracies. A large number of studies support this conclusion. This discussion will summarize only a few of the major studies to demonstrate the depth and variety of the research that has analyzed and validated the democratic peace principle. Later in the chapter we will consider challenges to the democratic peace principle.

In 1989 political scientists Zeev Maoz and Nasrin Abdolali published the results of a comprehensive study of the correlations between regime type and conflict involvement.[21] This study was intended to replicate previous research on the democratic peace principle and to analyze it by reformulating the test hypotheses and analyzing the previous research on a broader range of empirical data to assess the extent to which previous findings may be sensitive to differing research methodologies or to being limited to certain time periods and units of analysis.[22] The study used "two datasets, each covering nearly all independent political entities and nearly all militarized interstate disputes (including all wars) among these entities during the 1816–1976 period."[23]

The democratic peace principle proposes that democracies are more peaceful and less likely to initiate wars than nondemocracies (a national-level analysis) and that democracies do not fight other democracies (a dyadic-level analysis that compares democracies in pairs).[24] Maoz and Abdolali specifically analyze these two hypotheses and also add a hypothesis about the effect of democracies within the international system (a system-level analysis), which they believe is a logical extension of the first two: "If politically free states do not fight one another, then the more democracies, the less international conflict."[25] They analyzed wide-ranging statistical data relating to the democratic peace principle in the framework of the following three questions:

1. Are politically and economically free states less conflict prone than states that are not free? (national-level analysis)

2. Are politically and economically free states less likely to fight one another than those that are politically nonfree? Are politically free states less likely to initiate international conflicts in general than those that are nonfree? (dyadic-level analysis)

3. Does the level of conflict in the international system decline as the number of politically free states increases?[26] (system-level analysis)

The authors conclude that previous findings on the correlation between regime type and conflict involvement are "mixed"; however, the results are mixed primarily when considering the first question (national-level analysis) in the above list. Previous research does *not* demonstrate that democracies are *involved* in fewer conflicts than nonfree states.[27] Indeed, research suggests that free states "are neither more conflict prone nor less conflict prone than nonfree polities."[28] However, governments constrained by democratic political and economic structures *are less likely to initiate* violent conflicts than nonfree states.[29] Also, the proportion of disputes that democracies participate in "that escalate to war is significantly lower than that of nondemocratic polities."[30] Therefore, the authors' conclusions are consistent with the democratic peace principle. Although the answer to the first question (are free states more conflict prone?) is mixed, their conclusions with respect to the other questions (are free states less likely to fight each other? are free states less likely to initiate violent conflicts? does the level of conflict decline as the number of free states decreases?) nevertheless strongly and explicitly support the democratic peace principle.

With respect to the three questions addressed by their study, Maoz and Abdolali conclude:

1. There are no relations between regime type and conflict involvement measures when the unit of analysis is the individual polity (i.e., a state characterized by a certain regime type over a given time span); this finding is robust. . . .[31]

   . . .*The proportion of the disputes in which [democratic states] participate that escalate to war is significantly lower than that of nondemocratic polities. . . . Democracies tended to be less likely to get involved in ongoing disputes both on the initiator's side . . . and on the target's side.*[32] [emphasis added]

2. There is a significant relationship between the regime characteristics of a dyad and the probability of conflict involvement of that dyad: *Democracies rarely clash with one another, and never fight one another in war.*[33] [emphasis added]

51

3. Both the proportion of democratic dyads and the proportion of autocratic dyads in the international system significantly affect the number of disputes begun and under way. But *the proportion of democratic dyads in the system has a [significant] negative effect on the number of wars begun and on the proportion of disputes that escalate to war.*[34] [emphasis added]

Interestingly, Maoz and Abdolali also conclude that autocratic-autocratic polity interaction has "a significant negative effect on the number of wars begun."[35] Nevertheless, autocratic polities are not inherently peaceful and are involved in more conflicts than democracies. This comprehensive study unequivocally supports the proposition that democracies are more peaceful, less likely to initiate wars, and do not fight democracies.

In 1994 historian Spencer R. Weart conducted a detailed comparative case study of virtually all significant military confrontations between republics throughout history.[36] Weart concludes that a "striking lack of wars between well-established democracies prevailed not only among modern states but also among earlier regimes commonly described as democracies."[37]

Weart defines military confrontations as "state-supported organized violence across political boundaries,"[38] which is equivalent to the definition of war under modern international law: armed conflict between two or more governments or states.[39] Weart notes that the key dimension of this definition is the level of violence. Some studies have set a cutoff of 1,000 battle deaths to eliminate insignificant skirmishes. Weart concludes, however, that a cutoff as low as 200 battle deaths is enough to exclude such limited clashes.[40]

A standard definition of democracy spanning human history is more difficult. Weart recognizes that democracies have taken various forms throughout history and have not always been inclusive, denying voting rights to immigrants, transient laborers, women, and other groups; however, generally, Weart defines a democracy as a republic in which the body of citizens has decision-making rights.[41] In determining what governments should be included as a democracy in his comparative study of military confrontations, Weart was "generously inclusive" so that he could "severely test generalizations about wars between democracies."[42] He draws the following four conclusions from his study:

1. Well-established democracies have never made war on one another.

2. Well-established oligarchic republics have hardly ever made war on one another. (In an oligarchy, a small group of people or families rule. An oligarchic republic falls somewhere between democracies at one end of the continuum and totalitarian regimes at the other.[43])

3. Oligarchic republics do war with democracies.

4. Peace prevails only between the same kinds of republics, oligarchies, or democracies as the case may be.[44]

Weart thus arrives at two of the same conclusions as Maoz and Abdolali. First, similar republican regime types generally do not war with one another; that is, regimes are generally more peaceful in their relations with other states when based upon the principle that sovereignty resides in the citizenry. Second, in order to predict behavior based upon regime type, the regime must be "well-defined" and not "weakly and ambiguously defined or . . . undergoing transition,"[45] or, as Weart puts it, the regime must be "well-established."[46] Nevertheless, Weart concludes that it "is not some general concordance between two nations that makes for peace, but something directly related to the regime itself."[47] This "something," Weart explains, is a well-established political culture:

> We could thus define a "well-established" regime in the everyday sense: one that has existed long enough to demonstrate a stable, continuous character. . . .
>
> . . . [But the] duration of the regime has no obvious direct connection with war-making; it is presumably a surrogate for something more fundamental. . . .
>
> A well-established republic . . . is a regime where the political culture of the leaders . . . is such that they eschew lawless coercion of their fellow citizens, consistently tolerating dissent and negotiating compromises.[48]

Weart thus concludes that a noncoercive domestic political culture must be well-established in a republic before it can be predicted that such a regime is peaceful.[49] A well-established political culture results in national political leaders acting "toward their foreign counterparts in the same way they act towards rival domestic political leaders."[50] It is not enough for a regime to have constitutional mechanisms and other democratic characteristics if those features are overshadowed by coercion and domination by force. Weart observes the universal validity throughout history of the principle that "republics and only republics have tended to form durable, peaceful leagues."[51]

Bruce Russett, in one of the preeminent treatises on the democratic peace principle, observes that during Kant's lifetime the concept of a world of democratic, peaceful nations was simply a hope or theory without empirical basis; the "strong norm that democracies should not fight each other seems to have developed only toward the end of the nineteenth century."[52] However, the empirical fact that democracies have rarely, if ever, gone to war with each other went largely unnoticed during most of the twentieth century because democracies were a substantial minority in the world and geographically dispersed. As the number of democracies increased in the international community, the empirical fact that peace prevails among democracies became harder to ignore by the 1970s and widely accepted by the end of the 1980s. Russett warns, however, that wide acceptance is not synonymous with universal acceptance, and the concept of peace *among* democracies has become confused with the claim that democracies are in general more peaceful in their interactions with all kinds of states.[53]

Russett defines war as "large-scale institutionally organized lethal violence" between sovereign states that crosses the commonly accepted threshold of 1,000 battle fatalities (an arbitrary but reasonable figure).[54] A modern democracy is "usually identified with a voting franchise for a substantial fraction of citizens, a government brought to power in contested elections, and an executive either popularly elected or responsible to an elected legislature, often also with requirements for civil liberties such as free speech."[55] However, Russett cautions that a "simple dichotomy between democracy and autocracy of course hides" mixed systems that share features of both, and he reminds us that democracy did not mean the same to the ancient Greeks as it does to people in the twenty-first century. He notes that even in the nineteenth century, the United States, which was considered democratic by virtually any standard of the day, deprived women of the right to vote and disenfranchised blacks.[56]

To identify which states are democratic, Russett's study evaluates the degree to which a state meets the evolving definitions of democracy and considers the "minimal stability or longevity" of the political system.[57] In applying these criteria to approximately 71 interstate wars involving a total of nearly 270 participants since 1815, he concludes that it is "impossible to identify unambiguously *any* wars between democratic states."[58] He also observes that most of the "doubtful cases arise within a single year of the establishment of democratic government."[59] Notwithstanding differing definitions of war and democracy, Russett's analysis establishes that the "phenomenon of war between democracies [is] impossible or almost impossible to find."[60]

Russett establishes three main principles in his incisive political analysis:

> *First*, democratically organized political systems in general operate under restraints that make them more peaceful in their relations with other democracies. Democracies are not necessarily peaceful, however, in their relations with other kinds of political systems. *Second*, in the modern international system, democracies are less likely to use lethal violence toward other democracies than toward autocratically governed states or than autocratically governed states are toward each other. Furthermore, there are no clearcut cases of sovereign stable democracies waging war with each other in the modern international system. *Third*, the relationship of relative peace among democracies is importantly a result of some features of democracy, rather than being caused exclusively by economic or geopolitical characteristics correlated with democracy.[61] [emphasis added]

Russett's conclusions are consistent with the others discussed in this chapter and clearly support the democratic peace principle.

The most comprehensive analysis of the peaceful nature of democracies is found in the body of research by Rudolph Rummel, a political scientist nominated for the 1996 Nobel Peace Prize. Rummel defines war as "any military action in which at least 1,000 are killed in battle."[62] Similar to Weart and Russett,

Rummel defines democracy to include regimes with "periodic, competitive elections," so that the powerful can be removed from power and citizens have equal rights regardless of class or status.[63] He uses the term *democracy* to mean specifically a liberal democracy "where those who hold power are elected in competitive elections with a secret ballot and wide franchise (loosely understood as including at least two-thirds of adult males); where there is freedom of speech, religion, and organization; and a constitutional framework of law to which the government is subordinate and that guarantees equal rights."[64] However, Rummel explains that the definition of a democracy for previous centuries has been loosened by researchers to include those states such as the United States in the 1800s and democratic classical Athens that do not meet the contemporary definition of a liberal democracy.[65]

Rummel observes that most of the literature in the international community addresses only the "war version" of the democratic peace principle, that is, the "idea or fact that democracies do not (or virtually never) make war on each other."[66] Indeed his initial work also focused on the "war version"; however, in the 1980s Rummel discovered that "several times more people were killed in democide (genocide and mass murder) by governments than died in war."[67] Subsequently, his work expanded to include the study of violence within states as well as intrastate violence. Rummel's work now validates through theory, evidence, and analysis the "general version" of the democratic peace principle: "democracy is a general cure for political or collective violence of any kind—*it is a method of nonviolence.*"[68]

The entirety of Rummel's research through 1996 is summarized and documented in his 1997 book *Power Kills: Democracy as a Method of Nonviolence*, a powerful justification of the democratic peace principle. His book demonstrates that the realists—those who say foreign and domestic violence is in our blood and has always been and will always be with us—are simply wrong about war, lesser international violence, civil collective violence, genocide, and mass murder.[69] In rebutting the realists, Rummel concludes that "there is one solution to each [situation of violence] and the solution in each case is the same. It is to foster democratic freedom and to democratize coercive power and force. That is, mass killing and mass murder carried out by government is a result of indiscriminate, irresponsible Power at the center."[70] He goes on to say that "democracy is a practical solution to war and all other kinds of collective, that is, political regime, violence."[71]

Rummel posits six propositions supporting his conclusion that democracy is a method of nonviolence:

1. *Interdemocratic Peace Proposition*: Democracies do not make war on and rarely commit lesser violence against each other.

2. *Democracy/Dyadic Violence Proposition*: The more democratic two regimes, the less severe their violence against each other.

3. *Democracy/Foreign Violence Proposition*: The more democratic a regime, the less its foreign violence.

4. *Democracy/Internal Collective Violence Proposition*: The more democratic a regime, the less severe its internal collective violence.

5. *Democracy/Democide Proposition*: The more democratic a regime, the less its democide.

6. *Power Kills*: Nondemocracy is an engine of violence.

Interdemocratic Peace Proposition

To support his first proposition that democracies do not make war (and rarely commit lesser kinds of violence) on other democracies, Rummel reviews all the major twentieth century studies on the democratic peace principle.[72] A 1964 study by criminologist Dean Babst finds "that for 116 major wars of 438 countries from 1789 to 1941, not one war involved democracies on opposite sides."[73] Babst also finds that of "the thirty-three independent nations involved in World War I, ten were democracies and none fought against each other," and of "the fifty-two independent nations participating in World War II, fourteen democracies were on the same side and one, Finland, fought with Germany against the Soviet Union."[74] Babst concludes in his pioneering work that "this study suggests that the existence of independent nations with elective governments greatly increases the chances for the maintenance of peace. What is important is the form of government, not national character. Many nations, such as England and France, fought wars against each other before they acquired freely elected governments, but have not done so since."[75]

J. David Singer and Melvin Small examine the results of all 50 interstate wars among sovereign states between 1816 and 1965 for which there were at least 1,000 total battle dead by analyzing opposing pairs of nations (dyads). Singer and Small find "*no* wars between democracies, except for only two 'marginal exceptions,' which are an ephemeral republican France attacking an ephemeral republican Rome in 1849 and a rightward-drifting Finnish democracy joining Germany to attack Russia (and thus technically putting it at war with the Allied Nations in 1941)."[76] Based on these and other studies, such as the work of Maoz and Abdolali, Weart, and Russett, Rummel concludes that the "findings on the Interdemocratic Peace Proposition are robust, they are solid, they no longer can be denied."[77]

Democracy/Dyadic Violence Proposition

According to the second proposition, the more democratic two regimes are, the less severe their violence will be against each other.[78] To test this proposition, Rummel places nations on a continuum according to three basic types of political regime: democratic, authoritarian, and totalitarian. He observes that democracy-democracy pairs should tend to have no severe violence between them, democracy-authoritarian pairs should tend to have some severe violence, and so forth, with totalitarian-totalitarian pairs having the most severe violence. Rummel concludes that if his proposition is true, "just reforming regimes in the direction of greater civil rights and political liberties will promote less violence."[79] This proposition is an extension of the logic of the interdemocratic peace proposition but was not the subject of direct analysis until proposed by Rummel.

To initially test his proposition, Rummel uses the Freedom House 1976–80 ratings on civil liberties and political rights for each nation. Based on this limited study, Rummel concludes "there is a clear tendency for the violence to increase as the degree of democracy within the dyad decreases."[80] Rummel also reviews the work of other major studies, but since they measure force by a frequency count of wars and not severity of violence or the number of battle dead, these studies do not demonstrate any reliable proof of the democracy/dyadic violence proposition, although they are generally supportive.[81] Rummel, however, compiles data from these studies (1900–80) and adds two operational variables that permit him to test his hypothesis for six dyads.[82] The first variable is the "democraticness" of a dyad, which is the sum of the ratings of each dyad member, with democratic regimes having a value of zero, authoritarian regimes a value of one, and totalitarian regimes a value of two. The second variable is the sum of the number killed in battle for each member. Table 4 presents Rummel's results.

Table 4. Summary of Rummel's data on the democracy/dyadic violence proposition

Type of dyad	Democraticness	Battle dead[a]	Number of regimes[b]
democracy-democracy	0	0	c
democracy-authoritarian	1	567,108	66
democracy-totalitarian	2	940,796[d]	107[d]
authoritarian-authoritarian	2		
authoritarian-totalitarian	3	1,664,220	40
totalitarian-totalitarian	4	2,560,202	11

Adapted from R. J. Rummel, *Power Kills: Democracy as a Method of Nonviolence* (New Brunswick, NJ: Transaction Publishers, 1997), 58.

[a]Total battle dead for all regimes of the given dyad type that fought each other in wars.

[b]Total number of regimes analyzed for the given dyad.

[c]There was no war between any democracies.

[d]The data is combined for democracy-totalitarian and authoritarian-authoritarian dyads because they have the same democraticness factor.

Rummel concludes that his analyses, including the data presented in table 4, "well support" the democracy/dyadic violence proposition, and he observes that the absence of war within the democratic-democratic dyad also supports the interdemocratic peace proposition, which "has been established as a fact of international relations."[83]

Democracy/Foreign Violence Proposition

Rummel contends that the more democratic a regime, the less foreign violence it engages in, thus contradicting the belief among many experts that democracies are neither more nor less likely to make war or commit violence than other types of regimes.[84] According to Rummel, a careful reading of the relevant studies shows that this belief "does not well reflect the evidence" and instead reveals "that democracies are in fact the most pacific of regimes."[85] The fallacy of these studies is that they use the frequency of a democracy's involvement in war as an indicator of its propensity to engage in war. If the crucial variable is shifted to emphasize the severity of violence, then it can be empirically proved that democracies are less violent than nondemocracies.[86]

Democracy/Internal Collective Violence Proposition

Rummel shifts his analysis from foreign violence to internal collective violence in support of the proposition that the more democratic a regime, the less severe its collective internal violence.[87] Rummel is the first to correlate the form of government with the level of internal collective violence between a political regime and some opposing armed group.[88] Rummel analyzes 18 directly relevant quantitative studies—all conducted for purposes other than analysis of the democratic peace principle—that correlate or cross-tabulate measures of democracy with domestic violence. Of these, five studies strongly support the principle that democracy sharply reduces the severity of domestic collective violence, genocide, and mass murder by governments; 12 are supportive; and only one is negative, but not strongly so.[89]

Rummel also collects data on all incidents of internal conflict and violence for all nations from 1976 to 1980. Using the Freedom House ratings of civil liberties and political rights, he finds that the more democratic a regime, the lower its peak level of internal violence; Rummel calls his finding "robust and noncontroversial."[90] Rummel considers this principle an "even more important fact" about democracy and violence than the principle that democracies reduce interstate violence and concludes that "democracy is inversely related to the intensity of collective internal violence, such as revolutions, bloody coups d'etats, political assassinations, antigovernment terrorist bombings, guerrilla warfare, insurgencies, civil wars, mutinies, and rebellions."[91]

Democracy/Democide Proposition

Rummel continues his analysis of internal violence in his discussion of the democracy/democide proposition.[92] In contrast to the collective violence proposition, which addresses conflict between the government and armed groups, the democracy/democide proposition asserts that the more democratic a government, the less it commits democide, defined as genocide and mass murder by a regime.[93] After collecting data from a wide range of sources, Rummel conservatively estimates that governments murdered over 169 million people from 1900 to 1987. Higher estimates for specific regimes could push this figure up to nearly 341 million.[94] The statistics are overwhelming: "fifteen megamurderers alone have murdered over 151,000,000 people, *almost four times the almost 38,500,000 war dead for all this century's international and civil wars up to 1987.*"[95] Eight of the most totalitarian of these regimes account for nearly 128 million murders or 84 percent of the democide in the twentieth century.[96] Table 5 summarizes Rummel's data.

Table 5. Summary of Rummel's data on the democracy/democide proposition

Regimes	Years	Total democide
Megamurderers:	1900–87	151,491,000
USSR	1917–87	61,911,000
China (People's Republic)	1949–87	35,236,000
Germany	1933–45	20,946,000
China (Kuomintang)	1928–49	10,075,000
Japan	1936–45	5,964,000
China (Mao Soviets)	1923–49	3,466,000
Cambodia	1975–79	2,035,000
Turkey	1909–18	1,883,000
Vietnam	1945–87	1,670,000
North Korea	1948–87	1,663,000
Poland	1945–48	1,585,000
Pakistan	1958–87	1,503,000
Mexico	1900–20	1,417,000
Yugoslavia (Tito)	1944–87	1,072,000
Russia	1900–17	1,066,000
Lesser murderers	1900–87	17,707,000
World total	1900–87	169,199,000

Adapted from R. J. Rummel, *Power Kills: Democracy as a Method of Nonviolence* (New Brunswick, NJ: Transaction Publishers, 1997).

After studying over 200 regimes guilty of democide during the period 1900–87, Rummel concludes:

> The more totalitarian and less democratic a regime, the more its democide. A political regime's domestic democide in general and its genocide in particular can be predicted to the degree that Power is indiscriminate and irresponsible. Power is the means through which a regime can accomplish its goals or whims. When a regime's power is magnified through its forceful intervention in all aspects of society, including its control over religion, the economy, and even the family, then when conjoined with an absolutist ideology or religion, mass killing may appear to its rulers a practical and justified means of achieving their ends. . . . On the other hand, democratic elites generally lack the power to, and democratic culture anyway opposes, the outright extermination of people or social groups for whatever reason.[97]

Rummel also concludes that a nation's social diversity; ethnic, religious, racial, linguistic, or national divisions; the relative size of its minorities; cultural nature; and level of education or economic development are uncorrelated with and do not predict foreign or domestic democide.[98] The simple bottom line is that the "degree of a regime's power along a democratic to totalitarian scale is a direct underlying structural cause of domestic democide, including genocide."[99]

Power Kills

Rummel's first five propositions support his final one: power kills; that is, nondemocracy is an engine of violence.[100] His sixth proposition can be viewed as the deductive conclusion of the previous five. Rummel describes how behaviors between individuals and groups in a democratic regime "act to check and balance, to cross-cut and cross-pressure . . . and thus to severely limit the intensity of collective violence, and its spread across society."[101] In contrast, authoritarian and totalitarian regimes use violence to insure obedience and rule "by raw coercion and force; pervasive fear assures obedience."[102] Rummel presents overwhelming evidence in support of the principle that democracy is a method of nonviolence and concludes his book simply and eloquently with two words: "Power kills."[103]

Rummel's democratic peace clock reflects the world's movement toward universal peace. As democracy spreads, we come closer to eliminating war, collective violence, and democide. A 1 percent increase in the population living under democratic governance advances the clock 58.2 seconds. It was midnight, the darkest time of night, in the year 1900, when 0 percent of the world population lived under democratic governance. In 1950, when 31 percent of the world's population was under democratic governance, it was 3:43 a.m. In 2000, 58.2 percent of the world's population was under democratic governance, and the peace clock said 6:59 a.m. In 2006, Rummel advanced the clock to 8:15 a.m.—less than four hours to high noon, "when the sun shines full on the world, and when the entire world will be democratic, and therefore, the world will be at peace."[104]

Explanations for the Democratic Peace Principle

Democracy and free markets work, and the world knows it. And there is no finer example of this than America and her allies, who together comprise the strongest economies in the world, helping to reshape the entire world by [being] willing to trade openly and encourage others to do likewise. And there should be no question in any world leader's mind that the first and most essential ingredient for success in this 21st century is a free people and a government that derives its right to govern from the consent of such people.

—Secretary of State Colin L. Powell
Senate Confirmation Hearing
17 January 2001

Contemporary studies have demonstrated that democracies are inherently more peaceful than nondemocracies, which raises the question of *why* democracies are less prone to violence. Kant concludes in *Perpetual Peace* that the natural state of people living side by side is one of war and peace must therefore be established. A republican constitution can result in peace because the consent of the citizens is required to declare war.[105] Doyle observes that mutual respect among constitutionally secure liberal democracies that yields cooperative foundations for relations is one of the reasons why democracies do not go to war

63

with democracies, and heuristic evidence suggests a "significant predisposition against warfare between liberal states."[106]

Maoz and Abdolali rely heavily on Rummel's earlier works to provide theoretical underpinnings for their own study. They agree with Rummel that "the constraints imposed by political and economic structures on elites' expectations and behavior implies that politically free states should be less likely to *initiate* violent conflicts than nonfree states."[107] Their rationale is that open economies restrain conflicts between nations because, as Rummel suggests, open economies "tend to encourage exchange, rather than coercive and violent solutions."[108] Maoz and Abdolali also extend this logic to conclude that "politically free states will not initiate low-level conflicts that have a high potential to escalate into large-scale conflagrations, and in general, are less likely to initiate high-hostility conflicts."[109]

Weart observes that the democratic peace principle can be explained, in principle, by psychological, cultural, social, economic, or structural forces; however, he concludes that recent research casts doubt on most of these forces.[110] He believes the research shows that the democratic peace principle holds true because of the "bedrock characteristics of democracy itself: the formal structural mechanisms such as voting, and the political culture."[111] Other scholars using statistical analysis have concluded that the "inhibition against warfare is related to either constitutional structures or political culture."[112] Similarly, Weart and those scholars who have conducted comparative historical case studies have also concluded that democracies do not fight each other because domestically they have a shared republican political culture that channels direct pressure from the public, as well as bureaucratic and constitutional structures and social and economic systems which inhibit initiating war.[113]

Former Swedish deputy prime minister Per Ahlmark also echoes Rummel and others in his 1999 speech to the European Parliament:

> We must not deceive ourselves by suspecting that [the democratic peace principle] is a statistical error or just a lucky coincidence. Democratic leaders' freedom of action is limited by their citizens' resistance to bearing the burdens and accepting the deaths of war. Several of the leading scholars explain the peace between democracies by referring to the cross pressures in free societies (the checks and balances, and so on) or

to their political culture (debates, demonstrations, negotiations, compromises, tolerance, etc.). In a democracy it is impossible, or at least extremely difficult, to get enough support from the people to initiate a military confrontation with another democracy. Such people know each other too well. They trust each other too much. For democratic governments it is usually too easy and natural to talk and negotiate with one another—it would look and feel ridiculous or totally irresponsible to start shooting at a nation which is governed in the same way as your own country.[114]

Political scientist Charles Lipson believes that the war version of the democratic peace principle (democracies do not fight wars with each other) is "one of the most powerful findings in international politics and one of the most thoroughly tested. . . . [It is] now one of the best-established regularities in international politics, perhaps the best-established."[115] In *Reliable Partners: How Democracies Have Made a Separate Peace*, Lipson discusses three basic explanations advanced to date to explain the democratic peace principle:

1. Citizens' reluctance to bear the costs of war.

2. Shared values among democracies.

3. Unique domestic institutions, which restrain elected leaders.

According to the cost explanation, "citizens of a republic are less war-prone because they must bear the burdens themselves and can vote to avoid them. Monarchs and dictators, by contrast, can shift the costs of war onto their subjects, who have no voice in the decision." According to the normative explanation, "liberal democracies share certain basic values, grounded in their domestic political life. They settle disputes through neutral courts rather than through blunt force or status differences." Lipson says that the "institutional explanation underscores the constraints facing democratic policymakers. They face constitutional limits, must share power with other elected leaders, and can remain in office only by winning periodic elections, openly contested."[116]

Lipson, however, believes that these three explanations are incomplete because they focus on the individual properties of a democracy. Instead, Lipson argues, the "democratic peace is fundamentally an interactive phenomenon. It is not about why one democracy or another is peaceful. It is about why two democracies so seldom fight each other."[117] He explains the democratic peace principle by concluding that "because democracies have unique 'contracting advantages,' they can usually avert or settle conflicts with each other by reliable, forward-looking agreements that minimize the dead-weight costs of direct military engagement. To do that, states must be confident their partners will live up to their promises or, if they do not, that they can protect themselves from the risks."[118] These contracting advantages allow "democratic states to build stable, peaceful relations, based on multiple self-enforcing bargains."[119] Lipson's explanation is very helpful in that it further refines the contractual freedom inherent in the interplay between two democratic nations, but it does not add an additional explanation or rationale for the democratic peace principle. It simply helps us understand the democratic peace principle better.

Rummel recognizes Kant's explanation that the public will restrains decision makers from making war as probably the oldest and most persuasive.[120] He adopts it as the first of his three levels of explanation for the democratic peace principle:

- First-level explanation: the people's will

- Second-level explanation: cross-pressures, exchange culture, and in-group perception

- Third-level explanation, part 1: social field and freedom

- Third-level explanation, part 2: antifield and power

As Rummel reminds us, the democratic peace principle does not simply represent a dichotomous relationship between peaceful democracies and violent nondemocracies. Rather, there is a continuum of political regimes with totalitarian regimes at the most violent extreme, democratic regimes at the most peaceful, and authoritarian regimes in the middle.[121] An understanding of these three regime types and their respective power structures is central to understanding Rummel's three levels of explanation for the democratic peace principle.

Rummel defines three basic power structures in societies: coercive, authoritative, and bargaining. These three power structures, or some mix of them, regulate social relations between a government and its people. Coercive societies are commanded at gunpoint by totalitarian regimes who "use . . . threats of pain, negative deprivation, or some other negative outcome to get what is wanted."[122] These regimes are usually military dictatorships.[123] However, some totalitarian systems have some form of regular elections with universal franchise, but the elections offer no real competition for significant offices, so the ruling party gets over 95 percent of the vote. These sham elections are used to "periodically showcase and institutionally legitimize the leadership."[124] No law is "above the regime and that which is not permitted the citizen is forbidden."[125] The most egregious examples of twentieth-century totalitarian governments include those of Joseph Stalin (USSR), Mao Tse-tung (China), Pol Pot (Cambodia), Kim Il Sung (North Korea), and Enver Hoxha (Albania).[126]

In contrast, authoritative societies are "structured traditionally, according to customary rules and laws." Coercion exists, especially over cultural and religious norms, but the regime is seen as "legitimate, with a right to rule."[127] An authoritarian regime rules according to traditions and customs, such as power passing to the king's oldest son when the king dies.[128] Most authoritarian regimes usually have "no political parties, no elections, and no legislatures with meaningful power."[129] Almost all major national societies were authoritarian two centuries ago, ruled by monarchies or dynasties.[130] Examples of twentieth-century authoritarian governments include Nepal, Bhutan, Saudi Arabia, Kuwait, Bahrain, Qatar, and Oman.

Fascist regimes such as those of Juan Peron (Argentina), Francisco Franco (Spain), and Benito Mussolini (Italy) fall somewhere between totalitarian and authoritative forms of government on Rummel's continuum, and Adolf Hitler's form of fascism approaches a totalitarian form of government.[131] Other regimes that fall somewhere between totalitarian and authoritative forms of governments on Rummel's continuum include those of Idi Amin (Uganda), Augusto Pinochet (Chile), Muammar al-Qaddafi (Libya), and Park Chung Hee (South Korea).[132]

The bargaining power structure is a democracy where most relations between the regime and the society are based on exchange. Democracies are characterized by an economic free market as well as freedom of speech and the press, and people are free to oppose the regime and compete for power. Whereas totalitarian regimes are typically Communist and promise utopia and authoritarian regimes are typically monarchial and try to preserve traditions, democracies are libertarian. They are oriented to the present and try to respond to contemporary national problems and public demands.[133] Examples of twentieth-century democracies include Sweden, Switzerland, Belgium, Great Britain, Canada, and the United States. Oligarchic republics fall between democracies at one end of the continuum and totalitarian regimes at the other.[134]

Rummel's explanations for the democratic peace principle are rooted in the bargaining power structure that characterizes democracies. Rummel's first-level explanation, based upon the people's will, "has to do with the representative nature of democracies and the costs of violence."[135] In a society that embraces competitive and periodic elections, a wide franchise, a secret ballot, and freedom of speech, the popular will serves as a constraint that inhibits leaders' decisions to pursue violence because it is the people who bear the cost of violence, and it is the "natural desire of people to avoid the loss of their property, their loved ones, and their own lives."[136] However, Rummel finds that this explanation is "not sufficiently general to explain why democracy should be a method of nonviolence," nor does it explain why an oligarchic republic "should not make war on those of its own kind."[137]

Rummel's second-level explanation of cross-pressures, exchange culture, and in-group perception is based upon how democratic institutions and culture influence decision makers.[138] Generally, "democracy creates a political culture in which opposing groups and representatives must constantly make compromises. . . . [Where] by virtue of their institutions democratic people must, to maintain democracy, negotiate and compromise rather than fight, this becomes part of the cultural heritage."[139] Democracy creates an environment in which "people come to naturally behave, perceive, and expect" negotiation and compromise rather than violence. This behavior affects both domestic and international interactions of democratic peoples, thus creating a more peaceful environment within and between democracies.[140] According to Rummel, the second-level explanation also explains the lack of wars between oligarchic republics because their shared cultural and democratic norms create an expectation of reciprocal conciliatory behavior.[141]

There are many internal pressures and tensions that help keep democracies nonviolent. The social, economic, and political diversity of a democratic society, for example, acts to restrain and isolate violence. Other important factors in keeping democracies nonviolent include the public will speaking at election time, constraints such as institutional checks and balances within government, and the presence of special-interest groups that lobby for or against policies and laws. All of these domestic pressures are magnified when democratic states face each other in a possible dispute, and when these domestic pressures are combined with shared commercial and other societal exchange interests, they create powerful cultural, societal, and institutional expectations and pressures that push democratic governments toward a peaceful resolution.[142]

Rummel describes his third-level explanation as "the most encompassing and powerful explanation of why democracy is a method of nonviolence."[143] This two-part explanation contrasts how interactions among individuals in a free society create a peaceful social field (part 1) and interactions among individuals in an unfree society create violence-prone social antifields (part 2). Part 1 of Rummel's third-level explanation focuses on the importance of the individual in any explanation of democracy's effect on violence:[144]

> By social field I mean all the spontaneous social relations [of individuals] comprising a society (examples of societies are families, social and work groups, nations, international organizations, and international relations) and the underlying individual mentalities that gives [sic] them significance and importance. If we wish to be technical about this field we can conceive and indeed measure its dimensions in terms of the distinguishing psychological, cultural, and social characteristics of individuals in that society and the diverse behaviors they manifest.[145]

The concept of the social field shifts the focus away from direct cause-and-effect analysis of any single or multiple social, economic, or political characteristics. In analyzing a social field, the focus is instead on a "medium in which forces of some sort operate and [in] which forces continuously vary depending on the region of the field," allowing an observer to understand violence by considering the totality of the variables and how the effect of the variables is greater than simply the sum of their respective effects.[146]

Rummel explains how interactions within the social field take place in a free society:

> The [social] field is produced by individuals (including individuals acting in some authoritative capacity on behalf of groups) cooperating or conflicting according to *their* meanings, values, and norms. What gives specificity to these—and, thus, focus to the forces involved—is the *perceptions, expectations, disposition, capabilities, interests,* and *wills* of these individuals. *The field is thus a gestalt of a spontaneous society, one in which people are largely free to act as they see fit or wish. . . .*
>
> . . . [Within] such an exchange society, that is a social field, individuals and groups freely learn about and adjust to each other's interests, and expectations are developed that evolve and accrue to the society as a whole. . . . As a result *the social field is criss-crossed and cross-cut by the natural product of individuals acting spontaneously.* This is a great multitude of different corporations, partnerships, family businesses, churches, schools, unions, institutes, parties, leagues, clubs and other associations, institutions, and small groups. All are organized to satisfy or further the particular shared interests of individuals. . . . No one group wholly dominates this free society.[147]

The central conclusion of social field analysis is that the more freedom individuals have to pursue their own interests, the more peace and nonviolence will result.[148] This is true for a social field within a single nation, between two nations, and within the international community and applies equally to oligarchic republics.[149]

However, the dynamics within a social field are never static because a complete equilibrium of power among individuals does not always exist. Rummel uses the term *conflict helix* to describe the process of individuals seeking an equilibrium by adjustment and learning to find a simultaneous solution to their differing interests: "behavior between two people, groups, or regimes, cycles upward in mutual learning and successive adjustment, each cycle involving deeper cooperation and milder conflict, thus metaphorically creating the shape of a helix."[150] Rummel also notes that a "change in the power equations underlying a social relationship," a "conflict that serves to readjust expectations," or fundamental changes in relationships that alter "the process of adjustment itself" can also affect the peaceful equilibrium of a social field.[151]

In contrast, when governmental structures become less democratic and more authoritative or totalitarian, the freedom of individuals to pursue their own interests declines, and the social field of a society migrates toward a social antifield. A social antifield, the opposite of a social field, exists when a social field created by individual freedom has been "largely replaced by an organization of society built and structured by government."[152] A social antifield begins when an organization or government tries to "impose on a society some common goal or task, no matter what it may be."[153]

In part 2 of his third-level explanation (antifield and power), Rummel describes the Khmer Rouge, the notorious Cambodian ruling party from 1975 to 1979, as the strongest kind of social antifield. Under the leadership of Pol Pot, the Khmer Rouge wanted to create a true Communist society and eradicate the "mental and spiritual pollution" of capitalism.[154] During the pursuit of "communist nirvana," close to two million Cambodians, or nearly one-third of the population, were murdered by the Khmer Rouge or died of disease and starvation.[155]

In a social antifield such as the Khmer Rouge's Cambodia, the conflict helix collapses domestically, and international relations are reduced to the interaction between heads of state.[156] Rummel describes the conversion of a social field into an antifield:

> As social fields are converted into antifields a spontaneous society is turned into an organization. There is then a strict hierarchy of power, members are clearly divided into those who command and those who must obey, and coercion and force are the glue holding the organization together. By the very nature of this antifield, violence, democide, and war is [sic] its most likely outcome. Such is theory. The evidence supports this.[157]

Rummel's three-level explanation for the democratic peace principle thus shows how the social and political cultures of democracies promote nonviolence, while the coercive nature of nondemocracies makes violent conflicts more likely. He summarizes his explanation by reaffirming the demonstrable link between democracy and the absence of war:

> In sum, theoretical and empirical research establishes that democratic civil liberties and political rights promote nonviolence and is [sic] a path to a warless world. The clearest evidence of this is that there has never been a war between well-established democracies, while numer-

ous wars have occurred between all other political systems; and that of the near 170 million people that governments have murdered in our century, near 99 percent were killed by nondemocracies, and especially totalitarian ones.[158]

However, Rummel's most powerfully concise explanation of why democracies are a method of nonviolence is embedded in the two-word title of his text—power kills.

Challenges and Alternate Rationales

Wide recognition is not, however, synonymous with universal acceptance. It [the relative rarity of violent conflict between democracies] became confused with a claim that democracies are in general, in dealing with all kinds of states, more peaceful than are authoritarian or other nondemocratically constituted states.

—Bruce Russett
Grasping the Democratic Peace:
Principles for a Post-Cold War World

After almost a decade of research, specifically searching for data or studies that would contradict or undercut the democratic peace principle, I have yet to find any meaningful challenge to Rummel's six primary propositions that conclude democracy is a method of nonviolence. Some scholars have raised questions and challenges to the democratic peace principle, but no one has found any meaningful exception to the principle, such as a democracy dyad at war. When Per Ahlmark declared to the liberal democrats of the European Parliament that democracies do not fight democracies, he recognized that "some scholars have written articles (or chapters of books) claiming that there are such exceptions. But if you study those cases in detail you find either that the conflict is not an inter-state war but some sort of civil war; or that at least one of the participants is not a democracy; or that the number of people killed is very or fairly low, which means it is not a 'war' according to this definition [more than 1000 casualties]."[159]

Political scientist James Lee Ray conducted a detailed analysis of all consistently or prominently mentioned exceptions to the democratic peace principle. Of the 19 exceptions he studied, "only the American Civil War, the Spanish-American War, the Boer War, and the Turkish-Cypriot War come sufficiently close to being international wars between democratic states to require extended discussion."[160] However, even in these four examples, both parties in each dyad were not sufficiently close to being a liberal democracy to create an exception to the democratic peace principle.[161]

Some studies which have criticized the research methodologies used to prove the democratic peace principle nevertheless support the principle that democracies are less likely to fight with other democracies. For example, Nathaniel Beck, Jonathan N. Katz, and Richard Tucker have criticized the ways in which some studies on militarized conflict have handled the analysis of time. Nevertheless, when the authors apply their own data-analysis methods, they conclude that "democracy clearly inhibits conflict."[162]

Tucker and William Thompson evaluate two attacks on the democratic peace principle and conclude that the arguments do not hold up to scrutiny.[163] The first of these attacks, by Henry Farber and Joanne Gowa, argues that "for democratic dyads, the absence of war and the low probability of becoming involved in serious disputes are restricted to the post–World War II era and might be artifacts of the cold war."[164] The other, by Mansfield and Snyder, argues that "democracies eventually may become more peaceful but that, in their very early years, they are unusually prone to war involvement."[165]

Farber and Gowa believe that the explanations for the democratic peace principle are weak, and their study "retest[s] the central hypothesis relating regime type and war/militarized disputes."[166] They discover that findings supporting the democratic peace principle "are not consistent over time" and develop an alternative explanation "predicated on common interests, for conflictual behavior that has a different effect before World War I and after World War II."[167] If accurate, their conclusion would mean that democratization does not necessarily lead to a more peaceful world, but that common interests between states do lead to a more peaceful world.[168]

Mansfield and Snyder contend that spreading democracy is naive because it fails to take into account the short- to medium-term costs and risks since regime transition is unstable and may create an environment for war. They agree, however, that "well-established democracies (and stable autocracies) are less likely to fight within dyads consisting of similar type states."[169] They also conclude that in the "long run, the enlargement of the zone of stable democracy will probably enhance prospects for peace."[170]

Tucker and Thompson acknowledge that these criticisms of the democratic peace principle "certainly are strong, just as their empirical evidence seems compelling."[171] They conclude, however, that "neither the arguments nor the evidence holds up well to close scrutiny," and even though both studies help us to better understand the democratic peace principle, neither study "can undermine the premises that have served as a foundation for pursuing a better understanding of the democratic peace phenomenon."[172] However, Tucker and Thompson agree with the contention that regime transition creates an unstable environment in which war may occur.[173] Others also recognize the danger of a democracy in transition. For example, Doyle concludes that liberal states are predisposed not to go to war with each other, but exceptions exist when one or both of the parties in a conflict are in transition and the "pacifying effects of liberalism" are not yet deeply ingrained.[174]

In his review of Weart's *Never at War: Why Democracies Will not Fight One Another*, Stephen M. Walt claims that the evidence for the democratic peace principle is "ambiguous and its long-term validity uncertain."[175] Walt summarizes the two main challenges to the democratic peace principle. The first concludes that the "apparent pacifism between democracies may be a statistical artifact: because democracies have been relatively rare throughout history, the absence of wars between them may be due largely to chance."[176] Also the evidence supporting the democratic peace principle depends upon what time period is observed and how borderline cases are interpreted. The second challenge focuses on the causal logic of the democratic peace principle. Walt notes that when democratic states have come close to war, they have held back for "reasons that had more to do with strategic interests than shared political culture."[177] Walt criticizes Weart for selectively choosing which wars to analyze, not paying more attention to plausible alternative explanations, and dismissing a case that does not fit his thesis because one party did not perceive the other to be the right kind of republic.[178] Walt also argues that Weart's analysis cannot take into account what may happen when the entire world contains only one type of government or shared political culture. There is no way to predict, according to Walt, how a government will react when challenged by a similar government.[179]

The weakness of Walt's critique of the democratic peace principle, however, is that he focuses only on the similarity of political cultures as the predominant basis for why democracies do not fight democracies and are inherently nonviolent. He fails to consider key parts of the rationale for the democratic peace principle: the internal checks and balances in a democracy as well as the internal and external cross pressures on a mature democracy. He also fails to recognize the overwhelming statistical data collected in approximately 100 empirical studies during the twentieth century that validate the democratic peace principle. Walt does pose a very interesting hypothetical question: how might a democratic state interact with another democratic state in a world comprised predominantly or entirely of democracies? Russett also observes that a "system composed substantially of democratic states might reflect very different behavior than did the previous one composed predominantly of autocracies."[180] There is no empirical data based on a world that consists predominately or entirely of democracies; however, the nonviolent nature of democracies suggests that such a world would be more peaceful. Despite his pondering, Russett believes that a world of substantially democratic states would mean the end of wars and conquest as well as the reconstruction of the norms and rules of international order.[181]

Christopher Layne is also a critic of the democratic peace principle, which he claims rests on a shaky foundation:

> [Though the] democratic peace theory identifies a correlation between domestic structure and the absence of war between democracies, it fails to establish a causal link. . . . The statistical evidence that democracies do not fight each other seems impressive but in fact, it is inconclusive, because the universe of cases providing empirical support for democratic peace theory is small, and because several important cases of wars between democratic states are not counted for reasons that are not persuasive.[182]

75

Layne's criticism that the universe of cases supporting the democratic peace theory is small would be far more significant if those cases were a subset of the statistical evidence. However, contrary to Layne's conclusion, the principle that democracies do not fight each other is supported by the universe of all relevant conflicts.

Russett identifies five alternative explanations for the democratic peace principle and explains why they do not invalidate the principle:

1. Transnational and international institutions make peace.

2. Distance prevents war.

3. Alliances make peace.

4. Wealth makes peace.

5. Political stability makes peace.

According to the first alternative explanation, transnational and international institutions make peace by binding states through "common ties in a network of institutions crossing national boundaries."[183] Transnationalism, however, cannot be treated analytically or empirically as an independent cause of peace between democracies because it is substantially correlated with the open institutions of democracies. It is the "individual autonomy and pluralism within democratic states [that] foster the emergence of transnational linkages and institutions."[184]

Distance prevents war because historically most wars were fought between neighboring states since the closeness provided a greater capability to wage war and the constant contact facilitated the interaction that created reasons to go to war. Accordingly, since democracies were few and far between before World War II and even for much of the post-1945 period, it is not surprising that democracies did not end up at war with one another. However, the distance argument is weakened as modern contiguous democracies, such as those of the EU and the Western Hemisphere, remain at peace.[185]

Alliances are said to make peace because states choose alliances based on common interests or a common enemy and are thus already peacefully inclined toward each other. Another theory is that alliances are peaceful because of the "active policy of a dominant major power to keep peace within the alliance."[186] Historically though, the Soviet Union and its militarized allies were likely to fight each other, whereas democratic allied states have not been likely to fight each other.

Wealth is said to make peace because (1) the disincentive for politically stable, economically advanced, and rapidly growing countries to fight a war is too great; (2) wealth is a result of trade and investment between countries; and (3) rapidly growing democracies do not have an incentive for conflict between them. Wealth, however, cannot be viewed as an independent cause of peace between democracies because trade, investment, wealth, and growth are all substantially correlated with the open institutions of democracies.[187]

Political stability is said to make peace since countries with "stable and durable political systems will lack incentives to externalize domestic discontent into conflict with foreign countries."[188] Unstable governments have "more to gain from scapegoating and diversion, and are more likely to do so when they confront an adversary that faces substantial domestic political problems."[189] It is important to note, however, that twentieth-century democracies were generally more stable than were non-democracies.[190] Thus political stability also cannot be viewed as an independent cause of peace between democracies because it is substantially correlated to the democratic nature of the governments in question.

Although many scholars accept the premise that democracies do not make war *on each other*, they do not necessarily accept Rummel's proposition that democracies are less likely to make war or commit violence than other types of regimes. Rummel addresses those who say that democratic states are as aggressive and prone to war as other forms of government and argues that a careful examination of the relevant studies and their methodologies "shows that democracies are in fact the most pacific of regimes."[191] For example, some studies which conclude that democracies are as war-prone as other types of regimes fail to emphasize the *severity* of the violence as a crucial variable and instead count *frequency* of war involvement or other violence as a relevant variable.[192]

The Freedom House ratings of all nations on civil and political rights and liberties also strongly confirm Rummel's proposition that the more democratic a regime, the less its foreign violence. When Rummel rated conflicts by their level of violence and compared that data to the Freedom House democracy ratings, he found that the "highest levels of violence significantly increased as the level of freedom (for free, partially free and non-free regimes) decreased."[193]

Thus a careful review of the evidence strongly supports the democratic peace principle. Nondemocracies are more inclined to war and violent conflict; democracies are inherently more peaceful. The expansion of democracy and the concomitant decline of authoritarian and totalitarian regimes are therefore crucial objectives for the creating of lasting peace in the world.

Notes

1. Locke, *Two Treatises*, preface.
2. Ibid., preface and Book I, chapter XI.
3. Ravitch and Thernstrom, *The Democracy Reader*, 38.
4. Locke, *Two Treatises*, Book I, para. 106.
5. Ibid., Book II, 323.
6. Ibid., 177.
7. Doyle, "Kant," 225.
8. Ravitch and Thernstrom, *The Democracy Reader*, 41–42.
9. Doyle, "Kant," 225n.
10. Paine, *Rights of Man*, 156–62.
11. Ray, "Does Democracy Cause Peace?" 28.
12. Kant, *Perpetual Peace*, vii–viii.
13. Ibid., 3–9.
14. Kant, *Perpetual Peace*, 10.
15. Ibid., 10–23.
16. Ibid., 58.
17. Hamilton, Madison, and Jay, *Federalist Papers*, No. 6, 56.
18. Ibid., 56–59.
19. Per Ahlmark, former deputy prime minister of Sweden and co-chair of UN Watch, speech, 8 April 1999.
20. Ibid.
21. Maoz and Abdolali, "Regime Types," 33.
22. Ibid., 4.
23. Ibid., 10.
24. Ibid., 4–10.
25. Ibid., 8.
26. Ibid., 4.
27. Ibid., 4, 6, 8–20.
28. Ibid., 20.

29. Ibid., 6–8, 18.
30. Ibid., 18.
31. Ibid., 3.
32. Ibid., 18.
33. Ibid., 3.
34. Ibid., 3, 31.
35. Ibid., 31.
36. Weart, "Peace among Democratic and Oligarchic Republics," 299–316.
37. Ibid., 299, 302, 311–12.
38. Ibid., 301.
39. McDougal and Feliciano, *Law and Minimum World Public Order*, 97–98.
40. Weart, "Peace among Democratic and Oligarchic Republics," 301.
41. Ibid., 301–2.
42. Ibid., 302.
43. Rummel, *Power Kills*, 122.
44. Ibid., 302–3.
45. Maoz and Abdolali, "Regime Types," 31.
46. Weart, "Peace among Democratic and Oligarchic Republics," 304.
47. Ibid., 304.
48. Ibid., 305–6.
49. Ibid.
50. Ibid., 300.
51. Ibid., 305–9, 311.
52. Russett, *Grasping the Democratic Peace*, 5, 9.
53. Ibid., 9–11.
54. Ibid., 12–14.
55. Ibid., 14.
56. Ibid., 15.
57. Ibid., 15–16.
58. Ibid., 16.
59. Ibid.
60. Ibid., 20.
61. Ibid., 11.
62. Rummel, *Power Kills*, 10.
63. Rummel, "What Is the Democratic Peace?"
64. Rummel, *Power Kills*, 11.
65. Ibid., 12.
66. Rummel, "What Is the Democratic Peace?"
67. Rummel, *Power Kills*, ix.
68. Rummel, "What is the Democratic Peace?"
69. Rummel, *Power Kills*, 3.
70. Ibid.
71. Ibid., 6.
72. Ibid., 25–49.
73. Ibid., 26.
74. Ibid.
75. Quoted in ibid., 27.

76. Ibid., 28.
77. Ibid., 44.
78. Ibid., 51–61.
79. Ibid., 52.
80. Ibid.
81. Ibid., 53–57.
82. Ibid.
83. Ibid., 59.
84. Ibid., 63–83.
85. Ibid., 64.
86. Ibid., 64–80.
87. Ibid., 85–89.
88. Ibid., 85, 91.
89. Ibid., 85.
90. Ibid., 86–87.
91. Ibid., 85.
92. Ibid., 91–98.
93. Ibid., 91.
94. Ibid., 92.
95. Ibid.
96. Ibid.
97. Ibid., 93.
98. Ibid., 95–97.
99. Ibid., 97.
100. Ibid., 203–11.
101. Ibid., 203.
102. Ibid.
103. Ibid., 210.
104. Rummel, "Democratic Peace Clock."
105. Kant, *Perpetual Peace*, 10, 12–13.
106. Doyle, "Kant," 213.
107. Maoz and Abdolali, "Regime Types," 6.
108. Quoted in ibid.
109. Maoz and Abdolali, "Regime Types," 7.
110. Weart, "Peace among Democratic and Oligarchic Republics," 299.
111. Ibid.
112. Ibid., 300.
113. Ibid., 311–12.
114. Ahlmark, speech, 8 April 1999.
115. Lipson, *Reliable Partners*, 1.
116. Ibid., 2–4.
117. Ibid., 4.
118. Ibid.
119. Ibid., 1.
120. Rummel, *Power Kills*, 6.
121. Ibid., 117.
122. Ibid., 118.

123. Ibid., 204.
124. Ibid., 124.
125. Ibid., 118.
126. Ibid., 118–19.
127. Ibid., 119.
128. Ibid., 204.
129. Ibid., 124.
130. Ibid., 119.
131. Ibid., 121.
132. Ibid., 205–6.
133. Ibid., 120–21.
134. Ibid., 122.
135. Ibid., 129.
136. Ibid., 131, 149.
137. Ibid., 134.
138. Ibid., 6–7.
139. Ibid., 138.
140. Ibid., 138–39.
141. Ibid., 140.
142. Ibid., 143–50.
143. Ibid., 153.
144. Ibid., 11.
145. Ibid., 157.
146. Ibid., 159.
147. Ibid., 160–61.
148. Ibid., 168–69, 184.
149. Ibid., 168–83.
150. Ibid., 170, 189n43.
151. Ibid., 173.
152. Ibid., 157, 162–63.
153. Ibid., 194.
154. Ibid., 196.
155. Ibid., 197.
156. Ibid., 199.
157. Ibid., 200–201.
158. Ibid., 114.
159. Ahlmark, speech, 8 April 1999.
160. Ray, "Wars between Democracies," 269.
161. Ibid.
162. Beck, Katz, and Tucker, "Taking Time Seriously," 1284.
163. Thompson and Tucker, "A Tale of Two Democratic Peace Critiques," 428.
164. Ibid., 429.
165. Ibid.
166. Ibid.
167. Ibid.
168. Ibid., 430.
169. Ibid., 440.

170. Mansfield and Snyder, "Democratization and War," 97.
171. Thompson and Tucker, "A Tale of Two Democratic Peace Critiques," 451.
172. Ibid.
173. Ibid.
174. Doyle, "Kant," 213n7.
175. Walt, "Never Say Never," 146.
176. Ibid., 148.
177. Ibid.
178. Ibid., 148–49.
179. Ibid., 150.
180. Russett, *Grasping the Democratic Peace*, 138.
181. Ibid.
182. Layne, "Kant or Cant," 38–39.
183. Russett, *Grasping the Democratic Peace*, 25.
184. Ibid., 26.
185. Ibid., 26–27.
186. Ibid., 27.
187. Ibid., 28.
188. Ibid., 29.
189. Ibid.
190. Ibid.
191. Rummel, "Democracies ARE Less Warlike," 457–58.
192. Ibid., 459.
193. Ibid.

Chapter 4

War Avoidance through
Incentives and Deterrence

*As Helen was to the Trojans, so has that man been to
this [Roman] republic—the cause of war, the cause of
mischief, the cause of ruin.*

—Cicero
The Second Oration against
Mark Antony, 44 BC

In his four-term presidency (1933–45), Franklin D. Roosevelt
witnessed the domestic and international ravages of economic
depression as well as the devastation of a great world war,
which clearly confirmed for him the value of economic and human freedom, the benefits of democracy, and the role of America in maintaining international peace. In a letter of 2 December 1935, President Roosevelt wrote, "I do not know that the
United States can save civilization but at least by our example
we can make people think and give them the opportunity of
saving themselves. The trouble is that the people of Germany,
Italy and Japan are not given the privilege of thinking."[1] The
constriction of human freedom in Germany, Italy, and Japan
created the conditions for the ensuing war. During his annual
address to Congress on 6 January 1941, Roosevelt eloquently
captured his vision for a peaceful world, in which human freedom serves as the foundation of peace and prosperity:

> In the future days, which we seek to make secure, we look forward to
> a world founded upon four essential human freedoms. The first is free-
> dom of speech and expression—everywhere in the world. The second
> is freedom of every person to worship God in his own way everywhere
> in the world. The third is freedom from want, which, translated into
> world terms, means economic understandings which will secure to ev-
> ery nation a healthy peacetime life for its inhabitants—everywhere in
> the world. The fourth is freedom from fear, which, translated into world
> terms, means a world-wide reduction of armaments to such a point
> and in such a thorough fashion that no nation will be in a position to

commit an act of physical aggression against any neighbor—anywhere in the world.[2]

Roosevelt believed that human freedom is the foundation of world peace, and he attributed the cause of World War II, at least in part, to the fear, ignorance, and greed of Nazi Germany and Japan.[3]

There has never been a consensus on a single cause or explanation for war. Consequently, there has never been a consensus on a single approach to avoiding war.[4] Nevertheless, Roosevelt passionately believed that democracy and human freedom throughout the world are the foundation of peace. His words and actions echo the ideas of the political philosophers, such as Locke, Montesquieu, Paine, and Kant, who first articulated and developed the democratic peace principle. More recently, as we have seen, this principle has been validated by empirical studies and the work of historians and political scientists such as Rummel, whose six propositions declare that democracies do not make war on and rarely commit lesser violence against each other; the more democratic two regimes, the less severe their violence against each other; the more democratic a regime, the less its foreign violence; the more democratic a regime, the less severe its internal collective violence; the more democratic a regime, the less its democide; and nondemocracy is an engine of violence.[5] Rummel's overarching conclusion is that democracy is a method of nonviolence, while power kills. Democracies are inherently peaceful because their internal checks and balances prevent the aggressive use of force. In sharp contrast, these internal checks and balances are missing in nondemocracies. The greatest implication of Rummel's work is that "by creating democracies we create zones of peace"; a world of democracies is a world of peace, human freedom, and human development.

However, the world does not consist entirely of democracies and may not for many decades or even centuries, if ever. Accordingly, for the foreseeable future, the democratic peace principle can be only one "piece of the puzzle" to avoid war.[6] So an extraordinarily important question remains: how does the international community avoid war and maintain world peace in a mixed environment of democracies, governments in transition toward democracy but still politically unstable, and nondemocracies with no internal checks and balances to control the aggressive use of force? In short, how does the international community successfully avoid war in the twenty-first century? The solution to the "war puzzle" (what causes war and how can we avoid it?) has thus far eluded humankind, but scholars continue to pursue it. The remainder of this chapter will discuss one persuasive approach to solving the war puzzle: Moore's explanation for the cause of war and his strategies for avoiding it. Moore's incentive theory for war avoidance can be described by a mathematical formula that can be used to test the validity of the theory and ultimately to predict the probability of peace for a given nation.

Moore's Postulate on the Cause of War

The United States Institute of Peace (USIP) is an independent, nonpartisan federal institution established in 1984 to promote peace and reduce violent international conflicts.[7] The USIP educates the public, supports government policy makers, facilitates international dispute resolution, and trains personnel in conflict prevention and resolution. The founding chairman of the USIP board, John Norton Moore, has done extensive research on the cause of war and methods of war avoidance. The culmination of his research is his authoritative 2004 text *Solving the War Puzzle: Beyond the Democratic Peace.*

Moore also initiated one of the first efforts to demonstrate the full range of the correlative values of democracy with respect to human freedom and development. Democracy, in other words, is not valuable solely for its contributions to the prevention of war. Rather it helps to advance many objectives that contribute to human well-being, such as economic development, famine avoidance, and corruption avoidance:[8]

> This evidence of the relationship between government structures and performance on the principal goals of mankind . . . is so compelling that leaders all over the world now pepper their speeches with references to democracy and the rule of law. . . . For all its power, however, the democratic peace proposition is by itself incomplete. In its most common formulations, it focuses only on the correlation between democracy and war, and this in turn fails to capture the real strength of the case for

democracy, the rule of law, and human freedom across virtually all of the most commonly shared goals of mankind.[9]

In *Solving the War Puzzle*, Moore surveys the theories of great thinkers such as Paine and Kant on democracy and the cause of war; scientific and historical comparative studies on the origin of war; research on deterrence theory; and the contemporary empirical work of Singer and Small, Russett, and Rummel. Moore concludes that none of these important studies or empirical findings *by themselves* have "coalesced into a general theory about [the causes of] war."[10] However, when examined conjointly in the context of cognitive psychology, these theories and studies not only identify the cause of war but also reveal how to avoid war; that is, they are all indeed *pieces* of the war puzzle. In his own words, Moore's text "seeks to integrate the pieces of the puzzle now known into a broader and more predictive and workable theory about the causes of war."[11] In his preface, Moore modestly describes *Solving the War Puzzle* as likely an "incremental" contribution to the field that "may not have all of the pieces precisely in their final place";[12] however, this study will validate Moore's theories on the cause of war and war avoidance through analysis and application.

Elsewhere Moore has identified the two key factors that have led to modern wars:

> There is . . . significant evidence that major wars in the twentieth century have resulted in substantial part from a complex, interactive relationship between, on the one hand, a radical regime—typically but not inevitably of a non-democratic, single party, repressive, highly militarized nation—motivated and prepared to use force to achieve its objectives internationally, and, on the other hand, a failure of deterrence from the international system as a whole.[13]

Similarly, in a 1997 article, Moore identifies aggressive, non-democratic regimes combined with the absence of effective deterrence as the cause of war:

> Quite simply, I believe that the missing link that, in synergy with the democratic peace, largely explains major war, is deterrence, or more accurately, the system-wide absence of effective deterrence, in settings of major aggressive attack by non-democratic regimes. That is, major war is a synergy between aggressive attack (typically by a non-democratic regime prepared to undertake high risk aggression—but which does not

expect to lose), and an absence of effective system-wide deterrence that would have deterred a rational actor from the adventure. . . .

> Major wars occur as a synergy between a regime initiating an aggressive attack (typically non-democratic), and an absence of effective system-wide deterrence. If the theory is correct, one would not expect a major war if *either* factor is absent.[14]

This theory on the cause of war is the result of years of scholarly studies in which Moore validates the work of political scientists such as Rummel, developer of the democratic peace principle, and historians such as Kagan, who has concluded that war is caused during a competition for power by a failure of states to take appropriate actions to preserve the peace, that is, an absence or failure of deterrence.[15] Moore concludes, however, that while both of these approaches—the democratic peace principle and deterrence—are powerful correlates of the occurrence and nonoccurrence of war, neither, when taken alone, fully defines or explains the cause of war.[16] When taken in the aggregate, these two approaches do indeed define and explain the cause of war, according to Moore. Moore thus postulates that the cause of major international armed conflict is the synergy between the existence of a potentially aggressive nondemocratic (totalitarian) regime and the absence of effective systemwide deterrence.[17]

Thus the two core components of Moore's postulate on the cause of war are the democratic peace principle and effective systemwide deterrence. In his analysis of the democratic peace principle, Moore uses the accepted standard threshold of at least 1,000 battle-related casualties to define major international war, recognizing, however, that a standard of at least 2,000 likely yields equally robust findings.[18] International conflicts are between two or more sovereign nations; the category "does not include civil wars or colonial wars or those between a nation and a less than sovereign political entity."[19] He defines a liberal democracy as "a government of limited powers, operating under the rule of law in some meaningful system of checks and balances, which protects fundamental political, economic, and religious freedoms and in which minority rights are protected even from a majority."[20]

To explain the "principal *internal* mechanism responsible for the democratic peace" principle, Moore applies the theory of government failure, also known as public choice theory, which "posits that government decision makers will generally act rationally in pursuit of their interests, like actors elsewhere, and that the government setting, as with markets, provides mechanisms by which elites and special interest groups may be able to externalize costs on others."[21] In a democracy, internal checks and balances restrict the ability of leaders to externalize costs onto others. Nondemocracies, on the other hand, have no rule of law to act as a meaningful check on their national leaders, permitting those leaders to externalize costs on others and make decisions which benefit them personally:[22]

> Saddam Hussein, deciding on action against the State of Kuwait, is in a setting where he will personally reap the benefits of a successful takeover of Kuwaiti oil, while he is able to externalize the risks of the conflict onto draftees, many of whom are from groups in Iraq . . . who oppose him. He will stay in power win or lose, and the benefits of a win would inure to him directly, while the costs would be significant but largely borne by others. Notice that in totalitarian systems the incentive structures for high risk endeavors such as war operate on *both* the cost and benefit sides of the equation. That is, Saddam will personally reap the tangible rewards of success *and* he will be able to largely externalize the costs of failure on others, even his enemies.[23]

Moore notes that war, along with "terrorism, democide, famine, poverty, environmental degradation, corruption, narcotics trafficking, infant mortality, and refugees," is a characteristic failure of nondemocratic governments.[24]

If the theory of government failure holds true, then "one would expect to find that democracies are, in fact, getting into major wars principally, though not exclusively, as a result of aggression by nondemocratic states."[25] To test this theory, Moore conducted a study of major interstate wars since the adoption of the UN Charter in 1945 in which he concludes that "clear aggression by a democratic government in a major interstate war setting has been limited to a single instance out of approximately 29 major wars studied."[26] This instance occurred in 1956 when the United Kingdom, France, and Israel jointly attacked Egypt in the wake of Egypt's nationalization of the Suez Canal and continuing Fedayeen raids on Israel. However, Moore observes that the actions of the United Kingdom and France were aimed at restoring the status quo and were not aggression for territorial gain. Two additional cases reasonably characterized as aggression by a democracy are India's actions in the 1971 Bangladesh War and the actions of Turkey in a 1974 intervention. However, the first of these two could also reasonably be classified as a humanitarian intervention, and the second was in response to a coup against the government of Cyprus encouraged by Greece.[27] Moore concludes that "democratic nations predominantly get into major interstate war as a result of impermissible actions of nondemocratic nations rather than democratic nation aggression or simply through random distribution of blame or accident."[28]

Moore has also analyzed all major interstate wars in which the United States was involved and concludes that the United States was the aggressor in only three (the Mexican-American War of 1846–48, the Spanish-American War of 1898, and the Iraq War of 2003). The first two, however, have features that strongly suggest the United States was acting in self-defense, and the third was clearly motivated by defense and humanitarian concerns.[29] Moore's conclusion that "democracies are usually not the aggressor in the initiation of major international wars runs counter to a widely held assumption with the social science community"; however, that community either measures how frequently democracies are engaged in war and fails to distinguish between the aggressor and defender or is unable to demonstrate statistically that democracies are as aggressive as nondemocracies in major international wars.[30]

Democracies become involved in major international wars when they fail to deter a nondemocratic national leader from engaging in an aggressive use of military force.[31] We have already introduced the concept of deterrence and the importance of focusing deterrence on regime elites. Within the context of his postulate on the cause of war, Moore defines deterrence to include multiple tools and practices:

> [Deterrence is] the totality of positive and negative actions influencing expectations and incentives of a potential aggressor, including: potential military responses and security arrangements, relative power, level and importance of economic relations, effectiveness of diplomatic relations, effective international organizations (or lack thereof), effective

89

international law (or lack thereof), alliances, collective security, effects on allies, and the state of the political or military alliance structure, if any, of the potential aggressor and target state, etc. Most importantly, of course, there is a critical perception and communication component to deterrence since ultimately, it is the perception of the regime elite contemplating aggression that is most critical.[32]

More recently in *Solving the War Puzzle*, Moore has defined deterrence as a system of external incentives:

> Deterrence for our purposes is the totality of *external* incentives, that is, incentives from the international environment, which may be high or low, adequate or inadequate. Effective deterrence will be regarded as that aggregate of external incentives understood by a potential aggressor as adequate to prevent an aggressive action.[33]

Effective deterrence takes into account the culture of the potentially aggressive regime. It is "contextual, taking account of the myriad of relevant features affecting incentives and beliefs." Effective deterrence is also flexible to meet the demands of specific situations. It seeks a "realistic mix of incentives sufficient to produce the desired action or inaction and recognizes that in some settings, an absence of flexibility may produce a contrary result."[34]

Examining the level of deterrence that existed just prior to the principal wars of the twentieth century, Moore concludes that "in every case the potential aggressor made a rational calculation that the war would be won, and won promptly."[35] More specifically, "virtually all principal wars in the twentieth century, at least those involving conventional invasion, were preceded by . . . 'double deterrence absence' . . . [meaning that] the potential aggressor believed that they had the military force in place to prevail promptly *and* that nations that might have the military or diplomatic power to prevent this were not inclined to intervene."[36] This conclusion is supported by the work of historians such as Kagan, who analyzed the Peloponnesian War, World War I, Hannibal's War, and World War II and concluded that each war could have been prevented by achievable deterrence and that each occurred in the absence of such deterrence.[37]

In sum, Moore's postulate on the cause of war posits that the cause of major international armed conflict is the deadly synergy between the existence of a potentially aggressive non-democratic (totalitarian) regime and the absence of effective systemwide deterrence. Deterrence is the predominant theme: democratic regimes are deterred from aggressive action by their internal checks and balances, but nondemocratic regimes that lack internal checks and balances must be deterred from aggressive action by external incentives.

Moore's postulate provides an important insight for predicting the likelihood of war. For a given nation, the probability that it will go to war is a function of two variables: its form of government and the effectiveness of deterrence mechanisms targeted toward it. The less democratic the government and/or the less effective the systemwide deterrence, the greater the probability of war. The complex dynamics and subjectivities of this synergy do not lend themselves to precise quantitative analysis. However, it may be useful to express Moore's postulate as a formula that shows the relationship between the two variables or core components. In the equation below, the probability of war (P_W) is expressed as the sum of two factors: a nondemocratic form of government (G^{ND}) and a failure of effective systemwide deterrence ($-D^{SW}$).

A Formula for Representing Moore's
Postulate on the Cause of War

$$P_W = G^{ND} + (-D^{SW})$$

P_W	=	probability of war
G^{ND}	=	nondemocratic form of government
$-D^{SW}$	=	failure of effective systemwide deterrence

The likelihood of war increases as a government grows increasingly nondemocratic. The likelihood of war also increases as systemwide deterrence becomes less effective. However, highly effective systemwide deterrence mechanisms can reduce the probability of war even for a completely nondemocratic form of government. In the next section, a second formula based on Moore's incentive theory of war avoidance will refine the relationship among the form of government, deterrence, and the likelihood of war or peace. This formula will provide an analytical process for quantifying incentive and deterrence mechanisms, including those associated with the form of government, to predict the probability of peace for a given nation.

Moore's Incentive Theory of War Avoidance

The structure of world peace cannot be the work of one man, or one party, or one nation. . . . It must be a peace which rests on the cooperative effort of the whole world.

—Franklin Roosevelt
Address to Congress, 1 March 1945

More than an end to war, we want an end to the beginnings of all war.

—Franklin Roosevelt
Undelivered address

Moore's postulate on the cause of war serves as the foundation for his incentive theory of war avoidance, which describes the positive and negative incentives that can influence a regime's decision to pursue war. Introduced in *Solving the War Puzzle,* his incentive theory "blends the core elements of idealist and realist perspectives" and specifically incorporates "among many other factors, the importance of *form of government* from the idealist model and the importance of *deterrence* from the realist model."[38] The idealist perspective reflects relative optimism and emphasizes third-party dispute resolution, international organizations, trade, and democratic governments as ways to encourage peace. The realist perspective, on the other hand, emphasizes the security issues that emerge from competition and power struggles among the world's great powers.[39]

The conceptual and analytical framework for Moore's incentive theory is based, at least in part, on the insights of Kenneth Waltz's 1954 study that categorizes past explanations for the origins of war into three levels:

1. Individual level: violence, beliefs, and other subjectivities rooted in the individual

2. State or national level: variables accounting for war rooted in the form of government and other national variables

3. International level: variables rooted in the broader international system[40]

Idealists have traditionally focused on the national level "with
their interest in the form of government as a key variable" and
on the international level "with their interest in both trade and
international organization." In contrast, realists have traditionally focused on the international level with their interest in "the
anarchic international system, the security dilemma, great
power relations, deterrence, and the characteristics of varying
international systems."[41]

Moore concludes in *Solving the War Puzzle* that war arises
from the interaction of all three Waltzian levels (individual,
state or national, and international), whereas some proponents
of the democratic peace principle focus only on government
structures to explain war and some traditional realists focus
only on the international system. Both realists and democratic
peace proponents tend to emphasize institutions and systems,
whereas Moore reminds us that people—leaders—decide to
pursue war:

> Wars are not simply accidents. Nor, contrary to our ordinary language,
> are they made by nations. Wars are made by people; more specifically
> they are decided on by the leaders of nation states—and other non-
> national groups in the case of terrorism—who make the decision to
> commit aggression or otherwise use the military instrument. These
> leaders make that decision based on the totality of incentives affecting
> them at the time of the decision. . . .
>
> . . . [Incentive theory] tells us that we simply have a better chance of
> predicting war, and fashioning forms of intervention to control it, if we
> focus squarely on the effect of variables from all levels of analysis in
> generating incentives affecting the actual decisions made by those with
> the power to decide on war.[42]

Incentive theory focuses on the individual decisions that lead
to war and explains the synergistic relationship between the
absence of effective deterrence and the absence of democracy.
Together these three factors—the decisions of leaders made
without the restraining effects of deterrence and democracy—
are the cause of war:

> War is not strictly *caused* by an absence of democracy or effective deter-
> rence or both together. Rather war is *caused* by the human leadership

decision to employ the military instrument. The absence of democracy, the absence of effective deterrence, and most importantly, the synergy of an absence of both are conditions or factors that predispose to war. An absence of democracy likely predisposes by [its] effect on leadership and leadership incentives, and an absence of effective deterrence likely predisposes by its effect on incentives from factors other than the individual or governmental levels of analysis. To understand the *cause* of war is to understand the human decision for war; that is, major war and democide . . . are the consequence of individual decisions responding to a totality of incentives.[43]

Moore constructs his incentive theory of war avoidance within the analytical framework of Waltz's three levels of the origins of war: individual, state, and international. The first level of Moore's incentive theory analysis is at the individual level of the decision maker, which "includes personal subjectivities, beliefs, experience, and psychological factors [behavioral predispositions]."[44] The second level is at the state level and includes incentives that arise from different forms of government, such as the checks and balances inherent in democratic forms of government. The second level thus embraces the democratic peace principle.[45] The third level is at the international level and includes incentives that arise from the international system, such as systemwide deterrence, levels of contiguity, bilateral trade, and economic, military, and political incentives.[46] At the international level, systemwide deterrence is considered effective if it is capable of deterring a "rational actor."[47]

To fully understand the interrelationship among Moore's ideas about the cause of war and war avoidance, it is important to note that deterrence is the single variable that runs throughout all components and levels of his postulate on the cause of war and incentive theory of war avoidance. The second and third levels of his incentive theory of war avoidance, for example, embrace the two key components of his postulate on the cause of war: the democratic peace principle and systemwide deterrence. Moore emphasizes that the state of mind of a potential aggressor is based upon his or her perceptions of an aggregation of external incentives.[48] Effective deterrence must include those external incentives that will be perceived as persuasive by a specific potential aggressor. Therefore, the first level of Moore's incentive theory of war avoidance is an analysis of individualized incentives, motivations, and expectations, which will vary from decision maker to

94

decision maker. This level of analysis yields an individualized prism of behavioral, temperamental, emotional, and mental attributes through which the effect of incentives at the second and third levels must be analyzed. Table 6 summarizes the levels of analysis in Moore's incentive theory of war avoidance and shows their interrelationship with his postulate on the cause of war.

Table 6. Summary of Moore's incentive theory of war avoidance

Level of analysis in incentive theory of war avoidance	Elements	Corresponding component of postulate on the cause of war
Level 1: the individual	includes the individual's behavioral predispositions, personal subjectivities, beliefs, experience, and psychological factors	
Level 2: the state	includes incentives that arise from different forms of government	the democratic peace principle
Level 3: the international system	includes incentives that arise from the international system such as systemwide deterrence as well as levels of contiguity, bilateral trade, and economic, military, and political incentives	effective system-wide deterrence

Compiled from John Norton Moore's published works on the incentive theory of war avoidance. For references, see the bibliography.

Moore's postulate on the cause of war is described above as a formula $[P_W = G^{ND} + (-D^{SW})]$ showing that the probability of war (P_W) is based on two factors: the form of government and the effectiveness of systemwide deterrence. A nondemocratic form of government (G^{ND}) and a failure of effective systemwide deterrence $(-D^{SW})$ suggest a high probability for war (P_W). Moore's incentive theory of war avoidance can be described by a formula that provides an analytical process for determining the probability of peace for a given country. This predictive model, shown on the next page, quantifies and averages the multiple incentive and deterrence mechanisms that belong to the three levels of analysis in Moore's incentive theory of war avoidance. The probability of peace (P_P) is expressed as the integration of all applicable incentive and deterrence mechanisms (collectively referred to as factors [F]) at the individual (L_1), state (L_2), and international (L_3) levels. Integration denotes a greater interaction and synergy of complex variables than simple summation.

The variable L_1 includes the incentives and propensity that a national leader is believed to have or may have demonstrated toward war or peace based upon his or her "personal subjectivities, beliefs, experience, and psychological factors [behavioral predispositions]." The variable L_2 includes the checks and balances that are internal to that national leader's form of government. The variable L_3 includes the incentives that arise from the international system, such as systemwide deterrence, levels of contiguity, bilateral trade, and economic, military, and political incentives. The rationality factor (R) serves as a multiplier to take into account the rationality of the national leader.

Once quantified and indexed, each of these variables (L_1, L_2, and L_3) represents an average numerical value for a wide range of situational incentives and deterrence mechanisms (factors). The variable L_1 and the factored sum of L_2 and L_3 are then averaged to reflect the integration and complex synergy of the three levels of analysis of Moore's incentive theory of war avoidance.

A Mathematical Representation of Moore's Incentive Theory of War Avoidance

$$P_P = \frac{L_1 + R(L_2 + L_3)}{3}$$

P_P = probability of peace

Fn = all applicable incentive and deterrence mechanisms (factors)

L_1 = average of all applicable level 1 incentives and deterrence mechanisms

$$(L_1F1 + L_1F2 + L_1F3 + L_1F4 + L_1Fn)/n$$

L_2 = average of all applicable level 2 incentives and deterrence mechanisms

$$(L_2F1 + L_2F2 + L_2F3 + L_2F4 + L_2Fn)/n$$

L_3 = average of all applicable level 3 incentives and deterrence mechanisms

$$(L_3F1 + L_3F2 + L_3F3 + L_3F4 + L_3Fn)/n$$

R = rationality of national leader

The complex and subjective nature of incentives and deterrence mechanisms in any given situation is not conducive to *precise* quantitative analysis. However, the mathematical representation of the incentive theory of war avoidance is useful as a model for predicting the probability of peace. By assigning quantifiable variables to the elements of an abstract theory, the formula renders the theory more concrete and transparent. It concisely organizes the elements and levels of Moore's incentive theory into a working methodology that ensures all applicable factors are considered when evaluating the probability of peace or war. Most significantly, the mathematical formula compiles the subjective incentives and deterrence mechanisms and allows them to be quantified and indexed on a relative scale, yielding an indexed sum that can be averaged to measure the strength of a war avoidance strategy and predict the probability of peace or war.

A decimal (base 10) indexing system is applied to calculate the probability of peace (P_P) using the formula. The probability of peace (P_P) is indexed on a scale of 0–10. An index value of zero represents the greatest probability of war, and an index value of 10 represents the greatest probability of peace. For example, a war avoidance strategy that permits a totalitarian national leader to externalize the costs of war and fails to convince that leader that a state or group of states will respond to aggression with military force would have a very low index value after the calculations are completed. In contrast, a war avoidance strategy that fully embraces positive and negative incentives and deterrence mechanisms on the individual, state, and international level that personally target and encourage a national leader not to use aggressive force would have a very high index value after the calculations are completed.

The variable L_1 indexes an average value, on a scale of 0–10, for the relevant incentives, deterrence mechanisms, and propensity a national leader is believed to have toward war or peace based upon his or her behavioral predispositions. An index value of zero represents a great propensity toward war, and 10 represents a great propensity toward peace. For example, if a totalitarian national leader has resorted to the aggressive use of force for purposes of value extension, such as acquiring wealth or territory, a number of times in the past, the variable L_1Fn may be assigned a value of zero. In contrast, for an authoritarian national leader who has never resorted to the aggressive use of force in the past even when

97

repeatedly attacked, the variable L_1Fn may be assigned a value of 10. Similarly, a value of 10 may be assigned for a theocratic national leader whose religion strongly prohibits the aggressive use of force. All factors applicable at the individual level are indexed and averaged according to the formula $L_1 = (L_1F1 + L_1F2 + L_1F3 + L_1F4 + L_1Fn)/n$. For example, a theocratic leader whose religion discourages aggression may nevertheless have a record of initiating violent conflict. The factor representing his religious beliefs (L_1Fn) will be assigned a high number, while the factor representing his record of aggression (L_1Fn) will be assigned a low number. Both factors must be averaged into the value for L_1.

The variable L_2 indexes, on a scale of 0–10, the level of internal checks and balances inherent in the country's form of government. The form of government must be analyzed and indexed based upon the limits, if any, it imposes on its leader's options or ability to use aggressive military force. An index value of zero represents no internal checks and balances, and an index value of 10 represents the maximum number of checks and balances available in a form of government. For example, for totalitarian, dictatorial, and authoritarian forms of government, the variable L_2 would have an index value of zero after the calculations are completed since the national leaders maintain absolute, centralized political control and are subject to few, if any, internal checks and balances. In contrast, the variable L_2 for a model liberal democracy would have an index value of 10 after the calculations are completed since its constitutional form of government contains the maximum number of checks and balances available in a form of government. All other governments would have an L_2 value somewhere between zero and 10 after the calculations are completed. To calculate L_2, an index value of 0–10 must be assigned to each applicable factor or internal check and balance (Fn) for that form of government. Because a liberal democracy has the most limits and restraints on government power, the features that define the model liberal democracy, described in table 1 (chapter 1), can be used as factors for calculating L_2. If other level-two factors apply, they should be assigned an Fn value as well and included in calculating the average according to the formula $L_2 = (L_2F1 + L_2F2 + L_2F3 + L_2F4 + L_2Fn)/n$. An electoral democracy or a limited, transitional democracy, for example, would have some of the features characteristic of a liberal democracy but come up short with others, so it might receive an L_2 index value of five after the calculations are completed.

The variable L_3 indexes an average value, on a scale of 0–10, for the overall effectiveness of incentives that arise from the international system such as systemwide deterrence, levels of contiguity, bilateral trade, and economic, military, and political incentives. For example, the relationship between contiguous nations affects the likelihood of their fighting a war with each other. If two contiguous nations have no trade or economic ties, the factor L_3Fn may be assigned a value of zero. In contrast, where contiguous nations have very strong bilateral trade and economic ties, the factor L_3Fn may be assigned a value of 10. For nations that have a strong military alliance, the factor L_3Fn may be assigned a value of 10. All international-level factors are then averaged according to the formula $L_3 = (L_3F1 + L_3F2 + L_3F3 + L_3F4 + L_3Fn)/n$.

As the formula for P_P indicates, L_2 and L_3 must be factored by the rationality factor (R), which is indexed 0–1 to reflect the rationality of the national leader. The best indication of a leader's rationality is how he or she has reacted within the international community in the past. An index value of zero represents a completely irrational national leader that, for example, has responded to the actions of other states in an unpredictable or unreasonable way. If R has a value of zero, the variables L_2 and L_3 will become zero when factored by R, completely negating any value otherwise attributed to the incentive and deterrence mechanisms of levels two and three. In other words, a completely irrational leader might not be restrained by any conventional incentive or deterrence mechanism at the state or international levels. In contrast, a value of one represents a completely rational national leader who has responded to the actions of other states in a predictable and reasonable way. A value of one does not negate or diminish the value otherwise attributed to the incentive and deterrence mechanisms of levels two and three. For those national leaders that fall somewhere in between, a value must be assigned based on their demonstrated behavioral, temperamental, emotional, and mental attributes.

Table 7 summarizes the analytical process represented in the formula $P_P = [L_1 + R(L_2 + L_3)]/3$ and provides notional values for the baseline factors (Fn) of Moore's incentive theory of war avoidance. These factors are a starting point for analysis.

For specific countries, other factors may be relevant as well and should be included in the calculation of P_P.

Table 7. Notional values for the baseline factors of Moore's incentive theory of war avoidance

Level of analysis	Baseline factor used to determine P_P	Notional value
Level 1: the individual (L_1 = average of all applicable factors)	*Personal subjectivities*: wears a uniform and boasts of his or her warrior ethos	0
	Personal subjectivities: takes great pride in his or her diplomatic skills to resolve disputes	10
	Beliefs: strongly believes war is an extension of diplomacy	0
	Beliefs: strongly believes war is immoral and illegal	10
	Experience: has fought in and glorifies war	0
	Experience: has never fought in war and seems repulsed by its destruction	10
	Psychological factors (behavioral predispositions): seems predisposed to be aggressive and confrontational in all international interactions	0
	Psychological factors (behavioral predispositions): international interactions are very reserved, never confrontational	10
Level 2: the state (L_2 = the value attributed to the form of government)[a]	Totalitarian, dictatorial, and authoritarian forms of government	0
	Electoral democracy	5
	Limited, transitional democracy	5
	Model liberal democracy	10
Level 3: the international system (L_3 = average of all applicable factors)	*Level of contiguity*: nations are contiguous	0
	Level of contiguity: nations are thousands of miles apart and neither has means of power projection	10
	Bilateral trade and economic incentives: no trade exists	0
	Bilateral trade and economic incentives: nations strongly dependent on each other	10
	Political incentives: aggressive behavior would bolster leader's national image	0
	Political incentives: aggressive behavior may cause military coup	10
	Military incentives: potential victim of aggression has no security arrangements with major powers	0
	Military incentives: potential victim of aggression has strong security arrangements with major powers	10

Compiled from John Norton Moore's published works on the incentive theory of war avoidance. For references, see the bibliography.
[a]Like L_1 and L_3, L_2 is an average of multiple factors. For convenience, this table presents the final L_2 value (an average of multiple factors) for four forms of government.

Using the notional values in table 7 as a guide for analysis, the formula $P_P = [L_1 + R(L_2 + L_3)]/3$ can be used to calculate the probability of peace in a given scenario based upon Moore's incentive theory of war avoidance. This framework of analysis will be used in the next chapter to evaluate Moore's incentive theory both in general and in the specific context of the 1991 Persian Gulf War.

Notes

1. Roosevelt to Dodd, letter.
2. Roosevelt, "The Four Freedoms," speech.
3. Roosevelt, undelivered address. Roosevelt planned to deliver this speech on 13 April 1945, the day following his sudden death.
4. See the discussion in chapter 2.
5. See the extended discussion of the democratic peace principle in chapter 3.
6. Moore, *Solving the War Puzzle*, 1–2.
7. USIP Web site.
8. Moore, *Solving the War Puzzle*, xivn1, 2.
9. Ibid., 6–7.
10. Ibid., xviii–xix.
11. Ibid., xiii, xvii–xix.
12. Ibid., xiii.
13. Moore, *Crisis in the Gulf*, 337.
14. Moore, "Toward a New Paradigm," 811, 840.
15. Moore, *Solving the War Puzzle*, 1–8, 31; Kagan, *On the Origins of War*, 6, 68–74, 205–14, 269–74, 413–17, 546–48, 566–73.
16. Moore, "Toward a New Paradigm," 811, 838.
17. Moore, *Crisis in the Gulf*, 337; Moore, "Toward a New Paradigm," 811, 840; and Moore, *Solving the War Puzzle*, 39.
18. Moore, *Solving the War Puzzle*, 2, 94n8.
19. Ibid., 105–6n3.
20. Ibid., xxii.
21. Moore, "Toward a New Paradigm," 811, 833–34; and Moore, *Solving the War Puzzle*, 11. For previous discussions of Moore's application of the theory of government failure and public choice theory to the democratic peace principle, see Sharp, "International Obligations," 411, 414–16; and Sharp, "Revoking an Aggressor's License to Kill," 1, 60–61.
22. Moore, *Solving the War Puzzle*, 9–12.
23. Moore, "Toward a New Paradigm," 811, 834–35.
24. Moore, *Solving the War Puzzle*, 9.
25. Ibid., 13.
26. Ibid., 14.
27. Ibid.
28. Ibid., 15.

29. Ibid., 15–16.

30. Ibid., 16–24.

31. Ibid., 27.

32. Moore, "Toward a New Paradigm," 811, 841.

33. Moore, *Solving the War Puzzle*, 27.

34. Ibid., 28–29.

35. Ibid., 30.

36. Ibid.

37. Ibid., 31.

38. Ibid., xix. For a previous discussion of Moore's theory of war avoidance that focuses principally on democracy and deterrence, see Sharp, "Revoking an Aggressor's License to Kill," 1, 56–60.

39. Moore, *Solving the War Puzzle*, xvii–xviii.

40. Quoted in ibid., xix.

41. Moore, *Solving the War Puzzle*, xix–xx.

42. Ibid., xx–xxi.

43. Ibid., 66–67.

44. Ibid., xx, 145.

45. Ibid.

46. Ibid.

47. Moore, "Toward a New Paradigm," 811, 840; Moore, *Solving the War Puzzle*, 64.

48. Moore, *Solving the War Puzzle*, 28.

Chapter 5

A Validation of the Incentive
Theory of War Avoidance

*Power, geopolitical interests, and strategic calculations
greatly influence the decision-making calculus of all
states, democratic or not. But we contend that there
is a connection between democracy and foreign policy,
and that much of international relations cannot be explained without reference to domestic-level variables.*

—Miriam Elman
Paths to Peace: Is Democracy the Answer?

Moore's postulate on the cause of war attributes the cause of
major international armed conflict to the deadly synergy between
the existence of a potentially aggressive nondemocratic (totalitarian) regime and the absence of effective systemwide deterrence.
His incentive theory of war avoidance affirms that war is caused
by the decisions of human leadership and can therefore be prevented by positive and negative incentives at the individual,
state, and international levels that effectively discourage leaders
of nation-states from committing aggression. Deterrence is the
predominant variable that permeates Moore's theories. National
leaders of democratic regimes are deterred from aggressive action by the internal checks and balances of their respective governments, but national leaders of nondemocratic regimes that
lack internal checks and balances must be deterred from aggressive action by individual- and international-level incentives.
The role of deterrence in Moore's incentive theory of war avoidance will be analyzed and validated in this chapter by applying the mathematical formula for calculating the probability of
peace ($P_P = [L_1 + R(L_2 + L_3)]/3$) to the 1991 Persian Gulf War.[1]

Paths to Peace: Domestic and International
Factors in War Avoidance

In 1997, 10 scholars contributed to *Paths to Peace: Is Democracy the Answer?* an extensive critical examination of the

democratic peace principle that reaches a conclusion similar to Moore's incentive theory of war avoidance.[2] Among the contributors are both critics and proponents of the democratic peace principle. Moore's incentive theory of war avoidance blends the idealist and realist perspectives on international conflict: along with the idealists, Moore emphasizes the form of government and with the realists, the importance of deterrence.[3] Similarly, the contributors to *Paths to Peace* include both neoliberals who insist that "political ideologies and regime type determine states' threat perceptions and influence their propensity to wage war" and neorealists who believe that the "international system drives state behavior."[4] Editor Miriam Elman concludes that proponents of the democratic peace principle who believe democracy is the "best way to ensure international cooperation and the absence of war" have overstated their case.[5] She remains critical of the democratic peace principle:

> Under certain conditions liberal peace can break down, especially when external threats are severe. . . . Regime structure is frequently not the most important domestic political variable to influence war and peace decisions; the norms and institutions of democracy may not always prevent wars and ensure stable peace between democracies; the democratic process often generates aggressive foreign policies; and nondemocratic norms and institutions do not invariably increase the likelihood of war.[6]

Although she acknowledges that "domestic politics in general, and the democratic process in particular, crucially affect war and peace decision making," she argues that "peace among democracies can be attributed to influences other than shared democratic institutions and liberal norms."[7] Therefore, she believes "democracy [alone] may not be the answer we are looking for," and "power, geopolitical interests, and strategic calculations greatly influence the decision making calculus of all states, democratic or not."[8] The democratic peace principle "underemphasizes the importance of different leaders' views on national goals and the appropriate means to achieve them; that is, the theory neglects the role that extraordinary individuals often play in war and peace decision making."[9]

Elman argues that "both international and domestic factors influence state behavior in crisis, even among democracies."[10] For example, Christopher Layne concludes that as France and

Britain began to drift apart in the summer of 1839 over Near East interests involving Algeria, Egypt, and Syria in the Ottoman Empire, an Anglo-French war was avoided through a resolute British "deterrence model" which clearly communicated that any French actions in the Near East counter to British interests would be met by the use of a capable military force.[11] Arie Kacowicz provides two case studies of the 1932–33 territorial dispute between Peru and Colombia and the 1989–92 border dispute between Mauritania and Senegal. He concludes that an "unstable or fragile peace is usually maintained by threats, deterrence, or a lack of will or capabilities to engage in violent conflict."[12] Specifically, he observes that a fragile peace was maintained in these instances due to domestic and international factors such as "the lack of material means to wage international wars; sudden leadership changes; the pacifying role of regional hegemons . . . and of international institutions . . . and a normative regional consensus in favor of peaceful settlement of disputes and respect of the existing international borders."[13]

The extensive critical analysis provided by these scholars offers a strong validation of the major components of Moore's postulate on the cause of war and incentive theory of war avoidance. Collectively, the contributors to *Paths to Peace* conclude that peace is maintained by domestic democratic institutions and international factors that bear upon the calculations of decision makers. Elman suggests that additional research is needed and that "we may need to go beyond the democratic peace" to understand peace and conflict management.[14] Moore, to whom these scholars make no reference, provides this additional research. His body of research addresses the question "is democracy the answer?" by concluding that peace is a result of the checks and balances inherent in democratic regimes *and* effective systemwide deterrence and incentives at the individual, state, and international levels that affect the decisions of human leadership. Moore's theory thus goes beyond the democratic peace principle by arguing that where democracy does not exist, targeted deterrence can effectively minimize the occurrence of war.

An Analysis of the Role of Deterrence in the 1991 Persian Gulf War

We will persistently clarify the choice before every ruler and every nation.

—Pres. George W. Bush
Inaugural Address, 20 January 2005

The effect of deterrence can be expressed in the formula introduced in the previous chapter, which mathematically represents Moore's incentive theory of war avoidance and can be used to predict the probability of peace: $P_P = [L_1 + R(L_2 + L_3)]/3$. Applying this formula to a test case, the Gulf War, will demonstrate its utility as a predictive tool. This application is not intended to suggest mathematical precision in calculating the probability of peace or war because the dynamics of incentives and deterrence mechanisms are complex and not precisely predictable. However, the formula provides a working methodology to ensure all applicable factors are considered when evaluating the likelihood that a particular leader or nation will go to war. Since we know in hindsight that Saddam Hussein was, in fact, not effectively discouraged from committing aggression against Kuwait by the positive and negative incentives applied to him, we can compare the actual outcome to the outcome predicted by the peace-probability formula, thereby validating or refuting the accuracy of the formula and Moore's incentive theory of war avoidance. If Moore's theory is validated, then the outcome of future situations can be predicted by quantifying deterrence mechanisms (L_1, L_2, and L_3) and applying the formula to calculate the probability of peace.

The fundamental principles of deterrence must be incorporated into the analysis of incentives and deterrence mechanisms applicable to the Gulf War.[15] For deterrence to be effective, Kant concludes that despotic rulers must believe war is fatal to them.[16] According to Kagan, deterrence must "account for irrational thought" and "counterbalance passion with passion, fear with fear," and nations must take "responsibility" and "affirmative action" to deter war.[17] Moore emphasizes the singular importance of "military deterrence" and says that the "perception and communication" of the "totality of positive and negative actions influencing expectations and incentives" are fundamental elements of effective deterrence.[18] He identifies four key elements of military deterrence: "the ability to respond, the will to respond, effective communication of ability and will to the aggressive regime, and perception by the aggressive regime of deterrence ability and will."[19] Turner also emphasizes the importance of a potential aggressor's perception of "*strength* and *will*" and notes that "unenforced law is ineffective."[20] The DOD defines deterrence as a "state of mind,"[21] and US military strategy emphasizes that deterrence "rests on a potential adversary's perception of our capabilities and commitment."[22]

The types of factors that must be considered in this analysis of deterrence include jealousy, fear, resentment, greed, naiveté, desire for fame and glory, motivations for revenge, the level and importance of economic relations, the effectiveness of diplomatic relations, the effectiveness of international law (to include clear proscriptive norms) and international or regional organizations to maintain peace, consistency in condemning aggression and prosecuting war crimes, relative balance of power, potential military responses and security arrangements, alliances, collective security arrangements, effects on allies, and the perceived will to use military force in response to aggression. Each of these factors may influence the success of deterrence and incentive mechanisms. States must apply scenario-specific deterrence incentives at all levels—individual, state, and international—that target and personally affect potentially aggressive regime elites. Since wars always begin through the calculated decisions of leaders, the choice of incentives must be based on the perception and personality of the relevant decision maker. As the UNESCO constitution states, "Since wars begin in the minds of men, it is in the minds of men that the defences of peace must be constructed."[23]

Rummel too recognizes the premise that war is rooted in the minds of leaders:

> Conflict is formed in the minds of men. It is fought there; it ends there. And peace is a relationship between minds. All else—the noise, destruction, deaths, weapons—are [sic] the manifestation of conflict. They are either the tools of mental combat or the side effects. To understand con-

flict and peace is to then understand man's mind. It is, basically, under-standing yourself and what you share with others as a human being.[24]

Rummel defines a series of principles that assist in understand-ing the decision-making motivations and processes of leaders within the context of themselves, their interactions with oth-ers, interactions within their group (society), and interactions within their intergroups (international society). These five prin-ciples of self-knowledge are summarized in table 8.

Table 8. Rummel's principles of self-knowledge

Principle	Elements	Description
The subjectivity principle: perception is subjective	perception mental field balance	Perception is a balance between the powers of one's mental field and the outside world.
The intentionality principle: a person behaves to achieve	needs attitudes interests sentiments	A person's intentions gratify certain funda-mental needs: sex, hunger, sleep, gregari-ousness, protectiveness, curiosity, security, and self-assertion. An attitude is some latent (inactive) goal and means. An interest is the same as an attitude except that it is active, driven by stimulated needs. Sentiments are clusters of attitudes sharing a similar goal.
The self-esteem principle: a person strives for self-esteem	superego ego self will	The superego is the collection of attitudes we call morality. The ego is the organizing, administering aspect of one's relationships and interaction with the outside world. The self is one's total personality, integrated needs, attitudes, and sentiments. The will is one's ability to make conscious choices and act on them.
The expectations principle: expectations guide a person's behavior	prediction credibility	A person's expectations are really his or her predictions about the consequences of his or her actions. A person's credibility is the degree to which others can expect him or her to follow through on promises or threats.
The responsibility principle: an individual is responsible for his or her own behavior	free will morality choice	Free will means that an individual has the final responsibility for his or her actions. Mo-rality or superego is what a person believes he or she should, or should not, do. Choice means being able to choose from among a number of alternative behaviors and not being completely determined to select a particular one.

Compiled from R. J. Rummel, *In the Minds of Men: Principles Toward Understanding and Wag-ing Peace* (Seoul, South Korea: Sogang University Press, 1984), 13, 16, 23, 25–26, 31–33, 39–41, 45–46.

Rummel concludes that "groups and institutions and nations or governments do not perceive or have expectations. They are abstractions. . . . The core of any explanation of democracy's effect on violence, therefore, has to be the *individual*."[25] Thus deterrence incentives must be consistent with the principles of self-knowledge and target the perceptions and personality of the decision maker.

The military forces of Iraqi leader Saddam Hussein invaded Kuwait on 2 August 1990. In response, an international coalition force led by the United States liberated Kuwait in the Gulf War.[26] This discussion will identify and index known incentive and deterrence mechanisms, collectively referred to as factors (F), at the individual (L_1), state (L_2), and international (L_3) levels that were in place before Hussein's invasion of Kuwait. The analysis of the individual level will also index the rationality factor (R) for Hussein. The results will be compiled in table 9, and the formula $P_P = [L_1 + R(L_2 + L_3)]/3$ will be used to determine the probability of peace (P_P), which will either validate or repudiate Moore's incentive theory of war avoidance.

Individual-Level (L_1) Factors and the Rationality Factor (R)

The first level of analysis assigns a value to the individual incentives, motivations, and expectations (L_1), which vary from leader to leader. This analysis yields an individualized prism of behavioral, temperamental, emotional, and mental attributes— the rationality factor (R)—through which the effect of incentives at the second and third levels must be analyzed and weighted. The variable L_1 is an average of values assigned on a scale of 0–10 to each of the relevant incentives and deterrence mechanisms, as well as the propensity a national leader is believed to have toward war or peace based upon his or her behavioral predispositions. An index value of zero represents a great propensity toward or probability of war, and an index value of 10 represents a great propensity toward or probability of peace.

The capability of Iraq's military before the invasion was formidable, according to the DOD final report to Congress on the war:

> Iraq possessed the fourth largest army in the world, an army hardened in long years of combat against Iran. During that war Iraq killed hundreds

109

of thousands of Iranian soldiers in exactly the type of defensive combat it planned to fight in Kuwait. Saddam Hussein's forces possessed high-quality artillery, frontline T-72 tanks, modern MiG-29 and Mirage F-1 aircraft, ballistic missiles, biological agents and chemical weapons, and a large and sophisticated ground-based air defense system. His combat engineers . . . [were] rated among the best in the world.[27]

A potentially aggressive state with *no* military capability would receive an index value of 10. For states with a military capability, the relative strength of that capability must be taken into account: the greater the capability, the lower the index value. For example, the greatest military capability in the world would receive an index value of zero, and other world-class military capabilities would receive a very low index value. In 1990 the Iraqi battle-hardened military was the largest in the Persian Gulf and the fourth largest in the world, with an experienced combat soldier as its national leader.[28] The Iraqi military had an exceptionally strong capability to conduct aggressive war. Accordingly, for this factor (capability to engage in war, which is an indicator of the potentiality of war), Iraq should be assigned an index value of one.

Another factor to be quantified is a regime's history of aggression. Hussein previously ordered an aggressive attack on the neighboring country of Iran in September 1980, and after eight years of war, Hussein used chemical weapons on Iranian forces. Hussein's previous use of aggressive military force against a neighbor and his use of chemical weapons warrant an index value of zero.

Occupying Kuwait would significantly increase the financial resources and military power at Hussein's disposal; if unchecked, he could have easily moved against Saudi Arabia, seizing its vast oil resources. His occupation of Kuwait alone would have permitted Hussein to disrupt the world oil supply and the economies of industrialized nations. These economic and political advantages of invading Kuwait were very important because Hussein's million-member military was consuming enormous sums of money and by "mid-1990, Iraq had only enough cash reserves for three months of imports and an inflation rate of 40 percent."[29] Hussein was also in serious arrears with many international development loans that he had diverted to fund the Iraq-Iran war.[30] These economic and political factors provided a very strong incentive for Hussein to invade Kuwait, thus warranting a very low index value, possibly even a zero. However, a rational leader would always have in mind the possibility of losing the war, which would somewhat counteract the incentive for war. Accordingly, this factor—the leader's motivation—is assigned an index value of one.

Hussein "saw himself as the premier leader in (and of) the Arab world" and believed that his chemical-weapons capability balanced the power between Iraq and the Israeli nuclear-weapon capability. He also gave a number of threatening speeches just before his invasion of Kuwait and claimed that "Iraq alone had defended the 'Arab nation' against the age-old Persian threat."[31] Hussein's public threats, his perception of the regional balance of power, and his self-aggrandizement concerning the role of Iraq in the Arab world indicate a state of mind predisposed to war, thus warranting an index value of three.

Hussein rose to power predominantly through the use of force. He was involved in an aborted assassination attempt of the ruler of Iraq in 1959, was later involved in a successful Ba'ath coup in Baghdad, and then masterminded the July 1968 coup, after which he became the de facto ruler of Iraq by killing off any opposition.[32] Hussein also treated his own people brutally. His willingness to use military force domestically in multiple coups, openly murder for personal gain, and use brutality against his own people all reflect his tyrannical disregard for human rights and life, a factor that should be assigned an index value of zero. During the summer of 1990, Hussein escalated from making verbal threats to deploying massive forces north of Kuwait. He also demanded money and territory from Kuwait. When neighboring Arab leaders attempted to mediate and resolve the crisis peacefully, Hussein's representatives walked out of the meeting. Thus the use of diplomacy did not succeed in deterring Hussein from war. He continued to deploy the bulk of Iraq's best combat power to within hundreds of meters of the Kuwaiti border, which permitted an attack with virtually no warning.[33] Failed attempts to peacefully resolve the conflict, followed by significant troop movements, warrant an index value of zero.

These six factors are not the only incentives or deterrence mechanisms that may have been at work in the buildup to the Gulf War. However, they are representative and clearly demonstrate that even subjective quantifications such as these can be made with some reasonable accuracy, and they demonstrate the predictive value of this type of analysis. In this L_1 analysis, a clear pattern indicates a strong probability of war. The greater the number of factors that are considered, the greater weight and accuracy can be attributed to the L_1 analysis.

The rationality factor (R) takes into account the rationality of the national leader and is assigned an index value of 0–1. A value of zero represents a completely irrational leader, while a value of one represents a completely rational leader. Hussein has been described by political psychologists as a "malignant narcissist." The personality characteristics of a malignant narcissist include those of both the narcissist and sadist. A malignant narcissist has "an arrogant sense of grandiosity, sadistic cruelty, suspiciousness, and a lack of remorse." A malignant narcissist is usually hostile and malicious, as well as highly ambitious and self-promoting, with a keen sense of self-preservation.[34]

In December 1990, Dr. Jerrold Post testified before the House Armed Services Committee about Hussein's psychological profile:

> The record of Saddam Hussein's leadership . . . reveals a judicious political calculator, who is by no means irrational, but is dangerous to the extreme. . . . Saddam has been consumed by dreams of glory since his earliest days. He identifies himself with Nebuchadnezzar, the King of Babylonia who conquered Jerusalem (586 B.C.) and Saladin who regained Jerusalem in 1187 by defeating the Crusaders. . . . Commitments and loyalty are matter of circumstance, and circumstances change. If an individual, or a nation, is perceived as an impediment or a threat, no matter how loyal in the past, that individual or nation will be eliminated violently without a backward glance, and the action will be justified by "the exceptionalism of revolutionary needs."[35]

Post found no evidence that Hussein had a psychotic disorder and noted his patience and lack of impulsiveness. However, this conclusion does not mean that Hussein acted rationally:

While he is psychologically in touch with reality, he is often politically out of touch with reality. Saddam's world view is narrow and distorted, and he has scant experience out of the Arab world. His only sustained experience with non-Arabs was with his Soviet military advisors and he reportedly had one brief trip to France in 1976. . . . While Hussein is not psychotic, he has a strong paranoid orientation. . . . Saddam Hussein is so consumed with his messianic mission that he probably overreads the degree of his support in the rest of the Arab world. . . . Saddam Hussein is a ruthless political calculator who will go to whatever lengths are necessary to achieve his goals.[36]

The psychological insights and profiles of Hussein by psychologists such as Immelman and Post are important to an L_1 analysis and a determination of the rationality factor (R).[37] Given their conclusions that Hussein was rational and calculating, yet ruthless, willing to use force, and politically naive, Hussein should be assigned a rationality factor (R) of 0.6.

State-Level (L_2) Factors

The variable L_2 indexes on a scale of 0–10 the level of internal checks and balances imposed by the form of government in question on its leader's options or ability to use aggressive military force. An index value of zero represents no internal checks and balances, and a value of 10 represents the maximum number of checks and balances available in a form of government. In addition to evaluating the checks and balances available in a given form of government, an L_2 analysis considers how those checks and balances work in practice.

In its 2003 report *Freedom in the World*, Freedom House named Iraq as an authoritarian regime and one of the nine worst nations in the world for political rights and civil liberties.[38] When 193 countries or jurisdictions are ranked by an aggregated index value of democracy, Iraq is 190, meaning only three jurisdictions are less democratic than Iraq.[39] While the L_2 analysis for some countries would require an extensive review of the form of government and how its checks and balances work in practice, Hussein's Iraq is an extreme example and easy to index. Under Hussein, Iraq was an authoritarian regime that in practice did not follow its own constitution and laws, and its leader was a ruthless murderer who killed those who opposed him. Thus there were no functioning checks and balances in Hussein's Iraq, and the L_2 index value is zero.

An L_2 analysis must also consider the role of the legal system in explaining and predicting government behavior. Iraq had a customary-law legal system, which is more subject to the abusive use of power than civil-law and common-law systems. Given the demonstrated abuse of power by Hussein, this factor should also receive an index value of zero. The form of government and the legal system in Iraq before the Gulf War offered no checks and balances or restraints on Hussein's behavior.

International-Level (L_3) Factors

The variable L_3 indexes an average value on a scale of 0–10 for the overall effectiveness of incentives that arise from the international system, such as systemwide deterrence, levels of contiguity, bilateral trade, and economic, military, and political incentives. An index value of zero indicates the least effective incentives, while a value of 10 indicates the most effective. As with the L_1 analysis, a large number of factors can be considered, but only a few of the most significant ones will be addressed in this example to demonstrate the validity of incentive theory analysis.

There are clear proscriptive norms against the aggressive use of force by states. The UN Charter outlaws the aggressive use of force while recognizing a state's inherent right of individual and collective self-defense in Article 51 and the Security Council's obligation under Article 39 to maintain or restore international peace and security. If a state uses force against another state within the meaning of Article 2(4), that use of force is unlawful unless it is an exercise of that state's inherent right of self-defense or unless it is authorized by the Security Council under its coercive Chapter VII authority. While there is considerable debate within the international community concerning the meanings of Articles 2(4), 39, and 51 in the UN Charter, the blatantly illegal invasion and occupation of Kuwait by Iraq in 1990 was universally condemned by the international community as a clear violation of charter norms.[40] This factor—the existence of clear proscriptive norms—should be assigned an index value of 10.

The UN Charter also created an international collective-security alliance mechanism. However, leading up to the Gulf War, the international community had not formed a military coalition in the face of aggression since its response to the North Korean invasion of South Korea in 1950, and even then, just "five years after winning World War II, the United States was almost pushed off the Korean peninsula by the army of a third-rate country."[41] The effectiveness of the international collective-security mechanism in deterring aggression should be given an index value of three, given the relatively low likelihood of a UN military response to Iraq's invasion of Kuwait.

Since the Iraqi army was not only the fourth largest in the world but also the largest in the Persian Gulf area, a regional response by predominantly Arab nations was unlikely. As a potential deterrence mechanism, the military strength of the aggressor's neighbors should be assigned an index value of two. Similarly, since the Kuwaiti military forces were "hopelessly outmatched" by the battle-hardened Iraqi army,[42] an index value of one should be assigned to reflect the imbalance of military power between the two parties in a potential military conflict. Because Iraq and Kuwait are contiguous, Iraq could easily project military power into Kuwait; thus the factor of geography should be assigned an index value of zero.

The UN has had a practice of implementing trade sanctions, and it is likely that Hussein realized trade sanctions would be imposed if he invaded Kuwait. However, the deterrence value of trade sanctions is limited because their effect on the leader is usually minimal. In this case, the sanctions would have been felt primarily by the people of Iraq and may have caused domestic unrest, but the impact on Hussein would have been negligible, given the ruthless way in which he ruled Iraq. Accordingly, this factor should be given an index value of two.

There is considerable debate concerning how effectively the United States conveyed its willingness to defend Kuwait with military force in response to an Iraqi invasion. From 1980 through 1988, the United States provided substantial covert support to Iraq in its war with Iran even though Iraq had invaded Iran contrary to the same charter principles by which Iraq was later condemned when it invaded Kuwait. According to the *New York Times*, the United States never stated or even hinted that it would respond to Iraqi aggression with force, inadvertently giving Hussein "the green light to attack."[43] This absence of deterrence was reinforced with a conciliatory meeting between Hussein and US Ambassador April Glaspie on 25 July 1990.[44] According to a transcript published in a Pakistani newspaper, Glaspie told Hussein in their first and only meeting that the United States has "no opinion on your Arab-Arab conflicts, such as your dispute with Kuwait," and the "Kuwait issue is not associated with America."[45] Moreover, Bush administration officials testified before Congress on 31 July 1990, arguing against legislation to impose economic sanctions on Iraq. Hussein watched Washington very closely prior to his invasion of Kuwait and continued to receive very reassuring and conciliatory messages reinforcing his belief that the United States would not use military force to defend Kuwait.[46] While it would perhaps have departed from standard diplomatic practice, a clear signal that the United States would respond and destroy Iraq if it invaded Kuwait may have had considerable deterrence value.

The credibility of the Iraqi transcripts is questionable. What was actually said and, more importantly, what was perceived to have been said, given the previous US covert support for Iraq as well as language and cultural differences between two people who just met for the first time, will never really be known. Gen Colin Powell's assessment of the situation is that we "had Arab states saying nothing was going to happen, and the United States saying that if anything did, it was not our concern."[47] At one point before the invasion, reporters asked President Bush if he intended to send troops, and his response was that "I am not contemplating any such action."[48] Given the lack of clarity in US intentions and the standard diplomatic policy of not taking positions on border disputes between friendly countries, the highest value this factor—clear communication from the United States that it would respond with force—should be assigned is a three.

Table 9 summarizes the above incentive-theory analysis by collating the index values for the incentive and deterrence factors relevant to the Gulf War.

Table 9. Index values for incentive and deterrence factors for the 1991 Persian Gulf War

Level of analysis in Moore's incentive theory of war avoidance	Incentive and deterrence factor	Index value
Level 1: the individual (L_1 equals the average of the applicable factors)	Formidable Iraqi military capability	1
	Previous use of aggressive military force against a neighbor and use of chemical weapons	0
	Potentially bankrupt domestic economy in contrast to favorable economic and political advantages of going to war	1
	Perceived balance of regional power and self-aggrandizement of Iraq's role in the Arab world	3
	Willingness to use military force domestically, openly murder for personal gain, and brutalize his people	0
	Failed attempts at dispute resolution followed by significant escalation of massing troops on Kuwaiti border	0
	$L_1 = (L_1F1 + L_1F2 + L_1F3 + L_1F4 + L_1Fn)/n$	$L_1 = .833$
Level 2: the state (L_2 equals the average of factors associated with the form of government)	Authoritarian government with a national leader who does not follow the constitution or laws and murders his opposition	0
	Customary-law legal system	0
	$L_2 = (L_2F1 + L_2F2 + L_2F3 + L_2F4 + L_2Fn)/n$	$L_2 = 0$
Level 3: the international system (L_3 equals the average of the applicable factors)	Clear international prohibition on the aggressive use of military force to invade and occupy another nation	1 0
	Likelihood of an effective international collective-security response	3
	Likelihood of a regional collective-security response	2
	Imbalance of power between Iraq and Kuwait	1
	Level of contiguity between Iraq and Kuwait and Iraq's capability to project military power	0
	Effective implementation of trade sanctions	2
	Communication of the willingness of the United States to defend Kuwait with military force in response to an Iraqi invasion	3
	$L_3 = (L_3F1 + L_3F2 + L_3F3 + L_3F4 + L_3Fn)/n$	$L_3 = 3$

Using the analytical process captured in the formula $P_P = [L_1 + R(L_2 + L_3)]/3$, the variable L_1 and the sum of L_2 and L_3 factored by (R) can be averaged to determine the probability of peace (P_P) just prior to the Gulf War:

$$P_P = \frac{L_1 + R(L_2 + L_3)}{3}$$

$$.878 = \frac{.833 + .6(0 + 3)}{3}$$

According to this analysis, the probability of peace leading up to the Gulf War would have been .878 on a scale of 0–10, with zero representing the greatest probability of war and 10 representing the greatest probability of peace. A value of .878 is an extraordinarily strong indication that war is likely.

Additional Applications of the Peace-Probability Formula

The case of Iraqi aggression during the Gulf War was an extreme case. To further test Moore's analytical process as expressed in the formula $P_P = [L_1 + R(L_2 + L_3)]/3$, consider the opposite extreme: the probability that a completely rational US leader would use aggressive military force in a hypothetical border dispute between the United States and Canada over the drainage of brackish water. For analysis purposes, assume all factors are maximized for effective systemwide deterrence. Assume a rationality factor of one for a leader who behaves completely rationally. The analysis of individual-level (L_1) factors yields an index value of 10, and the index value of state-level (L_2) factors for a liberal democracy is also 10. Because the United States respects the constraints of international law and the UN Charter on the use of force, the international-level (L_3) factor has an index value of 10.

The probability of peace (P_P) for this hypothetical scenario is calculated as follows:

$$P_P = \frac{L_1 + R(L_2 + L_3)}{3}$$

$$10 = \frac{10 + 1(10 + 10)}{3}$$

The probability of peace is 10, indicating the greatest probability of peace.

The incentive theory analyses of the Gulf War and a hypothetical conflict between the United States and Canada validate the analytical process expressed in the peace-probability formula based on Moore's incentive theory of war avoidance. This analytical process can be used for general and specific deterrence applications. For general deterrence purposes, each national leader could be analyzed and assigned a value for individual-level (L_1) factors according to his or her propensity toward war or peace in an effort to identify systemic weaknesses in system-wide deterrence that could be addressed by international and regional organizations as well as nation-states. A comprehensive analysis that indexes multiple factors at the individual, state, and international levels could potentially identify other weaknesses or possible trouble spots that could be addressed by strengthening systemwide deterrence. For specific deterrence in potential war settings, the international community and nation-states could use the formula to calculate the probability of war or peace and identify weaknesses of deterrence incentives specific to that war setting. Both applications could be used by national leaders and policy makers at the international and national levels as a predictive tool to analyze and strengthen systemwide deterrence incentives. If deterrence and incentive indexes were created and maintained through detailed analysis, they could be a very meaningful and useful tool for maintaining international peace and security. The next chapter introduces indexes that could serve as a model for a deterrence index. These well-established indexes, maintained by internationally recognized organizations such as Freedom House and the Fraser Institute, measure the indicators of political freedom, economic freedom, and quality of life for all the nations and jurisdictions of the world. Similarly, a deterrence index that measures relevant factors for all jurisdictions could provide crucial data to support efforts to prevent war.

Notes

1. The formula for the probability of peace is introduced in chapter 4.
2. Elman, *Paths to Peace*.

3. Moore, *Solving the War Puzzle*, xix.
4. Elman, "Testing the Democratic Peace Theory," *Paths to Peace*, 473–74.
5. Ibid., "Preface," vii.
6. Ibid., "Testing the Democratic Peace Theory," 474.
7. Ibid., 474, 502.
8. Ibid., 503, 506.
9. Ibid., "Introduction," 36–37.
10. Ibid., 6.
11. Layne, "Lord Palmerston," *Paths to Peace*, 85–90.
12. Kacowicz, "Peru vs. Colombia," *Paths to Peace*, 335–36.
13. Ibid., 335.
14. Elman, "Testing the Democratic Peace Theory," 502–06.
15. See discussion in chapter 2.
16. Beck, introduction to *Perpetual Peace* by Kant, xiii.
17. Kagan, *On the Origins of War*, 73–74, 212–14, 567.
18. Moore, "Toward a New Paradigm," 811, 841.
19. Ibid.
20. Turner, "Deception and Deterrence," 23.
21. JP 1-02, *DOD Dictionary*, 157.
22. Joint Chiefs of Staff, *National Military Strategy*, 3.
23. UNESCO, *Constitution*, in *Manual of the General Conference*, 7.
24. Rummel, *In the Minds of Men*, 10.
25. Ibid., *Power Kills*, 154.
26. For a detailed account of the Iraqi invasion of Kuwait and the response of the international community, see US DOD, *Conduct of the Persian Gulf War*.
27. Ibid., ii.
28. Ibid., 9.
29. Ibid., 3.
30. Ibid., 4.
31. Ibid., 3.
32. Ibid., 5.
33. Ibid., 6–8.
34. Immelman, "The Clinton Chronicle."
35. Post, "Explaining Saddam Hussein."
36. Ibid.
37. Although these two references postdate Hussein's invasion of Kuwait in August 1990, they provide an example of the insights into the behavioral, temperamental, emotional, and mental attributes that can be used in incentive theory analysis.
38. Karatnycky, "Liberty's Expansion."
39. See chapter 6 for a discussion of legal systems. Table 11 ranks jurisdictions according to their aggregated index value of democracy, a value that is explained in chapter 6.
40. US DOD, *Conduct of the Persian Gulf War*, 21–31.
41. Ibid., xxv.
42. Ibid., 1.
43. Gelb, "A Bush Green Light to Iraq?"

44. Ibid.

45. The United States has not released any official transcripts of the meeting. For the transcript published in a Pakistani newspaper, see Omar, "Is the US State Department Still Keeping April Glaspie under Wraps?"

46. Gelb, "A Bush Green Light to Iraq?"

47. Powell, *My American Journey*, 462.

48. Quoted in ibid., 461.

Chapter 6

Correlative Values of Democracy

*Good governance is perhaps the single most important fac-
tor in eradicating poverty and promoting development.*

—Kofi Annan
Former UN Secretary-General, 1998

The significance of the democratic peace principle is inescap-
able, and it has extraordinary implications for humankind and
world peace. Since democracy is a method of nonviolence, Rummel argues, "by creating democracies we create zones of peace."[1]
Within these zones, "there is no war, virtually no military action,
the very least internal political violence, and almost no genocide
and mass murder."[2] Indeed, if "ever all nations were to become
democratic we have the promise of eliminating war and sharply
reducing the amount of political violence" throughout the world.[3]
A world of all democracies is a world of peace.

The value of democracy, however, extends beyond the prevention of war; the spread of democracy has implications for
human freedom and development as well. As Moore notes, government "structures rooted in democracy, the rule of law, and
human freedom perform impressively better than totalitarian
and authoritarian models" for a range of major human goals
such as improved human rights, economic development, environmental protection, famine avoidance, control of terrorism,
corruption avoidance, control of mass refugee flows, democide avoidance, reduction of infant mortality, and expansion of
women's rights. Simply stated, "democracy and the rule of law
are, quite centrally, a crucial goal for achieving common human aspirations."[4] Conversely, "nondemocratic structures and
a lack of human freedom go hand in hand with a wide variety
of [government] failures, including war, terrorism, democide,
famine, poverty, environmental degradation, corruption, narcotics trafficking, infant mortality, and refugees."[5] Not only is
a world of all democracies a world of peace, it is also a world of
human freedom and human development.

The Human-Development Benefits of Democracy

In terms of economic development, democracies "consistently outperform autocracies in the developing world," and "the most prosperous states in the world are well-established democracies."[6] Even low-income democracies perform better than low-income autocracies: citizens live an average of nine years longer, are 40 percent more likely to attend secondary school, benefit from 25 percent higher agricultural yields, have 20 percent fewer infant deaths, enjoy more stable annual gross domestic products with fewer large drops from year to year, live with less government corruption, and are less likely to experience humanitarian emergencies. For example, in 2003 80 percent of all "internally displaced persons" lived under authoritarian governments.[7] The fact is that poor democracies not only have fewer violent conflicts than poor authoritarian nations, they also "do a better job of generating material benefits for their citizens."[8] Democracies in the developing world outperform their authoritarian counterparts because their governmental institutions enable power to be shared, have internal checks and balances, spur the flow of information, are less corrupt, are adaptable, and adjust well to changing circumstances.[9]

For example, Nobel laureate economist Amartya Sen has shown that democracies usually act decisively when faced with crop failures and potential shortages in the food supply. Thus mass starvation due to famine has not occurred under any democratic government:

> One of the remarkable facts in the terrible history of famine is that no substantial famine has ever occurred in a country with a democratic form of government and a relatively free press. They have occurred in ancient kingdoms and in contemporary authoritarian societies, in primitive tribal communities and in modern technocratic dictatorships, in colonial economies governed by imperialists from the north and in newly independent countries of the south run by despotic leaders or by intolerant single parties. But famines have never afflicted any country that is independent, that goes to elections regularly, that has opposition parties to voice criticism, that permits newspapers to report freely and to question the wisdom of government policies without extensive censorship.[10]

Former deputy prime minister of Sweden and co-chair of UN Watch Per Ahlmark notes that "the crucial factor is freedom" because where "there is an active opposition and a free press, governments cannot neglect tens of thousands of people starving to death."[11] In contrast, when the "opposition is silenced and mass media give voice only to the propaganda of the dictator, the fate of millions of people dying from famine could be kept secret and ignored—because of ideology, incompetence, systematic lying and total lack of compassion."[12]

Johan Norberg's 2001 book *In Defence of Global Capitalism* validates the economic benefits of democracy. A former anarchist, Norberg has become a strong advocate of globalization, which he defines as the "process whereby people, communications, trade, investments, democracy and the market economy are tending more and more to cross national boundaries." He concludes that we "need a government which protects liberty and prevents the powerful from oppressing individuals" and that a "representative democracy is preferable to all other systems, for this very purpose of protecting the rights of the individual."[13] Norberg also concludes that democratic reforms and economic liberalization have improved the quality of life of the impoverished around the world. In India, for example, democracy and freedom of choice have empowered women and enabled a greater number of children to attend school.[14]

Norberg tells of a trip to a number of Asian countries in the 1960s by a Swedish author and a documentary filmmaker who observed "poverty, abject misery and imminent disaster" and left thinking there was no hopeful future for those people. Returning, however, to India and China in the 1990s, they saw how people had extricated themselves from poverty, hunger, and filth. The biggest change was in people's thoughts and dreams: television and newspapers had brought them ideas from around the world. Norberg attributes this development to the movement toward greater individual liberty. He describes how globalization has caused this change:

> The freedom to choose and the international exchange have grown, investments and development assistance have transmitted ideas and resources. In this way benefit has been derived from the knowledge, wealth and inventions of other countries. Imports of medicines and new health care systems have improved living conditions. Modern technology and new methods of production have moved production forward and improved the food supply. Individual citizens have become more and more free to choose their own occupations and to sell their products. We can tell from the statistics how this enhances national prosperity and reduces poverty among the population. But the most important thing of

all is liberty itself, the independence and dignity which autonomy confers on people who have been living under oppression.[15]

The average world citizen's income doubled between 1965 and 1998, and in the past half-century over 3 billion people were liberated from poverty. In fact, world poverty fell more during the past half-century than in the preceding 500 years. The average life expectancy of people in developing countries also more than doubled between 1900 and 1998, and infant mortality dropped by two-thirds between 1950 and 1995. Calorie intake in the developing world rose by 30 percent from the 1960s to the late 1990s. Global food production doubled in the last half-century, and world hunger declined by almost 25 percent from the 1970s to the late 1990s. Illiteracy also diminished by 55 percent in developing countries between 1926 and 1970. Norberg attributes all of these remarkable improvements in human development to globalization and the growth in individual liberty and parallels these developments with world democratization.[16]

Democratization and globalization have also challenged one of the "world's cruelest injustices"—the oppression of women.[17] The cultural contacts and interchange of ideas caused by globalization upset old traditions, habits, and laws whereby women in many parts of the world have been regarded as man's property and subjected to violence; have had little control over their lives; and have been unable to own or inherit property, file for divorce, and pursue the same education as men. Globalization allows women to become more prosperous and independent. Democratization "gives women a voice in politics, and in more and more countries the laws have been reformed in favour of greater equality between the sexes." The difference between the proportion of women and men enabled to attend school has "diminished by more than half in two decades," and on average worldwide, 46 percent of basic education pupils are now girls. The average life expectancy of women in the developing world has also "increased by 20 years during the past half-century."[18]

Economic freedom brings prosperity, growth, higher living standards, equality, and longer life expectancies, and it reduces government corruption. Capitalism and free trade also often cause improvements in environmental protection in developing countries.[19] Economic freedom and globalization have caused "communist dictatorships in the east and the military dictatorships of the Third World . . . and the walls they had raised against ideas, people and goods" to collapse.[20] However, while democracy and capitalism have reduced these and other enormous problems throughout the world, poverty and deprivation remain. In 2000, 3 million people died of a single disease—AIDS.[21] In 2001, approximately 20 million people lived as fugitives from oppression, conflicts, or natural disasters, and about 20 countries have grown poorer since 1965.[22] The 2004 report *The State of Food Insecurity in the World*, published by the UN Food and Agriculture Organization (FAO), estimates that 852 million people worldwide were undernourished in 2000–2002 (815 million in developing countries, 28 million in countries in transition, and 9 million in industrialized countries). During the second half of the 1990s, the number of chronically hungry people in developing countries increased at a rate of almost 4 million per year. Still today, over 5 million children die every year from undernourishment and deficiencies in essential vitamins and minerals.[23] The 2004–5 *World Employment Report* by the UN International Labour Organization (ILO) estimates that about half the world's workers—1.39 billion people—do not earn enough to lift themselves above the poverty line of two US dollars a day.[24] Nevertheless, where liberal policies have been allowed to operate the longest, poverty and deprivation have become the exception and not the rule.[25]

Rating Freedom and Human Development among the Nations

The correlative values of democracy can be validated by several well-established indexes or rating systems. Respected organizations such as Freedom House, the Heritage Foundation, the Fraser Institute, and the United Nations Development Programme (UNDP) have collected extensive data that evaluates and indexes various factors pertaining to democratic governance, economic freedom, and human development.

The Rating Organizations

Since 1972 Freedom House has published *Freedom in the World*, an annual assessment of political rights and civil liberties

127

for countries around the world; the survey is currently reporting on 193 countries and 15 territories.[26] While *Freedom in the World* analyzes freedom of the press as one of its criteria, since 1980 Freedom House has also completed a more extensive annual survey of media independence around the world; the current survey covers 194 countries and territories.[27] Similarly, from 1986 through 2006, Freedom House published an annual assessment of freedom of religion that covered over 90 percent of the world's population living in 74 countries and Tibet.[28]

The Heritage Foundation, a research and educational institute founded in 1973, conducts research to support conservative public policies that reflect its core principles of free enterprise, limited government, individual freedom, traditional American values, and a strong national defense.[29] Since 1994 the Heritage Foundation and the *Wall Street Journal* have jointly published an annual assessment of economic freedom for 161 countries. The *Index of Economic Freedom* measures 10 economic factors such as trade freedom, property rights, and freedom from government.[30]

The Fraser Institute is an independent, nonpartisan public policy organization that examines the impact of competitive markets and the effect of government interventions on markets.[31] It supports economic freedom and less government intervention. Since 1996 the Fraser Institute has coordinated the development of an annual economic freedom report that evaluates multiple measures to determine how well a nation's policies encourage economic freedom; the most recent report evaluated 141 countries.[32]

The UNDP is a UN organization that provides expertise and support services to governments and UN teams in five areas: democratic governance, poverty reduction, crisis prevention and recovery, energy and environment, and HIV/AIDS.[33] Since 1990 the UNDP has published an annual *Human Development Report* featuring the human development index, which measures a country's success in three dimensions of human development: long and healthy lives for its citizens, education, and a decent standard of living.[34] The *Human Development Report* highlights issues and policies that address economic, social, political, and cultural development challenges.[35] Each year the report focuses on a different issue. The 2003 report, which will be discussed here, analyzes the root causes of failed development by focusing on four sets of issues: the economic reforms

128

needed to create macroeconomic stability; the strong institutions and governance required to enforce the rule of law and control corruption; the need to provide social justice and involve people in decisions that affect them and their communities; and the need to address structural constraints that impede economic growth and human development.[36]

The Rating Data: Table A1

Table A1 (appendix A), Freedom and Human Development Ratings for 267 National and Territorial Jurisdictions, collates recent data from the four institutions described above to facilitate a comparative analysis of the data along with each jurisdiction's government type and legal system. This comparative analysis will present another perspective from which to evaluate the democratic peace principle. Because of its length, table A1 is provided in appendix A. Following is an explanation of each column in the table.

Column A. Column A identifies 267 jurisdictions found around the world. This list is primarily drawn from the CIA *World Factbook 2003*, with a few modifications. For example, the list of jurisdictions in table A1 includes the Socialist Federal Republic of Yugoslavia, which no longer exists and is not included in the 2003 *Factbook*. Table A1 also lists the Israeli-occupied territories of the West Bank and the Gaza Strip separately even though both are governed by the Palestinian Authority and usually listed as a single jurisdiction. Like the *Factbook*, the list in table A1 does not include Tibet, which is claimed by the People's Republic of China as one of its administrative subdivisions. Other lists of jurisdictions in the world may also vary from table A1, depending on how various jurisdictions are grouped and counted. A parenthetical date in column A identifies the date of admission to the UN for the 191 member states.[37]

Column B. Column B identifies the geographic region of each jurisdiction using the six regions of the world recognized by the US Department of State:[38]

1. Africa (AF): 59 jurisdictions (48 nations, 11 nonnations)

2. East Asia and the Pacific (EAP): 59 jurisdictions (30 nations, 29 nonnations)

3. Europe and Eurasia (EUR): 66 jurisdictions (52 nations, 14 nonnations)

4. Near East (NE): 21 jurisdictions (19 nations, two nonnations)

5. South Asia (SA): eight jurisdictions (eight nations, zero nonnations)

6. Western Hemisphere (WH): 54 jurisdictions (34 nations, 20 nonnations)

The State Department assigns some nonnation jurisdictions to the geographic region where the territory is located and some to the geographic region where its parent nation is located. For purposes of consistency and to maintain a geographic focus, all nonnation jurisdictions in table A1 are assigned to the geographic region where they are physically located.

Column C. Column C provides the Freedom House (FH) "state of freedom" country rating for 2004, which is based on data from 2003.[39] Jurisdictions are evaluated on a checklist of questions on political rights and civil liberties derived primarily from the Universal Declaration of Human Rights. Each jurisdiction is assigned a rating for political rights and a rating for civil liberties on a scale of 1–7, with one representing the highest degree of freedom and seven the lowest. The political-rights checklist asks detailed questions about the electoral process, political pluralism and participation, and the functioning of government. The civil-liberties checklist asks detailed questions about freedom of expression and belief, associational and organizational rights, the rule of law, and personal autonomy and individual rights. The average of the two ratings determines the overall status for a jurisdiction: free (F) for averages of 1.0–2.5, partly free (PF) for averages of 3.0–5.0, or not free (NF) for averages of 5.5–7.0.[40] For each jurisdiction reported on by Freedom House, column C shows the "state of freedom" country rating (F, PF, or NF), followed by its numerical rating for political rights and civil liberties.[41]

Column D. Column D shows the Freedom House country rating for media independence for 2003, based on data from 2002.[42] Jurisdictions are evaluated on the degree to which they permit the free flow of information. Each jurisdiction is assigned a rating for media independence on a scale of 1–100. Jurisdictions scoring 1–30 are regarded as having a free (F) media, 31–60 as having a partly free (PF) media, and 61–100 as having a not-free (NF) media. A rating of one thus represents the highest degree of freedom and 100 the lowest. To determine a jurisdiction's rating, Freedom House examines detailed criteria in three categories: the legal environment, political influences, and economic pressures on the media.[43]

Column E. Column E shows the Freedom House Center for Religious Freedom country rating for freedom of religion and belief in 2000, which is based on data from 1999. The report rates 74 countries which contain over 90 percent of the world's population on a scale of 1–7, with one representing the highest degree of religious freedom and seven the lowest. Jurisdictions with a rating of 1–3 are considered free (F), 4–5 are partly free (PF), and 6–7 are unfree (UF). The criteria used to rate freedom of religion are primarily developed from the International Covenant on Civil and Political Rights, the UN Declaration on the Elimination of All Forms of Intolerance and of Discrimination Based on Religion or Belief, and the European Convention on Human Rights.[44]

Column F. Column F shows the Heritage Foundation (HF) and *Wall Street Journal* country rating for 2004, which is based on data from 2003.[45] In the *2004 Index of Economic Freedom*, based on 2003 data, countries are evaluated and assigned an individual score on a scale of 1–5 for 10 factors of economic freedom. A score of one indicates the greatest degree of freedom for that factor, and five indicates the least. Then the 10 individual scores are averaged to yield an overall economic freedom score of 1–5. An overall score of one signifies "an economic environment or set of policies that are most conducive to economic freedom, while a score of five signifies a set of policies that are least conducive to economic freedom." Countries are then scored as free (F) if their average is 1.99 or less, mostly free (MF) if their average is 2.0–2.99, mostly unfree (MU) if their average is 3.0–3.99, and repressed (R) if their average is 4.0 or higher. For each jurisdiction reported on by the Heritage Foundation, Column F shows the 2003 "state of economic freedom" country rating (F, MF, MU, or R) and the overall numerical average, derived from the data provided by the Heritage Foundation.[46]

Column G. Column G provides the Fraser Institute (FI) country rating from the *Economic Freedom of the World: 2003 Annual*

Report, which presents data from 2001. Countries are indexed on a scale of 10–1 according to the degree of economic freedom in five major areas:

1. Size of government: expenditures, taxes, and enterprises

2. Legal structure and security of property rights

3. Access to sound money

4. Freedom to exchange with foreigners

5. Regulation of credit, labor, and business

Within these areas, the Fraser Institute compiles 38 distinct data points for each country. Each data point is assigned a value of 10–1, with 10 signifying the highest degree of economic freedom and one signifying the lowest. The data points within each area are then averaged to determine a rating for each area. The country rating is the average of the ratings for each of the five areas.[47] For each jurisdiction reported on by the Fraser Institute, Column G shows the 2001 "state of economic freedom" country rating, derived from the data provided by the Fraser Institute.

Column H. Column H identifies the UNDP Human Development Index (HDI) for 2001, which is published in the 2003 UNDP *Human Development Report*.[48] The index measures three dimensions of human development for 175 countries: "living a long and healthy life, being educated, and having a decent standard of living."[49] The index assigns a summary rating to each country on a scale of 1–0: a value of 0.8–1.0 represents high human development; 0.5–0.799 represents medium human development; and 0.0–0.499 represents low human development.[50] The *Human Development Report* compiles this data to better understand and analyze the root causes of failed development. One of its key conclusions is that "strengthening governance and institutions and adopting sound social and economic policies are all necessary," although far from sufficient by themselves, to achieve human development.[51]

Column I. Column I compares two sets of data. First, it classifies each of the 191 UN member states (as of 2003) and Taiwan according to political system, using the following schema:

1. Democracies (DEM): Political systems whose leaders are elected in competitive multiparty and multicandidate processes in which opposition parties have a legitimate chance of attaining power or participating in power. (119 countries, 62.0 percent of total world population governed by democracies)[52]

2. Restricted democratic practices (RDP): Primarily regimes in which a dominant ruling party controls the levers of power, including access to the media, and the electoral process in ways that preclude a meaningful challenge to its political hegemony. In the first half of the twentieth century, states with restricted democratic practices included countries which denied universal franchise to women, racial minorities, and the poor and landless. (16, 8.3 percent)

3. Monarchies (three types): Constitutional monarchies (CM), in which a constitution delineates the powers of the monarch and in which some power may have devolved to elected legislatures and other bodies (0, 0.0 percent); traditional monarchies (TM) (10, 5.2 percent); and absolute monarchies (AM), in which monarchic power is exercised in despotic fashion. (0, 0.0 percent)

4. Authoritarian regimes (AR): Typically one-party states and military dictatorships in which there are significant human rights violations. (40, 20.8 percent)

5. Totalitarian regimes (TOT): One-party systems that establish effective control over most aspects of information, engage in propaganda, control civic life, and intrude into private life. Typically, these have been Marxist-Leninist and national socialist regimes. (5, 2.6 percent)

6. Colonial and imperial dependencies (C): Territories that were under the domination of the large imperial systems that predominated in the first half of the century. (0, 0 percent)

7. Protectorates (P): Countries that have by their own initiative sought the protection of a more powerful neighboring state or are under the temporary protection and jurisdiction of the international community. (2, 1.0 percent)[53]

Second, column I identifies a more specific description of the government type, such as republic, constitutional monarchy, or military dictatorship, as classified by the CIA *World Factbook*.[54]

Columns J and K. Column J identifies whether a jurisdiction is one of the world's 121 civil-law jurisdictions (CI), 82 common-law jurisdictions (CO), or 64 customary-law jurisdictions (CU), as of 2003. This information is derived from an analysis of the more detailed description of a jurisdiction's legal system found in column K.[55]

The Rating Data: Table A2

While table A1 (columns C–H) collates six significant data points from Freedom House, the Heritage Foundation, the Fraser Institute, and the UNDP, these four institutions did not collect data on all 267 jurisdictions or even on all the same jurisdictions. Also the six data points from table A1 are indexed on five different scales: 1–7, 1–100, 1–5, 10–1, and 1–0. For some indexes, the lowest value represents the highest level of human freedom or development, and for others the highest value represents the highest level of human freedom or development. Accordingly, it is difficult to use table A1 for comparative analyses.

Table A2 (appendix A) provides a more convenient tool for comparative analyses by normalizing the data on a decimal (base 10) indexing system for Hong Kong, Taiwan, and all 191 UN member states, the great majority of which are indexed in table A1 by at least three sets of data points or ratings. For these 193 jurisdictions, the same information in table A1 is provided in table A2, Normalized Freedom and Human Development Ratings for 193 Selected Jurisdictions. Since the five different index or rating scales used in table A1 are linear, the data is normalized in table A2 by simply expanding or contracting each scale to correspond to a single indexed scale of 0–10, where a rating of zero represents the lowest level of human freedom or development and a rating of 10 represents the highest level of human freedom or development. In two cases, the original scale had to be inverted because zero represented the best rating or highest level of freedom. Table 10 shows how each scale used in table A1 is converted for table A2. For each scale used in table A1, the conversion factor (CF) is applied to the conversion equation to determine the scale for table A2.

134

Table 10. Conversion of scales used in table A1 to normalized scales used in table A2

Column C scale		Column D scale		Column E scale	
Table A1	Table A2	Table A1	Table A2	Table A1	Table A2
1	10[a]	1	10	1	10
2	8.3333	10	9.0909	2	8.3333
3	6.6666	20	8.0808	3	6.6666
4	4.9999	30	7.0707	4	4.9999
5	3.3333	40	6.0606	5	3.3333
6	1.6666	50	5.0505	6	1.6666
7	0	60	4.0404	7	0
		70	3.0303		
		80	2.0202		
		90	1.0101		
		100	0		
CF = 1.6666[b]		CF = .10101		CF = 1.6666 [b]	
A2 = (7-A1)CF		A2 = (100-A1)CF		A2 = (7-A1)CF	

Column F scale		Column G scale		Column H scale	
Table A1	Table A2	Table A1	Table A2	Table A1	Table A2
1	10	10	10	1	10
2	7.5	9	8.8888	.9	9
3	5.0	8	7.7777	.8	8
4	2.5	7	6.6666	.7	7
5	0	6	5.5555	.6	6
		5	4.4444	.5	5
		4	3.3333	.4	4
		3	2.2222	.3	3
		2	1.1111	.2	2
		1	0	.1	1
				0	0
CF = 2.5		CF = 1.1111		CF = 10	
A2 = (5-A1)CF		A2 = (A1-1)CF		A2 = (A1)CF	

[a]For each rating scale in table 2, a value of 10 represents the highest rating and 1 represents the lowest.
[b]The actual conversion factor is 1.6̄6̄ (a repeating decimal).

The normalized data is provided in columns C through H of table A2, and then each normalized rating is averaged to calculate an aggregated index value of democracy (D_a) for each jurisdiction, found in column K of table A2.

The Rating Data: Table A3

Table A3 (appendix A), Selected Jurisdictions Sorted by Aggregated Index Value of Democracy (D_a), sorts the jurisdictions by the D_a from highest to lowest or most democratic to least.

The aggregated index value of democracy (D_a) is an aggregate of as many as seven data points: Freedom House ratings on political rights, civil liberties, media independence, and freedom of religion; the Heritage Foundation ratings on economic freedom; the Fraser Institute ratings on economic freedom; and the UNDP index on human development. Accordingly, correlations and observations based on the ranking of jurisdictions by D_a must take into consideration the number of data points actually used to calculate D_a. A value for D_a based upon only a few data points should not be given as much weight as a D_a calculated on all seven data points. Table 11 provides a quick reference to all 193 jurisdictions, sorted by D_a. Column A shows the relative ranking of each jurisdiction identified in column B. Columns C and D identify the political and legal systems respectively. Column E identifies the number of data points used for the calculation of D_a, and Column F shows the D_a for each jurisdiction. The greater the number of data points used to calculate D_a, the greater relative relevance of D_a vis-à-vis other jurisdictions.

Table 11. Jurisdictions sorted by aggregated index value of democracy (D_a)

A = ranking   D = legal system
B = jurisdiction E = number of data points used to calculate D_a
C = political system F = D_a

A	B	C	D	E	F
1	Andorra	DEM	CI	3	9.76
2	Palau	DEM	CO	3	9.73
3	San Marino	DEM	CI	3	9.73
4	Marshall Islands	DEM	CO	3	9.69
5	Liechtenstein	DEM	CI	3	9.66

Table 11 (*continued*)

A	B	C	D	E	F
6	Tuvalu	DEM	CO	3	9.49
7	Micronesia	DEM	CO	3	9.46
8	Monaco	DEM	CI	3	9.18
9	Kiribati	DEM	CO	3	9.16
10	Nauru	DEM	CO	3	9.16
11	New Zealand	DEM	CO	6	9.12
12	Dominica	DEM	CO	4	9.11
13	United States	DEM	CO	7	9.11
14	Ireland	DEM	CO	7	9.10
15	Finland	DEM	CI	7	9.07
16	Switzerland	DEM	CI	6	9.01
17	Netherlands	DEM	CI	7	8.99
18	Australia	DEM	CO	6	8.94
19	Denmark	DEM	CI	6	8.94
20	Luxembourg	DEM	CI	6	8.94
21	Iceland	DEM	CI	6	8.92
22	Canada	DEM	CO	6	8.87
23	Norway	DEM	CI	7	8.86
24	United Kingdom	DEM	CO	7	8.85
25	Saint Lucia	DEM	CO	4	8.84
26	Sweden	DEM	CI	7	8.79
27	Saint Kitts and Nevis	DEM	CO	4	8.67
28	Estonia	DEM	CI	7	8.62
29	Grenada	DEM	CO	4	8.60
30	Austria	DEM	CI	7	8.58
31	Saint Vincent & Grenadines	DEM	CO	4	8.57
32	Portugal	DEM	CI	6	8.50
33	Belgium	DEM	CI	7	8.48
34	Cyprus	DEM	CI	6	8.43
35	Germany	DEM	CI	7	8.41
36	Bahamas	DEM	CO	6	8.37
37	Italy	DEM	CI	6	8.32
38	Malta	DEM	CO	6	8.26
39	Spain	DEM	CI	7	8.25
40	Barbados	DEM	CO	6	8.23

Table 11 (*continued*)

A	B	C	D	E	F
41	Chile	DEM	CI	7	8.23
42	Japan	DEM	CI	7	8.19
43	France	DEM	CI	7	8.08
44	Slovenia	DEM	CI	6	8.05
45	Samoa	DEM	CO	4	8.02
46	Lithuania	DEM	CI	7	7.99
47	Uruguay	DEM	CI	6	7.98
48	Costa Rica	DEM	CI	6	7.97
49	Czech Republic	DEM	CI	6	7.97
50	Cape Verde	DEM	CI	5	7.94
51	Sao Tome & Principe	DEM	CI	4	7.81
52	Poland	DEM	CI	7	7.78
53	Slovakia	DEM	CI	6	7.77
54	Latvia	DEM	CI	7	7.74
55	Hungary	DEM	CI	7	7.69
56	Taiwan	DEM	CI	6	7.65
57	Korea, Republic of	DEM	CI	7	7.64
58	Mauritius	AR	CU	6	7.64
59	Belize	DEM	CO	6	7.59
60	South Africa	DEM	CU	7	7.58
61	Vanuatu	DEM	CO	4	7.58
62	Panama	DEM	CI	6	7.53
63	Israel	DEM	CU	7	7.49
64	Greece	DEM	CI	7	7.34
65	Botswana	DEM	CU	7	7.30
66	Hong Kong	DEM	CO	5	7.29
67	Suriname	DEM	CI	5	7.21
68	Jamaica	DEM	CO	6	7.13
69	Guyana	DEM	CO	6	7.10
70	Serbia & Montenegro	DEM	CI	3	7.02
71	Trinidad & Tobago	DEM	CO	6	7.01
72	El Salvador	DEM	CI	7	6.99
73	Croatia	DEM	CI	6	6.98
74	Mongolia	DEM	CI	6	6.94
75	Bulgaria	DEM	CI	7	6.85

Table 11 (*continued*)

A	B	C	D	E	F
76	Argentina	DEM	CI	7	6.84
77	Peru	AR	CI	6	6.81
78	Solomon Islands	DEM	CO	4	6.81
79	Thailand	DEM	CI	6	6.80
80	Brazil	DEM	CI	7	6.78
81	Namibia	DEM	CI	7	6.77
82	Philippines	DEM	CI	7	6.77
83	Antigua & Barbuda	RDP	CO	4	6.72
84	Mexico	RDP	CI	7	6.71
85	Seychelles	DEM	CU	4	6.69
86	Bolivia	DEM	CI	6	6.54
87	Dominican Republic	DEM	CI	6	6.51
88	Ghana	DEM	CU	6	6.46
89	Romania	DEM	CI	7	6.40
90	Papua New Guinea	DEM	CO	5	6.34
91	Mali	DEM	CU	6	6.19
92	Benin	DEM	CU	6	6.18
93	Nicaragua	DEM	CI	6	6.16
94	Fiji	DEM	CO	6	6.15
95	Timor-Leste	P	CI	4	6.14
96	Singapore	AR	CO	7	6.06
97	Macedonia	DEM	CI	6	6.02
98	Senegal	RDP	CI	6	5.98
99	Lesotho	RDP	CU	5	5.94
100	Albania	DEM	CI	6	5.93
101	Sri Lanka	DEM	CO	7	5.89
102	Paraguay	DEM	CI	6	5.88
103	Ecuador	DEM	CI	6	5.76
104	Honduras	DEM	CI	6	5.72
105	Madagascar	DEM	CI	6	5.67
106	Tonga	RDP	CO	3	5.62
107	India	DEM	CO	7	5.59
108	Kuwait	TM	CU	6	5.58
109	Bosnia & Herzegovina	P	CI	5	5.43
110	Moldova	DEM	CI	6	5.43

139

Table 11 (*continued*)

A	B	C	D	E	F
111	Guatemala	DEM	CI	7	5.42
112	Bahrain	TM	CU	6	5.39
113	Kenya	AR	CU	6	5.34
114	Armenia	DEM	CI	6	5.29
115	Georgia	DEM	CI	6	5.24
116	Colombia	DEM	CI	7	5.16
117	Tanzania	RDP	CU	7	5.15
118	Uganda	AR	CU	6	5.14
119	Turkey	DEM	CI	7	5.09
120	Ukraine	DEM	CI	7	5.06
121	Jordan	RDP	CU	6	4.98
122	Mozambique	DEM	CI	5	4.98
123	Malaysia	RDP	CO	7	4.97
124	Indonesia	DEM	CI	7	4.93
125	Venezuela	DEM	CI	6	4.91
126	Comoros	RDP	CU	4	4.84
127	Burkina Faso	AR	CU	5	4.75
128	Malawi	DEM	CU	6	4.66
129	Morocco	TM	CU	7	4.65
130	Oman	TM	CU	6	4.65
131	Zambia	AR	CU	6	4.63
132	Gabon	AR	CU	6	4.62
133	United Arab Emirates	TM	CU	6	4.56
134	Niger	DEM	CU	6	4.45
135	Russia	DEM	CI	7	4.45
136	Sierra Leone	DEM	CU	6	4.37
137	Gambia	AR	CU	5	4.36
138	Nigeria	DEM	CU	7	4.35
139	Tunisia	AR	CU	6	4.29
140	Lebanon	AR	CU	6	4.19
141	Qatar	TM	CU	5	4.18
142	Nepal	DEM	CO	7	4.16
143	Congo, Republic of	AR	CU	6	4.09
144	Bangladesh	DEM	CO	7	4.08
145	Kyrgyzstan	DEM	CI	6	4.05

Table 11 (*continued*)

A	B	C	D	E	F
146	Brunei Darussalam	TM	CO	4	4.04
147	Maldives	AR	CO	4	4.04
148	Algeria	AR	CU	6	3.94
149	Kazakhstan	AR	CI	6	3.94
150	Cambodia	RDP	CI	5	3.89
151	Djibouti	DEM	CU	5	3.85
152	Azerbaijan	AR	CI	6	3.75
153	Côte d'Ivoire	AR	CU	6	3.69
154	Egypt	RDP	CU	7	3.67
155	Ethiopia	AR	CU	5	3.61
156	Yemen	RDP	CU	5	3.55
157	Pakistan	AR	CO	7	3.54
158	Guinea-Bissau	DEM	CI	6	3.49
159	Chad	RDP	CU	6	3.48
160	Burundi	AR	CU	5	3.40
161	Cameroon	RDP	CU	6	3.40
162	Togo	DEM	CU	6	3.39
163	Mauritania	AR	CU	6	3.38
164	Rwanda	AR	CU	6	3.33
165	Guinea	AR	CU	5	3.26
166	Tajikistan	RDP	CI	5	3.26
167	Swaziland	TM	CU	5	3.19
168	Belarus	AR	CI	6	3.13
169	Haiti	DEM	CI	6	3.12
170	Central African Republic	DEM	CU	6	3.11
171	China	AR	CI	7	2.99
172	Bhutan	TM	CO	5	2.96
173	Zimbabwe	RDP	CU	7	2.95
174	Angola	AR	CI	4	2.89
175	Iran	AR	CU	7	2.86
176	Syria	AR	CU	6	2.72
177	Equatorial Guinea	AR	CI	5	2.55
178	Saudi Arabia	TM	CU	6	2.43
179	Congo, Democratic Republic of the	AR	CU	5	2.40

141

Table 11 (continued)

A	B	C	D	E	F
180	Vietnam	TOT	CI	6	2.35
181	Uzbekistan	AR	CI	6	2.30
182	Cuba	TOT	CI	6	2.11
183	Lao People's Democratic Republic	TOT	CU	5	2.06
184	Libya	AR	CU	5	2.01
185	Afghanistan	TOT	CU	3	1.99
186	Eritrea	AR	CU	4	1.96
187	Liberia	DEM	CU	3	1.82
188	Turkmenistan	AR	CI	6	1.67
189	Myanmar	AR	CI	7	1.51
190	Iraq	AR	CU	3	1.28
191	Sudan	AR	CU	5	1.24
192	Somalia	AR	CU	3	1.23
193	Korea, Democratic People's Republic of	TOT	CI	5	0.08

Compiled from data in tables A1 and A2.

Correlation between Legal System and Form of Government

The data summarized in table 11 suggests a correlation between type of legal system and form of government. For example, of the five totalitarian regimes (TOT) listed in table 11, three have a civil-law (CI) system and two have a customary-law (CU) system; none have a common-law (CO) system. Of the 38 authoritarian regimes (AR), 10 have a civil-law system, and 25 have a customary-law system; only three have a common-law system. In contrast, only 15 of the 122 democracies have a customary-law system. Table 12 summarizes the relationship between legal systems and forms of government. For the purposes of this analysis, the two protectorates according to the 1999 Freedom House designations—Timor-Leste and Bosnia and Herzegovina—are counted as democracies. The international community recognized Timor-Leste as an independent

142

democratic state on 20 May 2002,[56] and Bosnia and Herzegovina continues making progress as an emerging federal democratic republic.[57]

Table 12. Legal systems and forms of government for 193 jurisdictions

Form of government	Legal system		
	Civil law	Common law	Customary law
Democracies (DEM): 124 (counting two protectorates)	75	34	15
Restricted democratic practices (RDP): 16	4	3	9
Traditional monarchies (TM): 10	0	2	8
Authoritarian regimes (AR): 38	10	3	25
Totalitarian regimes (TOT): 5	3	0	2
Total: 193 jurisdictions	92	42	59

Compiled from data presented in tables A1 and A2.

While almost 88 percent of all democracies have either a civil- or common-law system, the remaining 12 percent have a customary-law system. However, democracies with a customary-law system all have a very low or average D_a. In contrast, no totalitarian regime and only about 8 percent of all authoritarian regimes have a common-law system. Almost 63 percent of the 43 authoritarian and totalitarian regimes have a customary-law system.

Table 11 suggests another interesting correlation between type of legal system and value of D_a. For example, all governments with a D_a of 7.65 or higher are democracies and have either a civil-law or common-law system. When jurisdictions are ranked in order of D_a from highest to lowest, as in table 11, there are no customary-law systems in the top 56 jurisdictions (those with the highest D_a), and there are only 10 customary-law jurisdictions in the top 110 jurisdictions. The remaining 49 customary-law systems are found in jurisdictions with mostly authoritarian and totalitarian forms of government with a D_a of 5.39 or less.

A contemporary common-law legal system is generally an adversarial system of British heritage where law was developed by custom interpreted by courts. This system now relies upon legislation and court decisions as primary sources of law interpreted by judicial decision based upon custom and judicial precedent. A common-law system emphasizes the rights of individuals. A contemporary civil-law legal system is generally an inquisitorial system of Roman heritage where law was developed by adopting historic Roman codes. This system now relies upon legislation as the primary source of law, which is strictly interpreted by judicial decision. Although not controlling, judicial precedent is often considered and even sometimes cited in civil-law jurisdictions. Civil-law systems normally emphasize social stability.

A customary-law legal system, however, is "indigenous, fragmentary (on a geographical basis), binding only on those who accept it as the law applicable to them."[58] Customary law "emphasises status, duties, and community values, whereas human rights provisions emphasise individual rights and freedoms and equality and reflect internationally accepted value."[59] A customary-law system is a conservative, patriarchal legal system that is generally inconsistent with liberal, egalitarian principles.

The data in table 11 illustrates that civil-law and common-law systems are most often found in democracies. These systems are more conducive to the political and economic growth of democracies and are more compatible with democratic forms of government and economic freedom. Customary-law systems, on the other hand, are most often found in authoritarian and totalitarian regimes. These systems are more conducive to the political and economic stagnation of nondemocracies and are more compatible with nondemocratic forms of government. By their very nature, customary-law systems, which emphasize community values over individual rights, are not as conducive to political, economic, and religious freedom and are more subject to the abusive use of power than their civil-law and common-law counterparts.

Correlation between D_a and Economic Performance

Because democracies perform better than nondemocracies according to a number of quality-of-life indicators, we can expect that D_a—an aggregate of seven data points that measure political rights, civil liberties, media independence, freedom of religion, economic freedom, and human development—will have a strong correlation to indicators of human development such as economic achievement. For example, the top seven major industrialized nations, called the Group of Seven (G-7), account for about two-thirds of the world's economic output.[60] The G-7 members are, in order of size, the United States, Japan, Germany, the United Kingdom, France, Italy, and Canada. Not surprisingly, the G-7 members all have a high D_a. Russia officially became a member of the group in 1997, making it the Group of Eight (G-8); however, Russia has the G-8's smallest economy.

Table 13 shows the gross domestic product (GDP) in 1999 for the world's top 15 economies along with their percentage of the world's population (1999),[61] government type, legal system type, and D_a.

Table 13. GDP, population, and related data for the world's top 15 economies, sorted by D_a

Jurisdiction	GDP[a] (in millions)	Ranking by GDP	Percent of world population[b]	Government type[c]	Legal system type[c]	D_a[d]
United States (G-8)	9,152,098	1	4.60	DEM	CO	9.11
Australia	404,033	14	0.31	DEM	CO	8.94
Canada (G-8)	634,898	9	0.52	DEM	CO	8.87
United Kingdom (G-8)	1,441,787	4	0.98	DEM	CO	8.85
Germany (G-8)	2,111,940	3	1.40	DEM	CI	8.41
Italy (G-8)	1,170,971	6	0.96	DEM	CI	8.32
Spain	595,927	10	0.66	DEM	CI	8.25
Japan (G-8)	4,346,922	2	2.10	DEM	CI	8.19
France (G-8)	1,432,323	5	1.00	DEM	CI	8.08
Korea, Republic of	406,940	13	0.78	DEM	CI	7.64
Brazil	751,505	8	2.80	DEM	CI	6.78
Mexico	483,737	11	1.60	RDP	CI	6.71
India	447,292	12	16.7	DEM	CO	5.59
Russia (G-8)	401,442	15	2.50	DEM	CI	4.45
China	989,465	7	21.20	AR	CI	2.99

[a]US State Department. "The Size of the G-8 Economies." http://usinfo.state.gov/topical/econ/group8/g8size.htm.

[b]United Nations. 1999 population rankings for 20 most populous countries. http://www.un.org/esa/population/pubsarchive/india/20most.htm.

[c]See table A1.

[d]See table A2.

As table 13 shows, the G-8 member states, which were responsible for two-thirds of all of the world's economic output in 1999 despite representing only 14.06 percent of the world's population, are all democracies. Not only are they democracies, but they all have a D_a of greater than eight except for Russia, which has a D_a of 4.45. Also of significance, all 15 of the world's top economies are either common-law or civil-law jurisdictions. Even though the top four economic powers are common-law jurisdictions, 10 jurisdictions have civil-law systems; the other jurisdiction, India, has a common-law system.

China, an authoritarian regime with a D_a of 2.99, is the most notable exception in table 13 as the only nondemocracy among the top 15 world economic powers. However, China's performance in economic measures is better than in political measures. While China has an average normalized value of 1.34 for political rights, civil liberties, media independence, and freedom of religion in table A2 (an average of columns C, D, and E), it has an average normalized value of 4.2 for economic freedom (an average of columns F and G) and a normalized value of 7.21 for human development (column H). China was most likely the seventh largest economic power in the world in 1999, despite its largely nondemocratic practices, because it was the world's largest nation with 21.2 percent of the world population and because it started incorporating free market concepts into its domestic economic policies. China trailed six democracies that had almost 20 times the economic output of goods and services with almost half the population.

The 42 heavily indebted poor countries (HIPC) listed in table 14, identified by the World Bank in 2004, are neither predominantly nondemocratic nor democratic.[62] Thirty-four of these countries are from Africa, four from Latin America, three from Asia, and one from the Middle East. Table 14 sorts these countries by D_a.

Table 14. Heavily indebted poor countries sorted by D_a

Jurisdiction	Government type	Legal system	D_a
Sao Tome and Principe	DEM	CI	7.81
Guyana	DEM	CO	7.10
Bolivia	DEM	CI	6.54

Table 14 (continued)

Jurisdiction	Government type	Legal system	D_a
Ghana	DEM	CU	6.46
Mali	DEM	CU	6.19
Benin	DEM	CU	6.18
Nicaragua	DEM	CI	6.16
Senegal	RDP	CI	5.98
Honduras	DEM	CI	5.72
Madagascar	DEM	CI	5.67
Kenya	AR	CU	5.34
Tanzania	RDP	CU	5.15
Uganda	AR	CU	5.14
Mozambique	DEM	CI	4.98
Comoros	RDP	CU	4.84
Burkina Faso	AR	CU	4.75
Malawi	DEM	CU	4.66
Zambia	AR	CU	4.63
Niger	DEM	CU	4.45
Sierra Leone	DEM	CU	4.37
Gambia	AR	CU	4.36
Congo, Republic of	AR	CU	4.09
Côte d'Ivoire	AR	CU	3.69
Ethiopia	AR	CU	3.61
Yemen	RDP	CU	3.55
Guinea-Bissau	DEM	CI	3.49
Chad	RDP	CU	3.48
Burundi	AR	CU	3.40
Cameroon	RDP	CU	3.40
Togo	DEM	CU	3.39
Mauritania	AR	CU	3.38
Rwanda	AR	CU	3.33
Guinea	AR	CU	3.26
Central African Republic	DEM	CU	3.11
Angola	AR	CI	2.89
Congo, Democratic Republic of the	AR	CU	2.40
Vietnam	TOT	CI	2.35

Table 14 (*continued*)

Jurisdiction	Government type	Legal system	D_a
Lao People's Democratic Republic	TOT	CU	2.06
Liberia	DEM	CU	1.82
Myanmar	AR	CI	1.51
Sudan	AR	CU	1.24
Somalia	AR	CU	1.23

Compiled from data presented in tables A1 and A2.

Of these 42 HIPCs, 19 are either authoritarian or totalitarian, 17 are democratic, and six have restricted democratic practices. Also, 30 of these countries have a customary-law system, 11 have a civil-law system, and one has a common-law system. Table 15 summarizes the distribution of types of legal systems and governments for these 42 HIPCs.

Table 15. Legal systems and forms of government for HIPCs

Form of government	Legal system		
	Civil law	Common law	Customary law
Democracies (DEM): 17	7	1	9
Restricted democratic practices (RDP): 6	1		5
Authoritarian regimes (AR): 17	2		15
Totalitarian regimes (TOT): 2	1		1
Total: 42 regimes	11	1	30

Compiled from data presented in tables A1 and A2.

The nature of authoritarian and totalitarian regimes and the fact that they predominantly have customary-law systems explain why those 19 HIPCs are so poor. The remaining 23 governments, which are either democracies or have restricted democratic practices, could be poor because their transition to

148

democracy is too recent for democratic practices to encourage a thriving economy. For example, in table 14 the first 10 HIPC democracies or countries with restricted democratic practices all have values of D_a ranging from 5.67 through 7.81, which might suggest a productive economy. However, even though the democratic system is in place as evidenced by the relatively high D_a, it may not have had the time to work yet. These countries could also have small populations or populations that need the technical and educational skills to enter the international market, which take time to develop.

Alternatively, the 23 democratic or RDP governments could be so poor because of their respective legal systems. Fourteen of them have strong customary-law systems. Furthermore, the one common-law democracy and five of the remaining civil-law countries also have a strong customary- and religious-law influence. The remaining three—Honduras, Bolivia, and Nicaragua—have midlevel D_a values; however, all three of these countries have had very volatile political histories and have only recently developed democratic forms of government.[63] Ultimately, the explanation is likely a combination of all these dynamics, although the correlations discussed here do illustrate that civil-law and common-law systems are more conducive to liberal political and economic growth, while customary-law systems are more conducive to the political and economic stagnation of authoritarian and totalitarian regimes.

The World's Worst Governments

Freedom House lists Burma, China, Cuba, Equatorial Guinea, Eritrea, Iraq, Laos, Libya, North Korea, Saudi Arabia, Somalia, Sudan, Syria, Turkmenistan, Uzbekistan, and Vietnam as 16 of the worst governments in its 2003 report *The World's Most Repressive Regimes*.[64] Since the data for D_a is principally based on Freedom House data, it is no surprise that these 16 nations have the lowest D_a numbers. As table 16 shows, these 16 nations demonstrate the correlation between government type, legal system, and D_a. Nearly all have authoritarian or totalitarian governments; one has a traditional monarchy. None has a common-law system, and half have the least progressive of legal systems—customary law.

149

Table 16. Freedom House 16 worst regimes sorted by D_a

Jurisdiction	Government type	Type of legal system	Number of data points used to calculate D_a	D_a
China	AR	CI	7	2.99
Syria	AR	CU	6	2.72
Equatorial Guinea	AR	CI	5	2.55
Saudi Arabia	TM	CU	6	2.43
Vietnam	TOT	CI	6	2.35
Uzbekistan	AR	CI	6	2.30
Cuba	TOT	CI	6	2.11
Lao People's Democratic Republic	TOT	CU	5	2.06
Libya	AR	CU	5	2.01
Eritrea	AR	CU	4	1.96
Turkmenistan	AR	CI	6	1.67
Myanmar	AR	CI	7	1.51
Iraq	AR	CU	3	1.28
Sudan	AR	CU	5	1.24
Somalia	AR	CU	3	1.23
Korea, Democratic People's Republic of	TOT	CI	5	0.08

Compiled from data presented in tables A1 and A2.

Transparency International ranks 146 nations in its Corruption Perceptions Index (CPI), which surveys business people and country analysts to measure their perceptions of the degree of corruption in those nations.[65] A score of 10 means a nation is highly clean, and a score of zero means highly corrupt. In 2004 the 14 cleanest countries (in order of decreasing score) were Finland, New Zealand, Denmark, Iceland, Singapore, Sweden, Switzerland, Norway, Australia, the Netherlands, the United Kingdom, Canada, Austria, and Luxembourg—all with a CPI score of 8.4 or higher. These 14 nations also all have a D_a of 8.79 or higher except for Singapore, which has a D_a of 6.06. The 14 most highly corrupt nations (in order of decreasing score) were Angola, the Democratic Republic of the Congo,

Côte d'Ivoire, Georgia, Indonesia, Tajikistan, Turkmenistan, Azerbaijan, Paraguay, Chad, Myanmar, Nigeria, Bangladesh, and Haiti—all with a CPI score of 2.0 or lower. These 14 nations also have a D_a of 4.93 or lower except for Georgia and Paraguay, which have D_a values of 5.24 and 5.88 respectively.

In their 2003 *Trafficking in Persons Report*, the US Department of State places 15 countries in tier 3, which includes those countries "whose governments do not fully comply with the minimum standards [for eliminating trafficking of persons] and are not making significant efforts to do so": Belize, Bosnia and Herzegovina, Burma, Cuba, Dominican Republic, Georgia, Greece, Haiti, Kazakhstan, Liberia, North Korea, Sudan, Suriname, Turkey, and Uzbekistan.[66] Eleven of these countries have a D_a of 5.43 or less. However, one common-law and three civil-law democracies are also in tier 3 and have a D_a of 6.51 or higher.

In the 2003 report, the State Department also designates seven countries as state sponsors of terrorism: Cuba, Iran, Iraq, Libya, North Korea, Sudan, and Syria.[67] These seven countries all have a D_a of 2.86 or less; five are authoritarian regimes with customary-law systems, and two are totalitarian regimes with civil-law systems.

This chapter validates the correlations between democracy and a wide range of major human goals. The degree to which a government protects political rights, civil liberties, media independence, freedom of religion, and economic freedom—the core elements of a liberal democracy—is an important indicator of its association with nonviolence, peace, human freedom, and human development. The correlations established in this chapter also demonstrate the important role of the legal system in explaining and predicting government behavior. Civil-law and common-law systems can be found in all forms of government, but are most often found in democracies, where they foster political and economic growth. Customary-law systems, however, are more conducive to the political and economic stagnation of nondemocracies and are more subject to the abusive use of power than their civil-law and common-law counterparts. Not surprisingly, customary law is the most common legal system for authoritarian and totalitarian regimes. Democracy and the rule of law are valuable not only for their ability to reduce the occurrence of war. Good governance, which can be equated by and large with democratic governance, is indeed the key factor for promoting human development.

Notes

1. Rummel, *Power Kills*, 23.
2. Ibid.
3. Ibid. See also Maoz and Abdolali, "Regime Types," 3–35. They observe that if "politically free states do not fight one another then the more democracies, the less international conflict."
4. Moore, *Solving the War Puzzle*, xxii, 2, 60.
5. Ibid., 9. Moore also notes that "preliminary evidence suggests that the principal problem nations with respect to trafficking in illegal drugs have been nondemocratic" (102n1).
6. Siegle, Weinstein, and Halperin, "Why Democracies Excel," 58–59.
7. Ibid., 59–66.
8. Ibid., 62.
9. Ibid., 63–66.
10. Sen, "Freedom and Needs."
11. Ahlmark, speech, 8 April 1999.
12. Ibid.
13. Norberg, *In Defence of Global Capitalism*, 8.
14. Ibid., 12–13.
15. Ibid., 21–23.
16. Ibid., 23–39, 58–63.
17. Ibid., 40.
18. Ibid., 40–43.
19. Ibid., 63–67, 81, 221–22.
20. Ibid., 58.
21. Ibid., 55–56. Liberal democracies have not purged themselves of pandemics such as HIV/AIDS. It is estimated that over 1 million people (approximately one out of every 250 people) in the United States have the HIV infection or AIDS. See the Web site of the American Foundation for AIDS Research at http://www.amfar.org.
22. Ibid., 55.
23. UN FAO, *The State of Food Insecurity in the World 2004*, 6, 8.
24. UN ILO, *World Employment Report 2004–05*, 24.
25. Norberg, *In Defence of Global Capitalism*, 56.
26. Freedom House, "Freedom in the World (About the Survey)."
27. Ibid., "Freedom of the Press."
28. Ibid., "A History." This religious freedom report is now being published by the Hudson Institute.
29. The Heritage Foundation, "About Us."
30. Ibid., *2007 Index*.
31. The Fraser Institute, Web site.
32. Ibid., "The Economic Freedom of the World Project."

33. UN, "United Nations Development Programme."

34. UNDP, *Human Development Report 2003*, 2.

35. Ibid., "Human Development Reports."

36. Ibid., *Human Development Report 2003*, 1.

37. UN, "Member States." In 2003, there were 191 member states in the UN. However, the Freedom House reports used in this study refer to 192 states because they include Taiwan.

38. US Department of State, "Countries."

39. A spreadsheet containing all the *Freedom in the World* country ratings from 1972 through 2007 is available at http://www.freedomhouse.org/uploads/fiw/FIWAllScores.xls.

40. Freedom House, "Methodology," *Freedom in the World 2004*.

41. The ratings for each jurisdiction as well as a discussion of specific conditions in that jurisdiction can be found in Freedom House, "Country Reports," *Freedom in the World 2004*.

42. Freedom House, *Freedom of the Press 2003*.

43. Ibid., "Methodology," *Freedom of the Press 2003*.

44. Marshall, *Religious Freedom in the World*.

45. Miles, Feulner, and O'Grady, *2004 Index of Economic Freedom*.

46. Ibid., 51.

47. Gwartney and Lawson, *Economic Freedom of the World: 2003 Annual Report*, 6.

48. UNDP, *Human Development Report 2003*, 237.

49. Ibid., 60.

50. Ibid., 237–39.

51. Ibid., vi.

52. At the end of 2000.

53. Freedom House, *Democracy's Century*.

54. CIA, *World Factbook 2003*.

55. Ibid.

56. CIA, "East Timor," *World Factbook 2003*. See also the official government Web site of Timor-Leste at http://www.timor-leste.gov.tl/, which proudly declares it to be the "world's newest democracy" after 450 years of continuous foreign occupation.

57. CIA, "Bosnia and Herzegovina," *World Factbook 2003*.

58. Care, "Conflict between Customary Law and Human Rights in the South Pacific."

59. Ibid.

60. US Department of State, "The Group of Seven and the Group of Eight."

61. UN Population Division, "The Twenty Most Populous Countries."

62. The list of countries eligible for debt relief under the HIPC Initiative changes. The current list can be found on the World Bank Web site at http://www.worldbank.org/hipc/.

63. CIA, "Bolivia," "Honduras," and "Nicaragua," *World Factbook 2003*.

64. Freedom House, *The World's Most Repressive Regimes*, vii.

65. Transparency International, *Corruptions Perception Index 2004*.

66. US Department of State, *Trafficking in Persons Report 2003*, 15, 21.

67. US Department of State, *Patterns of Global Terrorism 2003*, ix. As a result of Operation Iraqi Freedom, President Bush formally rescinded Iraq's status as a state sponsor of terrorism on 24 September 2004.

Chapter 7

Conclusion: Democracy and Deterrence in the Twenty-First Century

There are those, I know, who will reply that the liberation of humanity, the freedom of man and mind, is nothing but a dream. They are right. It is the American Dream.

—Archibald MacLeish
A Continuing Journey

Americans are one of the most religious peoples on Earth. Because they know that liberty, just as life itself, is not earned but a gift from God, they seek to share that gift with the world.

—Pres. Ronald Reagan
Moscow State University, 1988

The sole duty for all governments is to care for their people. Good governance and a national legal system that embodies the rule of law and permits robust economic development are the keys to the future of any sovereign nation and the future of human liberty and development as well. To govern successfully, national leaders must earn the trust of their people and the international community. Leaders must represent their people, treat them justly, and protect their liberty, standard of living, health, and economic condition. The people of a nation are the economic engine in a free market that builds the nation through domestic commerce and international exports. The people of a nation serve as the potential market base that attracts imports and business development by the international community. National leaders must do everything within their power to establish and preserve an honest and transparent government and legal system that includes a constitution and a set of laws empowering all the men and women of their nation to reach their full human potential. Leaders must guarantee all citizens, including all minorities, extensive human rights and civil liberties. This is an extraordinary vision and challenge, but the peoples of the world—regardless of their heritage, culture, religion, nationality, gender, or race—deserve no less. Some leaders, however, fall short in this duty, and some abuse their power. Thus leaders must be held accountable by domestic and international incentives that ensure meaningful checks and balances for governmental power.

The United States is the greatest political achievement in human history. It has adopted the extraordinary vision and challenge of preserving human rights and civil liberties domestically and abroad. Pres. George W. Bush's second inaugural address embraces the theme of promoting and protecting human liberty around the world and acknowledges the role of human liberty in US national security and international peace. The speech echoes the work of Locke, Montesquieu, Paine, Kant, Russett, Rummel, and Moore and is consistent with the core principles of this study. Bush's words attest to the real-world implications of Moore's postulate on the cause of war and incentive theory of war avoidance:

> There is only one force of history that can break the reign of hatred and resentment, and expose the pretensions of tyrants, and reward the hopes of the decent and tolerant, and that is the force of human freedom. . . .

> The survival of liberty in our land increasingly depends on the success of liberty in other lands. The best hope for peace in our world is the expansion of freedom in all the world. . . .

> Across the generations we have proclaimed the imperative of self-government, because no one is fit to be a master, and no one deserves to be a slave. Advancing these ideals is the mission that created our nation. It is the honorable achievement of our fathers. Now it is the urgent requirement of our nation's security, and the calling of our time. So it is the policy of the United States to seek and support the growth of democratic movements and institutions in every nation and culture, with the ultimate goal of ending tyranny in our world. This is not primarily the task of arms, though we will defend ourselves and our friends by force of arms when necessary. . . .

> We will persistently clarify the choice before every ruler and every nation: The moral choice between oppression, which is always wrong, and freedom,

156

which is eternally right. America will not pretend that jailed dissidents pre-fer their chains, or that women welcome humiliation and servitude, or that any human being aspires to live at the mercy of bullies. . . .

All who live in tyranny and hopelessness can know: the United States will not ignore your oppression, or excuse your oppressors. When you stand for your liberty, we will stand with you.[1]

Bush's speech recognizes one of the basic principles ex-pressed in this study and incorporates it as a central element of US foreign policy: the spread of democracy is a strategy of war avoidance, and the free world must actively facilitate the growth of democracy to ensure its own security.[2] Bush high-lights the importance of human freedom, self-governance, and deterrence in shaping peace in today's world. The president's theme is consistent with Moore's postulate on the cause of war, which argues that war is caused by the synergy between the existence of a potentially aggressive nondemocratic (totalitar-ian) regime and the absence of effective systemwide deterrence. To avoid war, as Moore's incentive theory suggests, positive and negative incentives must be used to discourage leaders from committing aggression. Thus Bush asserts the role of the United States in seeking, supporting, and defending human freedom and the growth of democracies in every nation and culture as a means to end tyranny in our world.

Moore's incentive theory of war avoidance is an important ana-lytical tool and framework to accomplish the foreign-policy ob-jectives of securing peace and liberty in the world. This study validates Moore's theory and advocates both general and specific deterrence applications of the theory. The analytical formula for calculating the probability of peace in specific crisis settings along with the indexing and rating of each national leader in the world according to his or her propensity for aggression can serve as a predictive tool to analyze and strengthen systemwide deterrence incentives generally as well as in a specific crisis setting. The ret-rospective analysis of Saddam Hussein's behavior leading up to the Gulf War can serve as a model for analyzing and predicting the behavior of other national leaders. The analytical process pro-posed in this study can be applied to highly individualized situa-tions and personalities, making it an ideal tool for the threats of the twenty-first century, which are more changeable and unconventional than the threats of the Cold War era.

Moore's incentive theory can be used to guide the foreign and national-security policy of nations and the charter principles of regional and international organizations. Democracies are inherently peaceful because of internal checks and balances that discourage the aggressive use of force; however, nondemocracies need external checks and balances—effective systemwide deterrence measures—to prevent aggression. Thus the more democracies in the world, the greater the level of international peace and security. Similarly, the more incentives that provide systemwide deterrence at the individual, state, and international levels, the greater the level of international peace and security.

Democracies also promote human freedom and development. Most people naturally migrate toward democratic forms of government if allowed to choose, or at least they desire to choose the form of government under which they live. However, throughout the world, many nondemocratic rulers use force to assume power and then harshly abuse the law, using military and police forces to suppress the freedom and diminish the well-being of their peoples. In these cases, democracy is not able to develop naturally through the free choice of the people. Sometimes democracy must be encouraged through the actions of other free nations within the international community, who must actively facilitate, through military intervention when necessary, the political environment in which people can freely choose their form of government and new democracies can develop. Free nations must make an active effort to promote global democratization and strengthen systemwide deterrence at the individual, state, and international levels.

Actively promoting democracy includes providing incentives for nondemocratic forms of government to transition toward democracy, creating an environment for democracies to develop in ways consistent with diverse religions and cultures, and assisting willing governments in their transition to democracy. All democratic states, prodemocracy regional and international organizations, and the UN should be actively engaged in developing comprehensive strategies to promote democratic forms of government. Where that is not possible, they should work to establish systemwide deterrence incentives at all levels. This is the path to international peace. Moore concludes that enhancing deterrence against war and terrorism "requires a focus on all elements of deterrence, from maintenance of a strong military to appropriate . . . advance communication about unacceptable actions."[3] He also argues that we should enhance collective security; strengthen the UN; focus deterrence on all levels, especially regime elites; and perhaps designate a special representative to the president to more effectively coordinate US democracy-assistance programs.[4]

Free nations must also work to solidify and spread the rule of law, which is essential to maintaining peace in the world. International legal scholar Philip Allott describes the transformative power of law:

> In the making of the human world, nothing has been more important than what we call *law*. Law is the intermediary between human power and human ideas. Law transforms our natural power into social power, transforms our self-interest into social interest, and transforms social interest into self-interest. . . .
>
> Law is a wonderful, and insufficiently appreciated, human invention. . . . The hallowed ideal characteristics of democracy are all better seen as ingenious methods for using law to restrain law.[5]

Supreme Court Justice Sandra Day O'Connor has observed that the "rule of law is fundamental to the existence of a free society. . . . [It] secures our liberty and separates civilization from anarchy."[6] She concludes:

> To preserve liberty, then, we must preserve the rule of law, we must hold those who violate it accountable. But holding these individuals "accountable" does not necessarily mean prosecution. There is a tension between the international obligation to prosecute certain crimes and the countervailing interests of national sovereignty in choosing to pursue accountability through some combination of amnesty and public acknowledgment of the crimes. Neither approach will be appropriate for all situations; indeed, it is doubtful that there can be any adequate response to mass atrocities. . . .
>
> Instead, we must take the route that best vindicates the rule of law in each situation, pursuing justice while nurturing burgeoning democracies.[7]

The rule of law is the key underpinning of human liberty and democracy; it restrains, channels, and transforms natural power in socially beneficial ways. Law is also a key component of effective deterrence because it creates incentives for individuals, including national leaders, to behave in certain ways and holds accountable those who violate social and legal norms. As O'Connor notes, law can be used to enforce international standards of behavior in ways that also nurture the growth of democracy.

The spread of democracy encourages peace and human development. Should free states therefore take up arms to achieve these clearly desirable ends? Rummel asks similar questions: "To wage peace you should foster freedom. But how? Encourage revolution? Intervene in dictatorships and throw out tyrants? Make war for democracy?" He answers those questions with a resounding *no*:

> People should be left alone to form their own communities or states, to live their own lives. If they prefer to live in authoritarian societies (as many do) or under totalitarian governments, that is their choice. . . .

> Promoting freedom does not mean, then, forcibly converting others into accepting an exchange society and libertarian government; nor does it mean waging a crusade against other societies or governments or ideologies. Instead, fostering freedom means to facilitate *procedurally and institutionally* people making their own choices about how they want to live, whether with freedom or not, as long as they do not try to impose their choice on others.[8]

Rummel is correct. People should, in general, be left alone to organize their communities according to their own values and customs, and it should not be US national policy to promote freedom through the use of force. However, under extreme situations such as democide and genocide, military intervention may be necessary when deterrence fails. While people should be able to choose their own form of government, and some may freely choose to live in authoritarian societies, it is doubtful that they choose to be slaughtered, and military intervention may be necessary to protect a population from megamurderers. It should not, however, be the primary tool for spreading democracy.

Instead Rummel defines 10 "vectors of action" that facilitate freedom, five at the state level and five at the international level:

State Level

1. Enhance and guarantee freedom of choice and mobility of citizens and groups.

2. Decentralize government power.

3. Expand the horizontal distribution of power.

4. Increase the political participation of communities and peoples.

5. Decrease government's social and economic control and intervention.

International Level

1. Facilitate and guarantee through the United Nations a right to emigrate.

2. Encourage and aid efforts through the United Nations for national self-determination and independence.

3. Represent people in the United Nations, as well as states.

4. Gradually strengthen United Nations peacekeeping and peacemaking machinery.

5. Increase the global power of the United Nations (transform the United Nations into a minimum libertarian government monopolizing force).[9]

Rummel's "grand master principle" for waging peace is "whether at the state or international level, promote the maximum freedom of individuals, groups, and states, consistent with a like freedom for others."[10]

After more than a decade of research on the interrelationship between government, law, and war in the work of scholars and philosophers from Kant to Moore and Rummel, it is evident to this author that promoting democracy, human freedom, economic freedom, and the rule of law are the significant contributing factors in promoting world peace and human development. The absence of any meaningful argument to the contrary is remarkable. Where democracy, freedom, and the rule of law do not prevail, deterrence mechanisms must be erected against the aggressive tendencies of many nondemocratic leaders. These conclusions are consistent with Moore's work on the cause of war and war avoidance. His many decades spent sorting through and analyzing the complexities of empirical data, economic theory, metaphysical reasoning, and the dynamics of human behavior as they relate to international peace and security have revealed how democracy, human freedom, economic freedom, and the rule of law interact to promote world peace and human development. The implications of Moore's theory of war avoidance are profound. If the premise of Moore's theory had been actively embraced by the United States and other democratic nations as a major foreign policy strategy 100 years ago, as it is now by the United States, one wonders how many of the 169 million murders of innocent people by their own government (using Rummel's conservative estimates) could have been prevented and how many of the 38.5 million war deaths during the twentieth century could have been avoided. For example, Hussein's aggression against Kuwait and the subsequent Gulf War demonstrate a failure of systemwide deterrence. Had Moore's principles for effective, targeted deterrence measures been adopted, particularly the requirement to clearly communicate the consequences of unacceptable actions, the invasion and war might have been prevented.

Wars and their attendant human misery begin in the minds of national leaders whose power is unchecked by incentives and deterrence mechanisms. Because such restraints are inherent in democratic forms of government, war is comparatively rare where human freedom, economic freedom, and the rule of law thrive. The spread of democracy in the twenty-first century is therefore of utmost importance in advancing human welfare. Actively encouraging the expansion of freedom is the responsibility of democratic nations. Democracy is, as Bush stated in his first inaugural address, "a seed upon the wind, taking root in many nations. Our democratic faith is more than the creed of our country, it is the inborn hope of our humanity, an ideal we carry but do not own, a trust we bear and pass along. . . . If our country does not lead the cause of freedom, it will not be led."[11]

Though democracy is indeed taking root in many nations, the free world cannot rest. For all the progress made in the democratization of the former Soviet bloc and in other parts of the world, a recent Freedom House study reports that democracy and good governance are threatened or unattainable in many places. Russia can "no longer be considered a democracy at all" by most standards, and democratic development in smaller countries such as Thailand and Bangladesh has been derailed.[12] These disturbing developments underscore the significance of the war avoidance strategies outlined in this study: encourage the spread of democracy and the rule of law while establishing positive and negative incentive and deterrence mechanisms to restrain those who govern nondemocratic nations.

Notes

1. Pres. George W. Bush, second inaugural address.

2. The spread of democracy has not always been an imperative of US foreign policy. Appendix B traces the history of American foreign policy from a position of isolationism to the proactive stance held by recent presidential administrations.

3. Moore, *Solving the War Puzzle*, 87.

4. Ibid., 87–89.

5. Allott, "Law and the Re-Making of Humanity," 19–20, 27.

6. O'Connor, "Vindicating the Rule of Law," 31.

7. Ibid., 38.

8. Rummel, *In the Minds of Men*, 281.

9. Ibid., 283.

10. Ibid., 285.

11. Pres. George W. Bush, first inaugural address.

12. Freedom House, country reports, *Countries at the Crossroads 2007*.

Appendix A

Freedom, Human Development, and Democracy Ratings

Note: The tables in this appendix present data discussed in chapter 6, which explains the purposes and sources of this data.

Acronyms and Abbreviations in Tables A1–A3

AF	Africa
AM	absolute monarchy
AR	authoritarian regime
C	colonial and imperial dependency
CI	civil law
CM	constitutional monarchy
CO	common law
CU	customary law
D_a	aggregated index value of democracy
DEM	democracy
EAP	East Asia and the Pacific
EUR	Europe and Eurasia
F	free
FH	Freedom House
FI	Fraser Institute
HDI	Human Development Index
HF	Heritage Foundation
M	monarchy
MF	mostly free
MU	mostly unfree
NE	Near East
NF	not free
P	protectorate
PF	partly free
R	repressed
RDP	restricted democratic practices
SA	South Asia
SAR	special administrative region
TM	traditional monarchy
TOT	totalitarian regime
UF	unfree
UNDP	United Nations Development Programme
WH	Western Hemisphere

Table A1. Freedom and human development ratings for 267 national and territorial jurisdictions

A Jurisdiction (date admitted to UN)	B Region	C FH rating: political/ civil (1–7)	D FH rating: media (1–100)	E FH rating: religion (1–7)	F HF rating: economic (1–5)	G FI rating: economic (10–1)	H UNDP HDI (1–0)	I Government type	J Type of legal system	K Description of legal system
Afghanistan[a] (19 Nov 1946)	SA	NF, 6/6	NF, 74					TOT, transi- tional	CU	The Bonn Agreement calls for a judicial commission to rebuild the justice system in accordance with Islamic principles, international standards, the rule of law, and Afghan legal traditions
Albania (14 Dec 1955)	EUR	PF, 3/3	PF, 50		MU, 3.10	5.6	M, .735	DEM, emerging democracy	CI	
Algeria (8 Oct 1962)	NE	NF, 6/5	NF, 62		MU, 3.31	4.2	M, .704	AR, republic	CU	Socialist, based on French and Islamic law; judicial review of legislative acts in ad hoc constitutional council composed of various public officials, including several supreme court justices
American Samoa (US territory)	EAP								CO	
Andorra (28 Jul 1993)	EUR	F, 1/1	F, 8					DEM, par- liamentary democracy	CI	Based on French and Spanish civil codes; no judicial review of legislative acts

[a]Most data in table A1 is from 2003. An explanation of each column is provided in chapter 6.

Table A1 (continued)

A Jurisdiction (date admitted to UN)	B Region	C FH rating: political/ civil (1–7)	D FH rating: media (1–100)	E FH rating: religion (1–7)	F HF rating: economic (1–5)	G FI rating: economic (10–1)	H UNDP HDI (1–0)	I Government type	J Type of legal system	K Description of legal system
Angola (1 Dec 1976)	AF	NF, 6/5	NF, 72		Not graded in 2003[b]		L, .377	AR, republic; nominally a multiparty democracy with a strong presidential system	CI	Based on Portuguese civil-law system and customary law; recently modified to accommodate political pluralism and increased use of free markets
Anguilla (UK territory)	WH								CO	Based on English common law
Antarctica (administered by member nations of the 1951 Antarctic Treaty)	WH							Consultative management by parties to the Antarctic Treaty	CU	Administered through meetings of the consultative member nations of the Antarctic Treaty. Decisions from these meetings are carried out by these member nations (within their areas) in accordance with their national laws
Antigua and Barbuda (11 Nov 1981)	WH	PF, 4/2	PF, 45				M, .798	RDP, constitutional monarchy with UK-style parliament	CO	Based on English common law
Argentina (24 Oct 1945)	WH	F, 2/2	PF, 39	F, 3	MU, 3.48	6.5	H, .849	DEM, republic	CI	Mixture of US and West European legal systems

[b]The Heritage Foundation has suspended the evaluation of some countries because deteriorating conditions prevent the collection of accurate or measurable data.

Table A1 (continued)

A Jurisdiction (date admitted to UN)	B Region	C FH rating: political/ civil (1–7)	D FH rating: media (1–100)	E FH rating: religion (1–7)	F HF rating: economic (1–5)	G FI rating: economic (10–1)	H UNDP HDI (1–0)	I Government type	J Type of legal system	K Description of legal system
Armenia (2 Mar 1992)	EUR	PF, 4/4	NF, 65	PF, 4	MF, 2.63		M, .729	DEM, republic	CI	Based on civil-law system
Aruba (part of the Netherlands)	WH							Parliamentary democracy	CI	Based on Dutch civil-law system, with some English common law influence
Ashmore and Cartier Islands (Australian territory)	EAP								CO	The laws of the Commonwealth of Australia and the Northern Territory of Australia valid where applicable
Australia (1 Nov 1945)	EAP	F, 1/1	F, 14		F, 1.88	8.0	H, .939	DEM, democratic, federal-state system recognizing the British monarch as sovereign	CO	Based on English common law
Austria (14 Dec 1955)	EUR	F, 1/1	F, 23	F, 2	MF, 2.08	7.6	H, .929	DEM, federal republic	CI	Civil-law system of Roman origin; judicial review of legislative acts by the Constitutional Court; separate administrative and civil/penal supreme courts
Azerbaijan (2 Mar 1992)	EUR	NF, 6/5	NF, 73	PF, 5	MU, 3.39		M, .744	AR, republic	CI	Based on civil-law system

Table A1 (continued)

A Jurisdiction (date admitted to UN)	B Region	C FH rating: political/civil (1–7)	D FH rating: media (1–100)	E FH rating: religion (1–7)	F HF rating: economic (1–5)	G FI rating: economic (10–1)	H UNDP HDI (1–0)	I Government type	J Type of legal system	K Description of legal system
Azores (autonomous region of Portugal)	EUR								CI	
Bahamas (18 Sep 1973)	WH	F, 1/1	F, 11		MF, 2.25	6.6	H, .812	DEM, constitutional parliamentary democracy	CO	Based on English common law
Bahrain (21 Sep 1971)	NE	PF, 5/5	NF, 68		MF, 2.08	7.1	H, .839	TM, constitutional hereditary monarchy	CU	Based on Islamic law and English common law
Baker Island (US territory)	EAP								CO	US laws valid where applicable
Bangladesh (17 Sep 1974)	SA	PF, 4/4	NF, 65	UF, 6	MU, 3.70	5.6	M, .502	DEM, parliamentary democracy	CO	Based on English common law
Barbados (9 Dec 1966)	WH	F, 1/1	F, 14		MF, 2.41	5.8	H, .888	DEM, parliamentary democracy; independent sovereign state within the Commonwealth	CO	English common law; no judicial review of legislative acts
Bassas da India (possession of France)	AF								CI	Laws of France valid where applicable

Table A1 (*continued*)

A Jurisdiction (date admitted to UN)	B Region	C FH rating: political/ civil (1–7)	D FH rating: media (1–100)	E FH rating: religion (1–7)	F HF rating: economic (1–5)	G FI rating: economic (10–1)	H UNDP HDI (1–0)	I Government type	J Type of legal system	K Description of legal system
Belarus (Byelorussia) (24 Oct 1945)	EUR	NF, 6/6	NF, 82	PF, 5	R, 4.09		H, .804	AR, republic	CI	Based on civil-law system
Belgium (27 Dec 1945)	EUR	F, 1/1	F, 9	F, 3	MF, 2.19	7.4	H, .937	DEM, federal parliamentary democracy under a constitutional monarch	CI	Civil-law system influenced by English constitutional theory; judicial review of legislative acts
Belize (25 Sep 1981)	WH	F, 1/2	F, 23		MF, 2.69	6.3	M, .776	DEM, parliamentary democracy	CO	English law
Benin (20 Sep 1960)	AF	F, 2/2	F, 28		MU, 3.44	5.6	L, .411	DEM, republic under multiparty democratic rule	CU	Based on French civil law and customary law
Bermuda (UK territory)	WH							Parliamentary British overseas territory with internal self-government	CO	English law
Bhutan (21 Sep 1971)	SA	NF, 6/5	NF, 70	UF, 6			M, .511	TM, monarchy; special treaty relationship with India	CO	Based on Indian law and English common law

171

Table A1 (continued)

A Jurisdiction (date admitted to UN)	B Region	C FH rating: political/ civil (1–7)	D FH rating: media (1–100)	E FH rating: religion (1–7)	F HF rating: economic (1–5)	G FI rating: economic (10–1)	H UNDP HDI (1–0)	I Government type	J Type of legal system	K Description of legal system
Bolivia (14 Nov 1945)	WH	PF, 3/3	F, 30		MF, 2.59	6.5	M, .672	DEM, republic	CI	Based on Spanish law and Napoleonic Code
Bosnia and Herzegovina (22 May 1992)	EUR	PF, 4/4	PF, 49		MU, 3.30		M, .777	P, emerging federal democratic republic	CI	Based on civil-law system
Botswana (17 Oct 1966)	AF	F, 2/2	F, 30	F, 2	MF, 2.55	7.1	M, .614	DEM, parliamentary republic	CU	Based on Roman-Dutch law and local customary law; judicial review limited to matters of interpretation
Bouvet Island (territory of Norway)	AF								CI	Laws of Norway valid where applicable
Brazil (24 Oct 1945)	WH	F, 2/3	PF, 38	F, 2	MU, 3.10	5.8	M, .777	DEM, federative republic	CI	Based on Roman codes
British Indian Ocean Territory (UK territory)	AF								CO	UK laws valid where applicable
British Virgin Islands (UK territory)	WH								CO	English law
Brunei Darussalam (21 Sep 1984)	EAP	NF, 6/5	NF, 76				H, .872	TM, constitutional sultanate	CO	Based on English common law; for Muslims, Islamic Sharia law supersedes civil law in a number of areas

172

Table A1 (continued)

A Jurisdiction (date admitted to UN)	B Region	C FH rating: political/civil (1–7)	D FH rating: media (1–100)	E FH rating: religion (1–7)	F HF rating: economic (1–5)	G FI rating: economic (10–1)	H UNDP HDI (1–0)	I Government type	J Type of legal system	K Description of legal system
Bulgaria (14 Dec 1955)	EUR	F, 1/2	F, 30	PF, 4	MU, 3.08	5.3	M, .795	DEM, parliamentary democracy	CI	Civil law and criminal law based on Roman law
Burkina Faso (20 Sep 1960)	AF	PF, 4/4	PF, 39		MU, 3.28		L, .330	AR, parliamentary republic	CU	Based on French civil-law system and customary law
Burundi (18 Sep 1962)	AF	PF, 5/5	NF, 76		Not graded in 2003	5.1	L, .337	AR, republic	CU	Based on German and Belgian civil codes and customary law
Cambodia (14 Dec 1955)	EAP	NF, 6/5	NF, 64		MF, 2.90		M, .556	RDP, multi-party democracy under a constitutional monarchy established in September 1993	CI	Primarily a civil-law mixture of French-influenced codes from the UN Transitional Authority in Cambodia, royal decrees, and acts of the legislature, with influences of customary law and remnants of Communist legal theory; increasing influence recently of common law
Cameroon (20 Sep 1960)	AF	NF, 6/6	NF, 65		MU, 3.63	5.6	L, .499	RDP, unitary republic; multiparty presidential regime	CU	Based on French civil-law system, with common-law influence

173

Table A1 (continued)

A Jurisdiction (date admitted to UN)	B Region	C FH rating: political/ civil (1–7)	D FH rating: media (1–100)	E FH rating: religion (1–7)	F HF rating: economic (1–5)	G FI rating: economic (10–1)	H UNDP HDI (1–0)	I Government type	J Type of legal system	K Description of legal system
Canada (9 Nov 1945)	WH	F, 1/1	F, 17		F, 1.98	8.1	H, .937	DEM, confederation with parliamentary democracy	CO	Based on English common law, except in Quebec, where civil-law system based on French law prevails
Cape Verde (16 Sep 1975)	AF	F, 1/1	F, 30		MF, 2.86		M, .727	DEM, republic	CI	Derived from the legal system of Portugal
Cayman Islands (UK territory)	WH							British crown colony	CO	British common law and local statutes
Central African Republic (20 Sep 1960)	AF	NF, 7/5	NF, 67		MU, 3.38	4.9	L, .363	DEM, republic	CU	Based on French law
Chad (20 Sep 1960)	AF	NF, 6/5	NF, 67		MU, 3.54	5.6	L, .376	RDP, republic	CU	Based on French civil-law system and Chadian customary law
Channel Islands (consists of British Crown dependencies of Guernsey and Jersey)	EUR								CO	

Table A1 (continued)

A Jurisdiction (date admitted to UN)	B Region	C FH rating: political/ civil (1–7)	D FH rating: media (1–100)	E FH rating: religion (1–7)	F HF rating: economic (1–5)	G FI rating: economic (10–1)	H UNDP HDI (1–0)	I Government type	J Type of legal system	K Description of legal system
Chile (24 Oct 1945)	WH	F, 1/1	F, 22	F, 3	F, 1.91	7.3	H, .831	DEM, republic	CI	Based on Code of 1857 derived from Spanish law and subsequent codes influenced by French and Austrian law; judicial review of legislative acts in the Supreme Court
China, People's Republic of (24 Oct 1945)	EAP	NF, 7/6	NF, 80	UF, 6	MU, 3.64	5.5	M, .721	AR, Communist state	CI	A complex amalgam of custom and statute, largely criminal law; rudimentary civil code in effect since 1 January 1987; new legal codes in effect since 1 January 1980; continuing efforts are being made to improve civil, administrative, criminal, and commercial law
Christmas Island (territory of Australia)	EAP								CO	Under the authority of the governor general of Australia and Australian law
Clipperton Island (possession of France)	WH								CI	Laws of France valid where applicable

175

Table A1 (continued)

A Jurisdiction (date admitted to UN)	B Region	C FH rating: political/ civil (1–7)	D FH rating: media (1–100)	E FH rating: religion (1–7)	F HF rating: economic (1–5)	G FI rating: economic (10–1)	H UNDP HDI (1–0)	I Government type	J Type of legal system	K Description of legal system
Cocos (Keeling) Islands (territory of Australia)	EAP								CO	Based on the laws of Australia and local laws
Colombia (5 Nov 1945)	WH	PF, 4/4	NF, 63	PF, 4	MU, 3.13	5.4	M, .779	DEM, republic; executive branch dominates government structure	CI	Based on Spanish law; a new criminal code modeled after US procedures was enacted in 1992–93; judicial review of executive and legislative acts
Comoros (12 Nov 1975)	AF	PF, 5/4	PF, 43				M, .528	RDP, independent republic	CU	French and Sharia (Islamic) law in a new consolidated code
Congo, Democratic Republic of the (formerly Zaire) (20 Sep 1960)	AF	NF, 6/6	NF, 82		Not graded in 2003	3.9	L, .363	AR, dictatorship; presumably undergoing a transition to representative government	CU	Based on Belgian civil-law system and tribal law
Congo, Republic of the (20 Sep 1960)	AF	PF, 5/4	PF, 55		MU, 3.90	4.5	M, .502	AR, republic	CU	Based on French civil-law system and customary law

176

Table A1 (continued)

A Jurisdiction (date admitted to UN)	B Region	C FH rating: political/civil (1–7)	D FH rating: media (1–100)	E FH rating: religion (1–7)	F HF rating: economic (1–5)	G FI rating: economic (10–1)	H UNDP HDI (1–0)	I Government type	J Type of legal system	K Description of legal system
Cook Islands (self-governing in free association with New Zealand)	EAP							Self-governing parliamentary democracy	CO	Based on New Zealand law and English common law
Coral Sea Islands (territory of Australia)	EAP								CO	Laws of Australia valid where applicable
Costa Rica (2 Nov 1945)	WH	F, 1/2	F, 14		MF, 2.71	7.1	H, .832	DEM, democratic republic	CI	Based on Spanish civil-law system; judicial review of legislative acts in the Supreme Court
Côte d'Ivoire (Ivory Coast) (20 Sep 1960)	AF	NF, 6/5	NF, 68		MU, 3.18	5.9	L, .396	AR, republic; multiparty presidential regime established 1960	CU	Based on French civil-law system and customary law; judicial review in the constitutional chamber of the Supreme Court
Croatia (22 May 1992)	EUR	F, 2/2	PF, 33		MU, 3.11	6.0	H, .818	DEM, presidential parliamentary democracy	CI	Based on civil-law system
Cuba (24 Oct 1945)	WH	NF, 7/7	NF, 94	UF, 6	R, 4.08		H, .806	TOT, Communist state	CI	Based on Spanish and American law, with large elements of Communist legal theory

Table A1 (continued)

A Jurisdiction (date admitted to UN)	B Region	C FH rating: political/ civil (1–7)	D FH rating: media (1–100)	E FH rating: religion (1–7)	F HF rating: economic (1–5)	G FI rating: economic (10–1)	H UNDP HDI (1–0)	I Government type	J Type of legal system	K Description of legal system
Cyprus (20 Sep 1960)	EUR	F, 1/1	F, 18		F, 1.95	6.2	H, .891	DEM, republic	CI	Based on common law, with civil-law modifications
Czech Republic (19 Jan 1993)	EUR	F, 1/2	F, 23		MF, 2.39	6.9	H, .861	DEM, parliamentary democracy	CI	Civil-law system based on Austro-Hungarian codes; legal code modified to bring it in line with Organization on Security and Cooperation in Europe obligations and to expunge Marxist-Leninist legal theory
Denmark (24 Oct 1945)	EUR	F, 1/1	F, 11		F, 1.80	7.6	H, .930	DEM, constitutional monarchy	CI	Civil-law system; judicial review of legislative acts
Djibouti (20 Sep 1977)	AF	PF, 5/5	NF, 65		MU, 3.23		L, .462	DEM, republic	CU	Based on French civil-law system, traditional practices, and Islamic law
Dominica (18 Dec 1978)	WH	F, 1/1	F, 14				M, .776	DEM, parliamentary democracy; republic within the Commonwealth	CO	Based on English common law

Table A1 (continued)

A Jurisdiction (date admitted to UN)	B Region	C FH rating: political/ civil (1–7)	D FH rating: media (1–100)	E FH rating: religion (1–7)	F HF rating: economic (1–5)	G FI rating: economic (10–1)	H UNDP HDI (1–0)	I Government type	J Type of legal system	K Description of legal system
Dominican Republic (24 Oct 1945)	WH	F, 3/2	PF, 33		MU, 3.51	6.6	M, .737	DEM, rep- resentative democracy	CI	Based on French civil codes
Ecuador (21 Dec 1945)	WH	PF, 3/3	PF, 41		MU, 3.60	5.0	M, .731	DEM, republic	CI	Based on civil-law system
Egypt (24 Oct 1945)	NE	NF, 6/6	NF, 79	PF, 5	MU, 3.28	6.5	M, .648	RDP, republic	CU	Based on English common law, Islamic law, and Napoleonic codes; judicial review by Supreme Court and Council of State (oversees validity of administrative decisions)
El Salvador (24 Oct 1945)	WH	F, 2/3	PF, 38	F, 3	MF, 2.24	7.2	M, .719	DEM, republic	CI	Based on civil and Roman law, with traces of common law; judicial review of legislative acts in the Supreme Court
Equatorial Guinea (12 Nov 1968)	AF	NF, 7/6	NF, 81		MU, 3.69		M, .664	AR, republic	CI	Partly based on Spanish civil law and tribal custom

179

Table A1 (continued)

A Jurisdiction (date admitted to UN)	B Region	C FH rating: political/ civil (1–7)	D FH rating: media (1–100)	E FH rating: religion (1–7)	F HF rating: economic (1–5)	G FI rating: economic (10–1)	H UNDP HDI (1–0)	I Government type	J Type of legal system	K Description of legal system
Eritrea (28 May 1993)	AF	NF, 7/6	NF, 83				L, .446	AR, transitional government	CU	Primary basis is the Ethiopian legal code of 1957, with revisions; new civil, commercial, and penal codes have not yet been promulgated; also relies on customary and post-independence laws and, for civil cases involving Muslims, Sharia law
Estonia (17 Sep 1991)	EUR	F, 1/2	F, 17	F, 1	F, 1.76	7.5	H, .833	DEM, parliamentary republic	CI	Based on civil-law system; no judicial review of legislative acts
Ethiopia (13 Nov 1945)	AF	PF, 5/5	NF, 64		MU, 3.33		L, .359	AR, federal republic	CU	Currently transitional mix of national and regional courts
Europa Island (possession of France)	AF								CI	Laws of France valid where applicable
Falkland Islands (Islas Malvinas) (UK territory; also claimed by Argentina)	WH								CO	English common law
Faroe Islands (part of Denmark)	EUR								CI	Danish law

Table A1 (continued)

A Jurisdiction (date admitted to UN)	B Region	C FH rating: political/ civil (1–7)	D FH rating: media (1–100)	E FH rating: religion (1–7)	F HF rating: economic (1–5)	G FI rating: economic (10–1)	H UNDP HDI (1–0)	I Government type	J Type of legal system	K Description of legal system
Fiji (13 Oct 1970)	EAP	PF, 4/3	F, 29		MU, 3.06	6.1	M, .754	DEM, republic	CO	Based on British system
Finland (14 Dec 1955)	EUR	F, 1/1	F, 10	F, 1	F, 1.95	7.7	H, .930	DEM, republic	CI	Civil-law system based on Swedish law; Supreme Court may request legislation interpreting or modifying laws
France (24 Oct 1945)	EUR	F, 1/1	F, 17	F, 3	MF, 2.63	6.7	H, .925	DEM, republic	CI	Civil-law system with indigenous concepts; review of administrative but not legislative acts
French Guiana (department of France)	WH								CI	French legal system
French Polynesia (territory of France)	EAP								CI	Based on French system
French Southern and Antarctic Lands (territory of France)	AF								CI	Laws of France valid where applicable

181

Table A1 (continued)

A Jurisdiction (date admitted to UN)	B Region	C FH rating: political/ civil (1–7)	D FH rating: media (1–100)	E FH rating: religion (1–7)	F HF rating: economic (1–5)	G FI rating: economic (10–1)	H UNDP HDI (1–0)	I Government type	J Type of legal system	K Description of legal system
Gabon (20 Sep 1960)	AF	PF, 5/4	PF, 58		MU, 3.43	5.2	M, .653	AR, republic; multiparty presidential regime	CU	Based on French civil-law system and customary law; judicial review of legislative acts in Constitutional Chamber of the Supreme Court
Gambia (21 Sep 1965)	AF	PF, 4/4	NF, 65		MU, 3.54		L, .463	AR, republic under multiparty democratic rule	CU	Based on a composite of English common law, Koranic law, and customary law
Gaza Strip (governed by the Palestinian Authority)	NE		NF, 86				M, .731		CU	Treaty with Israel permits self-government of West Bank and Gaza Strip by Palestinian Authority
Georgia (31 Jul 1992)	EUR	PF, 4/4	PF, 54	PF, 4	MU, 3.19		M, .746	DEM, republic	CI	Based on civil-law system
Germany (18 Sep 1973)	EUR	F, 1/1	F, 15	F, 3	MF, 2.03	7.3	H, .921	DEM, federal republic	CI	Civil-law system with indigenous concepts; judicial review of legislative acts in the Federal Constitutional Court
Ghana (8 Mar 1957)	AF	F, 2/2	F, 30		MU, 3.40	5.8	M, .567	DEM, constitutional democracy	CU	Based on English common law and customary law

Table A1 (continued)

A Jurisdiction (date admitted to UN)	B Region	C FH rating: political/civil (1–7)	D FH rating: media (1–100)	E FH rating: religion (1–7)	F HF rating: economic (1–5)	G FI rating: economic (10–1)	H UNDP HDI (1–0)	I Government type	J Type of legal system	K Description of legal system
Gibraltar (UK territory)	EUR								CO	English law
Glorioso Islands (possession of France)	AF								CI	Laws of France valid where applicable
Greece (25 Oct 1945)	EUR	F, 1/2	F, 28	PF, 4	MF, 2.80	6.7	H, .892	DEM, parliamentary republic	CI	Based on codified Roman law; judiciary divided into civil, criminal, and administrative courts
Greenland (part of Denmark)	EUR							Parliamentary democracy within a constitutional monarchy	CI	Danish law
Grenada (17 Sep 1974)	WH	F, 1/2	F, 14				M, .738	DEM, constitutional monarchy with Westminster-style parliament	CO	Based on English common law
Guadeloupe (department of France)	WH								CI	French legal system
Guam (US territory)	EAP								CO	Modeled on United States; US federal laws apply

Table A1 (continued)

A Jurisdiction (date admitted to UN)	B Region	C FH rating: political/ civil (1–7)	D FH rating: media (1–100)	E FH rating: religion (1–7)	F HF rating: economic (1–5)	G FI rating: economic (10–1)	H UNDP HDI (1–0)	I Government type	J Type of legal system	K Description of legal system
Guatemala (21 Nov 1945)	WH	PF, 4/4	PF, 58	F, 3	MU, 3.16	6.3	M, .652	DEM, constitutional democratic republic	CI	Civil-law system; judicial review of legislative acts
Guernsey (British Crown dependency)	EUR								CO	English law and local statute; justice is administered by the Royal Court
Guinea (12 Dec 1958)	AF	NF, 6/5	NF, 74		MU, 3.24		L, .425	AR, republic	CU	Based on French civil-law system, customary law, and decree; legal codes currently being revised
Guinea-Bissau (17 Sep 1974)	AF	PF, 6/4	PF, 60		MU, 3.90	4.4	L, .373	DEM, republic, multiparty since mid-1991	CI	
Guyana (20 Sep 1966)	WH	F, 2/2	F, 21		MU, 3.13	6.3	M, .740	DEM, republic within the Commonwealth	CO	Based on English common law with certain admixtures of Roman-Dutch law
Haiti (24 Oct 1945)	WH	NF, 6/6	NF, 79		MU, 3.78	6.0	L, .467	DEM, elected government	CI	Based on Roman civil-law system
Heard Island and McDonald Islands (territory of Australia)	EAP								CO	Laws of Australia valid where applicable

Table A1 (continued)

A *Jurisdiction (date admitted to UN)*	B *Region*	C *FH rating: political/ civil (1–7)*	D *FH rating: media (1–100)*	E *FH rating: religion (1–7)*	F *HF rating: economic (1–5)*	G *FI rating: economic (10–1)*	H *UNDP HDI (1–0)*	I *Government type*	J *Type of legal system*	K *Description of legal system*
Holy See (Vatican City) (established as an independent state in 1929)	EUR							Ecclesiastical	CU	Based on code of canon law and revisions to it
Honduras (17 Dec 1945)	WH	PF, 3/3	PF, 51		MU, 3.53	6.1	M, .667	DEM, democratic constitutional republic	CI	Rooted in Roman and Spanish civil law with increasing influence of English common law; recent judicial reforms include abandoning Napoleonic legal codes in favor of the oral adversarial system
Hong Kong (special administrative region [SAR] of China)	EAP	PF, 5/3			F, 1.34	8.6	H, .889	DEM, limited democracy	CO	Based on English common law
Howland Island (US territory)									CO	US laws valid where applicable
Hungary (14 Dec 1955)	EUR	F, 1/2	F, 23	F, 3	MF, 2.60	7.0	H, .837	DEM, parliamentary democracy	CI	Rule of law based on Western model
Iceland (19 Nov 1946)	EUR	F, 1/1	F, 8		MF, 2.00	7.6	H, .942	DEM, constitutional republic	CI	Civil-law system based on Danish law

Table A1 (continued)

A Jurisdiction (date admitted to UN)	B Region	C FH rating: political/ civil (1–7)	D FH rating: media (1–100)	E FH rating: religion (1–7)	F HF rating: economic (1–5)	G FI rating: economic (10–1)	H UNDP HDI (1–0)	I Government type	J Type of legal system	K Description of legal system
India (30 Oct 1945)	SA	F, 2/3	PF, 45	PF, 5	MU, 3.53	6.1	M, .590	DEM, federal republic	CO	Based on English com- mon law; limited judicial review of legislative acts
Indonesia (28 Sep 1950)	EAP	PF, 3/4	PF, 56	PF, 5	MU, 3.76	5.6	M, .682	DEM, republic	CI	Based on Roman- Dutch law, substantially modified by indigenous concepts and by new criminal-procedures code
Iran, Islamic Republic of (24 Oct 1945)	NE	NF, 6/6	NF, 76	UF, 7	R, 4.26	5.7	M, .719	AR, theocratic republic	CU	Constitution codifies Islamic principles of government
Iraq (21 Dec 1945)	NE	NF, 7/5	NF, 95		Not graded in 2003			AR, transi- tional	CU	In transition following 2003 defeat of Saddam Hussein regime by US- led coalition
Ireland (14 Dec 1955)	EUR	F, 1/1	F, 16	F, 1	F, 1.74	8.0	H, .930	DEM, republic	CO	Based on English com- mon law, substantially modified by indigenous concepts; judicial re- view of legislative acts in Supreme Court
Isle of Man (British Crown dependency)	EUR							Parliamen- tary democ- racy	CO	English common law and Manx statute

Table A1 (continued)

A Jurisdiction (date admitted to UN)	B Region	C FH rating: political/civil (1-7)	D FH rating: media (1-100)	E FH rating: religion (1-7)	F HF rating: economic (1-5)	G FI rating: economic (10-1)	H UNDP HDI (1-0)	I Government type	J Type of legal system	K Description of legal system
Israel (11 May 1949)	NE	F, 1/3	F, 27	F, 3	MF, 2.36	6.5	H, .905	DEM, parliamentary democracy	CU	Mixture of English common law, British Mandate regulations, and, in personal matters, Jewish, Christian, and Muslim legal systems
Italy (14 Dec 1955)	EUR	F, 1/1	F, 28		MF, 2.26	7.0	H, .916	DEM, republic	CI	Based on civil-law system; appeals treated as new trials; judicial review under certain conditions in Constitutional Court
Jamaica (18 Sep 1962)	WH	F, 2/3	F, 20		MF, 2.81	7.0	M, .757	DEM, constitutional parliamentary democracy	CO	Based on English common law
Jan Mayen (territory of Norway)	EUR								CI	Laws of Norway valid where applicable
Japan (18 Dec 1956)	EAP	F, 1/2	F, 17	F, 2	MF, 2.53	7.1	H, .932	DEM, constitutional monarchy with a parliamentary government	CI	Modeled after European civil-law system, with English-American influence; judicial review of legislative acts in the Supreme Court
Jarvis Island (US territory)	EAP								CO	US laws valid where applicable

187

Table A1 (continued)

A Jurisdiction (date admitted to UN)	B Region	C FH rating: political/civil (1–7)	D FH rating: media (1–100)	E FH rating: religion (1–7)	F HF rating: economic (1–5)	G FI rating: economic (10–1)	H UNDP HDI (1–0)	I Government type	J Type of legal system	K Description of legal system
Jersey (British Crown dependency)	EUR								CO	English law and local statute; justice is administered by the Royal Court
Johnston Atoll (US dependency)	EAP								CO	US laws valid where applicable
Jordan (14 Dec 1955)	NE	PF, 5/5	NF, 65		MF, 2.73	6.9	M, .743	RDP, constitutional monarchy	CU	Based on Islamic law and French codes; judicial review of legislative acts in a specially provided high tribunal
Juan de Nova Island (possession of France)	AF								CI	Laws of France valid where applicable
Kazakhstan (2 Mar 1992)	EUR	NF, 6/5	NF, 73	PF, 4	MU, 3.70		M, .765	AR, republic	CI	Based on civil-law system
Kenya (16 Dec 1963)	AF	PF, 3/3	NF, 68		MU, 3.26	6.6	L, .489	AR, republic	CU	Based on Kenyan statutory law, Kenyan and English common law, tribal law, and Islamic law; judicial review in High Court; constitutional amendment of 1982 making Kenya a de jure one-party state repealed in 1991

Table A1 (continued)

A Jurisdiction (date admitted to UN)	B Region	C FH rating: political/ civil (1–7)	D FH rating: media (1–100)	E FH rating: religion (1–7)	F HF rating: economic (1–5)	G FI rating: economic (10–1)	H UNDP HDI (1–0)	I Government type	J Type of legal system	K Description of legal system
Kingman Reef (US territory)	EAP								CO	US laws valid where applicable
Kiribati (14 Sep 1999)	EAP	F, 1/1	F, 26					DEM, republic	CO	
Korea, Democratic People's Republic of (17 Sep 1991)	EAP	NF, 7/7	NF, 96	UF, 7	R, 5.00			TOT, authoritarian socialist; one-man dictatorship	CI	Based on German civil-law system with Japanese influences and Communist legal theory; no judicial review of legislative acts
Korea, Republic of (17 Sep 1991)	EAP	F, 2/2	F, 29	F, 2	MF, 2.69	7.1	H, .879	DEM, republic	CI	Combines elements of continental-European civil-law systems, Anglo-American law, and Chinese classical thought
Kuwait (14 May 1963)	NE	PF, 4/5	PF, 54		MF, 2.70	6.9	H, .820	TM, nominal constitutional monarchy	CU	Civil-law system, with Islamic law significant in personal matters
Kyrgyzstan (2 Mar 1992)	EUR	NF, 6/5	NF, 71	PF, 4	MU, 3.36		M, .727	DEM, republic	CI	Based on civil-law system
Lao People's Democratic Republic (formerly Laos) (14 Dec 1955)	EAP	NF, 7/6	NF, 80		R, 4.45		M, .525	TOT, Communist state	CU	Based on traditional customs, French legal norms and procedures, and socialist practice

189

Table A1 (continued)

A Jurisdiction (date admitted to UN)	B Region	C FH rating: political/civil (1–7)	D FH rating: media (1–100)	E FH rating: religion (1–7)	F HF rating: economic (1–5)	G FI rating: economic (10–1)	H UNDP HDI (1–0)	I Government type	J Type of legal system	K Description of legal system
Latvia (17 Sep 1991)	EUR	F, 1/2	F, 18	F, 3	MF, 2.36	6.6	H, .811	DEM, parliamentary democracy	CI	Based on civil-law system
Lebanon (24 Oct 1945)	NE	NF, 6/5	NF, 71	PF, 4	MU, 3.13		M, .752	AR, republic	CU	Mixture of Ottoman law, canon law, Napoleonic code, and civil law; no judicial review of legislative acts
Lesotho (17 Oct 1966)	AF	F, 2/3	PF, 42		MU, 3.50		M, .510	RDP, parliamentary constitutional monarchy	CU	Based on English common law and Roman-Dutch law; judicial review of legislative acts in High Court and Court of Appeal
Liberia (2 Nov 1945)	AF	NF, 6/6	NF, 79					DEM, republic	CU	Dual system of statutory law based on Anglo-American common law for the modern sector and customary law based on unwritten tribal practices for indigenous sector
Libyan Arab Jamahiriya (14 Dec 1955)	NE	NF, 7/7	NF, 89		R, 4.55		M, .783	AR, military dictatorship (in theory, governed by the populace through local councils)	CU	Based on Italian civil-law system and Islamic law; separate religious courts; no constitutional provision for judicial review of legislative acts

Table A1 (continued)

A Jurisdiction (date admitted to UN)	B Region	C FH rating: political/ civil (1–7)	D FH rating: media (1–100)	E FH rating: religion (1–7)	F HF rating: economic (1–5)	G FI rating: economic (10–1)	H UNDP HDI (1–0)	I Government type	J Type of legal system	K Description of legal system
Liechtenstein (18 Sep 1990)	EUR	F, 1/1	F, 11					DEM, hereditary constitutional monarchy on a democratic, parliamentary basis	CI	Local civil and penal codes
Lithuania (17 Sep 1991)	EUR	F, 1/2	F, 18	F, 2	MF, 2.19	6.2	H, .824	DEM, par- liamentary democracy	CI	Based on civil-law system; legislative acts can be appealed to the constitutional court
Luxembourg (24 Oct 1945)	EUR	F, 1/1	F, 14		F, 1.71	7.7	H, .930	DEM, constitutional monarchy	CI	Based on civil-law system
Macau (SAR of China)	EAP	PF, 6/4						Limited democracy	CI	Based on Portuguese civil-law system
Macedonia, the former Yugoslav Republic of (8 Apr 1993)	EUR	PF, 3/3	PF, 50	PF, 4	MU, 3.04		M, .784	DEM, par- liamentary democracy	CI	Based on civil-law system; judicial review of legislative acts
Madagascar (20 Sep 1960)	AF	PF, 3/3	PF, 38		MU, 3.14	5.6	L, .468	DEM, republic	CI	Based on French civil- law system and tradi- tional Malagasy law

191

Table A1 (continued)

A Jurisdiction (date admitted to UN)	B Region	C FH rating: political/ civil (1–7)	D FH rating: media (1–100)	E FH rating: religion (1–7)	F HF rating: economic (1–5)	G FI rating: economic (10–1)	H UNDP HDI (1–0)	I Government type	J Type of legal system	K Description of legal system
Malawi (1 Dec 1964)	AF	PF, 3/4	PF, 57		MU, 3.46	4.8	L, .387	DEM, multiparty democracy	CU	Based on English common law and customary law; judicial review of legislative acts in the Supreme Court of Appeal
Malaysia (17 Sep 1957)	EAP	PF, 5/4	NF, 71	PF, 4	MU, 3.16	6.4	M, .790	RDP, constitutional monarchy	CO	Based on English common law; judicial review of legislative acts in the Supreme Court at request of supreme head of the federation
Maldives (21 Sep 1965)	SA	NF, 6/5	NF, 64				M, .751	AR, republic	CO	Based on Islamic law with admixture of English common law primarily in commercial matters
Mali (28 Sep 1960)	AF	F, 2/2	F, 24		MU, 3.34	5.8	L, .337	DEM, republic	CU	Based on French civil-law system and customary law; judicial review of legislative acts in Constitutional Court (formally established on 9 March 1994)
Malta (1 Dec 1964)	EUR	F, 1/1	F, 13		MF, 2.51	6.4	H, .856	DEM, republic	CO	Based on English common law and Roman civil law

Table A1 (continued)

A Jurisdiction (date admitted to UN)	B Region	C FH rating: political/ civil (1–7)	D FH rating: media (1–100)	E FH rating: religion (1–7)	F HF rating: economic (1–5)	G FI rating: economic (10–1)	H UNDP HDI (1–0)	I Government type	J Type of legal system	K Description of legal system
Marshall Islands (17 Sep 1991)	EAP	F, 1/1	F, 10					DEM, constitutional government in free association with the United States	CO	Based on adapted Trust Territory laws; acts of the legislature; and municipal, common, and customary laws
Martinique (department of France)	WH								CI	French legal system
Mauritania (27 Oct 1961)	AF	NF, 6/5	NF, 61	UF, 6	MF, 2.94		L, .454	AR, republic	CU	Combination of Sharia (Islamic law) and French civil law
Mauritius (24 Apr 1968)	AF	F, 1/2	F, 24		MF, 2.99	7.3	M, .779	AR, parliamentary democracy	CU	Based on French civil-law system with elements of English common law in certain areas
Mayotte (territorial collectivity of France)	AF								CI	French law
Mexico (7 Nov 1945)	WH	F, 2/2	PF, 38	PF, 4	MF, 2.90	6.2	H, .800	RDP, federal republic	CI	Mixture of US constitutional theory and civil-law system; judicial review of legislative acts

193

Table A1 (continued)

A Jurisdiction (date admitted to UN)	B Region	C FH rating: political/ civil (1–7)	D FH rating: media (1–100)	E FH rating: religion (1–7)	F HF rating: economic (1–5)	G FI rating: economic (10–1)	H UNDP HDI (1–0)	I Government type	J Type of legal system	K Description of legal system
Micronesia, Federated States of (17 Sep 1991)	EAP	F, 1/1	F, 17					DEM, constitutional government in free as- sociation with the United States	CO	Based on adapted Trust Territory laws; acts of the legislature; and municipal, common, and customary laws
Midway Islands (US territory)	EAP								CO	US laws valid where applicable
Moldova, Republic of (2 Mar 1992)	EUR	PF, 3/4	PF, 59	PF, 4	MU, 3.09		M, .700	DEM, republic	CI	Based on civil-law system; Constitutional Court reviews legality of legislative acts and governmental decisions of resolution
Monaco (28 May 1993)	EUR	F, 2/1	F, 9					DEM, constitutional monarchy	CI	Based on French law
Mongolia (27 Oct 1961)	EAP	F, 2/2	PF, 36	F, 3	MF, 2.90		M, .661	DEM, parlia- mentary	CI	Blend of Soviet, Ger- man, and US systems of law that combines aspects of a parliamen- tary system with some aspects of a presiden- tial system; constitution ambiguous on judicial review of legislative acts

194

Table A1 (continued)

A Jurisdiction (date admitted to UN)	B Region	C FH rating: political/civil (1–7)	D FH rating: media (1–100)	E FH rating: religion (1–7)	F HF rating: economic (1–5)	G FI rating: economic (10–1)	H UNDP HDI (1–0)	I Government type	J Type of legal system	K Description of legal system
Montserrat (UK territory)	WH								CO	English common law and statutory law
Morocco (12 Nov 1956)	NE	PF, 5/5	PF, 57	PF, 4	MF, 2.93	5.8	M, .606	TM, constitutional monarchy	CU	Based on Islamic law and French and Spanish civil-law system; judicial review of legislative acts in Constitutional Chamber of Supreme Court
Mozambique (16 Sep 1975)	AF	PF, 3/4	PF, 47		MU, 3.28		L, .356	DEM, republic	CI	Based on Portuguese civil-law system and customary law
Myanmar (formerly Burma) (19 Apr 1948)	EAP	NF, 7/7	NF, 94	UF, 7	R, 4.45	3.8	M, .549	AR, military regime	CI	
Namibia (23 Apr 1990)	AF	F, 2/3	PF, 37	F, 2	MF, 2.96	6.7	M, .627	DEM, republic	CI	Based on Roman-Dutch law and 1990 constitution
Nauru (14 Sep 1999)	EAP	F, 1/1	F, 26					DEM, republic	CO	Acts of the Nauru Parliament and British common law
Navassa Island (US territory)	WH								CO	US laws valid where applicable
Nepal (14 Dec 1955)	SA	PF, 5/4	NF, 65	PF, 5	MU, 3.53	5.7	L, .499	DEM, parliamentary democracy and constitutional monarchy	CO	Based on Hindu legal concepts and English common law

195

Table A1 (continued)

A Jurisdiction (date admitted to UN)	B Region	C FH rating: political/ civil (1–7)	D FH rating: media (1–100)	E FH rating: religion (1–7)	F HF rating: economic (1–5)	G FI rating: economic (10–1)	H UNDP HDI (1–0)	I Government type	J Type of legal system	K Description of legal system
Netherlands (10 Dec 1945)	EUR	F, 1/1	F, 15	F, 1	MF, 2.04	7.8	H, .938	DEM, constitutional monarchy	CI	Civil-law system incorporating French penal theory; constitution does not permit judicial review of acts of the States General
Netherlands Antilles (part of the Netherlands)	WH							Parliamentary	CI	Based on Dutch civil-law system, with some English common-law influence
New Caledonia (territory of France)	EAP								CI	1988 Matignon Accords grant substantial autonomy to the islands; formerly under French law
New Zealand (24 Oct 1945)	EAP	F, 1/1	F, 8		F, 1.70	8.2	H, .917	DEM, parliamentary democracy	CO	Based on English law, with special land legislation and land courts for the Maori
Nicaragua (24 Oct 1945)	WH	PF, 3/3	PF, 40		MF, 2.94	6.4	M, .643	DEM, republic	CI	Civil-law system; Supreme Court may review administrative acts
Niger (20 Sep 1960)	AF	PF, 4/4	PF, 53		MU, 3.43	5.6	L, .292	DEM, republic	CU	Based on French civil-law system and customary law

Table A1 (continued)

A Jurisdiction (date admitted to UN)	B Region	C FH rating: political/ civil (1–7)	D FH rating: media (1–100)	E FH rating: religion (1–7)	F HF rating: economic (1–5)	G FI rating: economic (10–1)	H UNDP HDI (1–0)	I Government type	J Type of legal system	K Description of legal system
Nigeria (7 Oct 1960)	AF	PF, 4/4	PF, 53	PF, 5	MU, 3.95	5.6	L, .463	DEM, republic transitioning from military to civilian rule	CU	Based on English common law, Islamic Sharia law (only in some northern states), and traditional law
Niue (self-governing in free association with New Zealand)	EAP							Self-governing parliamentary democracy	CO	English common law; self-governing, with the power to make its own laws
Norfolk Island (territory of Australia)	EAP								CO	Based on the laws of Australia, local ordinances and acts; English common law applies in matters not covered by either Australian or Norfolk Island law
Northern Marianas (commonwealth in political union with United States)	EAP							Commonwealth; self-governing with locally elected governor, lieutenant governor, and legislature	CO	Based on US system, except for customs, wages, immigration laws, and taxation

197

Table A1 (continued)

A Jurisdiction (date admitted to UN)	B Region	C FH rating: political/ civil (1–7)	D FH rating: media (1–100)	E FH rating: religion (1–7)	F HF rating: economic (1–5)	G FI rating: economic (10–1)	H UNDP HDI (1–0)	I Government type	J Type of legal system	K Description of legal system
Norway (27 Nov 1945)	EUR	F, 1/1	F, 9	F, 1	MF, 2.35	7.1	H, .944	DEM, constitutional monarchy	CI	Mixture of customary law, civil-law system, and common-law traditions; Supreme Court renders advisory opinions to legislature when asked
Oman (7 Oct 1971)	NE	NF, 6/5	NF, 73		MF, 2.80	7.4	M, .755	TM, monar-chy	CU	Based on English com-mon law and Islamic law; ultimate appeal to the monarch
Pakistan (30 Sep 1947)	SA	NF, 6/5	PF, 58	UF, 6	MU, 3.40	5.4	L, .499	AR, federal republic	CO	Based on English common law with provi-sions to accommodate Pakistan's status as an Islamic state
Palau (15 Dec 1994)	EAP	F, 1/1	F, 9					DEM, constitutional government in free as-sociation with the United States	CO	Based on Trust Terri-tory laws; acts of the legislature; and mu-nicipal, common, and customary laws
Palmyra Atoll (US territory)	EAP								CO	US laws valid where applicable
Panama (13 Nov 1945)	WH	F, 1/2	PF, 34		MF, 2.83	7.2	M, .788	DEM, constitutional democracy	CI	Based on civil-law system; judicial review of legislative acts in the Su-preme Court of Justice

198

Table A1 (continued)

A Jurisdiction (date admitted to UN)	B Region	C FH rating: political/ civil (1–7)	D FH rating: media (1–100)	E FH rating: religion (1–7)	F HF rating: economic (1–5)	G FI rating: economic (10–1)	H UNDP HDI (1–0)	I Government type	J Type of legal system	K Description of legal system
Papua New Guinea (10 Oct 1975)	EAP	PF, 3/3	F, 25			5.8	M, .548	DEM, constitutional monarchy with parliamentary democracy	CO	Based on English common law
Paracel Islands (occupied by China but claimed by Vietnam and Taiwan)	EAP								CI	
Paraguay (24 Oct 1945)	WH	PF, 3/3	PF, 55		MU, 3.39	6.3	M, .751	DEM, constitutional republic	CI	Based on Argentine codes, Roman law, and French codes; judicial review of legislative acts in Supreme Court of Justice
Peru (31 Oct 1945)	WH	F, 2/3	PF, 35		MF, 2.83	6.7	M, .752	AR, constitutional republic	CI	Based on civil-law system
Philippines (24 Oct 1945)	EAP	F, 2/3	F, 30	F, 3	MU, 3.05	6.6	M, .751	DEM, republic	CI	Based on Spanish and Anglo-American law
Pitcairn Islands (UK territory)	EAP								CO	Local island bylaws

Table A1 (continued)

A Jurisdiction (date admitted to UN)	B Region	C FH rating: political/ civil (1–7)	D FH rating: media (1–100)	E FH rating: religion (1–7)	F HF rating: economic (1–5)	G FI rating: economic (10–1)	H UNDP HDI (1–0)	I Government type	J Type of legal system	K Description of legal system
Poland (24 Oct 1945)	EUR	F, 1/2	F, 18	F, 2	MF, 2.81	6.0	H, .841	DEM, republic	CI	Mixture of continental (Napoleonic) civil law and holdover Communist legal theory; changes being gradually introduced as part of broader democratization process; limited judicial review of legislative acts, but rulings of the Constitutional Tribunal are final; court decisions can be appealed to the European Court of Justice in Strasbourg
Portugal (14 Dec 1955)	EUR	F, 1/1	F, 15		MF, 2.38	7.2	H, .896	DEM, parliamentary democracy	CI	Civil-law system; the Constitutional Tribunal reviews the constitutionality of legislation
Puerto Rico (commonwealth associated with United States)	WH	F, 1/2						Commonwealth	CI	Based on Spanish civil code; within the US federal system of justice
Qatar (21 Sep 1971)	NE	NF, 6/6	NF, 61		MF, 2.86		H, .826	TM, traditional monarchy	CU	Discretionary system of law controlled by the amir, although civil codes are being implemented; Islamic law dominates family and personal matters

200

Table A1 (continued)

A Jurisdiction (date admitted to UN)	B Region	C FH rating: political/ civil (1–7)	D FH rating: media (1–100)	E FH rating: religion (1–7)	F HF rating: economic (1–5)	G FI rating: economic (10–1)	H UNDP HDI (1–0)	I Government type	J Type of legal system	K Description of legal system
Reunion (department of France)	AF								CI	French law
Romania (14 Dec 1955)	EUR	F, 2/2	PF, 38	F, 3	MU, 3.66	4.7	M, .773	DEM, republic	CI	Former mixture of civil-law system and communist legal theory; now based on the constitution of France's Fifth Republic
Russian Federation (24 Oct 1945)	EUR	PF, 5/5	NF, 66	PF, 4	MU, 3.46	5.0	M, .779	DEM, federation	CI	Based on civil-law system; judicial review of legislative acts
Rwanda (18 Sep 1962)	AF	NF, 6/5	NF, 80		MU, 3.36	5.2	L, .422	AR, republic; presidential, multiparty system	CU	Based on German and Belgian civil-law systems and customary law; judicial review of legislative acts in the Supreme Court
Saint Helena (UK territory)	AF								CO	
Saint Kitts and Nevis (23 Sep 1983)	WH	F, 1/2	F, 18				H, .808	DEM, constitutional monarchy with Westminster-style parliament	CO	Based on English common law

Table A1 (continued)

A Jurisdiction (date admitted to UN)	B Region	C FH rating: political/ civil (1–7)	D FH rating: media (1–100)	E FH rating: religion (1–7)	F HF rating: economic (1–5)	G FI rating: economic (10–1)	H UNDP HDI (1–0)	I Government type	J Type of legal system	K Description of legal system
Saint Lucia (18 Sep 1979)	WH	F, 2/1	F, 8				M, .775	DEM, West-minster-style parliamentary democracy	CO	Based on English common law
Saint Pierre and Miquelon (self-governing territorial collectivity of France)	WH								CI	French law with special adaptations for local conditions, such as housing and taxation
Saint Vincent and the Grena-dines (16 Sep 1980)	WH	F, 1/2	F, 17				M, .755	DEM, par-liamentary democracy; independent sovereign state within the Common-wealth	CO	Based on English common law
Samoa (formerly West-ern Samoa) (15 Dec 1976)	EAP	F, 2/2	F, 24				M, .775	DEM, constitutional monarchy under native chief	CO	Based on English common law and local customs; judicial review of legislative acts with respect to fundamental rights of the citizen
San Marino (2 Mar 1992)	EUR	F, 1/1	F, 9					DEM, independent republic	CI	Based on civil-law system with Italian law influences

Table A1 (continued)

A Jurisdiction (date admitted to UN)	B Region	C FH rating: political/civil (1–7)	D FH rating: media (1–100)	E FH rating: religion (1–7)	F HF rating: economic (1–5)	G FI rating: economic (10–1)	H UNDP HDI (1–0)	I Government type	J Type of legal system	K Description of legal system
Sao Tome and Principe (16 Sep 1975)	AF	F, 2/2	F, 19				M, .639	DEM, republic	CI	Based on Portuguese legal system and customary law
Saudi Arabia (24 Oct 1945)	NE	NF, 7/7	NF, 80	UF, 7	MU, 3.05		M, .769	TM, monarchy	CU	Based on Islamic law, several secular codes have been introduced; commercial disputes handled by special committees
Scotland (administrative division of the UK)	EUR								CO	
Senegal (28 Sep 1960)	AF	F, 2/3	PF, 38		MU, 3.00	5.8	L, .430	RDP, republic under multiparty democratic rule	CI	Based on French civil-law system; judicial review of legislative acts in Constitutional Court; the Council of State audits the government's accounting office
Serbia and Montenegro (1 Nov 2000)	EUR	F, 3/2	PF, 40		Not graded in 2003			DEM, republic	CI	Based on civil-law system
Seychelles (21 Sep 1976)	AF	PF, 3/3	PF, 50				H, .840	DEM, republic	CU	Based on English common law, French civil law, and customary law

Table A1 (continued)

A Jurisdiction (date admitted to UN)	B Region	C FH rating: political/ civil (1–7)	D FH rating: media (1–100)	E FH rating: religion (1–7)	F HF rating: economic (1–5)	G FI rating: economic (10–1)	H UNDP HDI (1–0)	I Government type	J Type of legal system	K Description of legal system
Sierra Leone (27 Sep 1961)	AF	PF, 4/3	NF, 61		MU, 3.73	5.2	L, .275	DEM, constitutional democracy	CU	Based on English law and customary laws indigenous to local tribes
Singapore (21 Sep 1965)	EAP	PF, 5/4	NF, 66	PF, 4	F, 1.61	8.5	H, .884	AR, parliamentary republic	CO	Based on English common law
Slovakia (19 Jan 1993)	EUR	F, 1/2	F, 21		MF, 2.44	6.0	H, .836	DEM, parliamentary democracy	CI	Civil-law system based on Austro-Hungarian codes; legal code modified to comply with the obligations of Organization on Security and Cooperation in Europe and to expunge Marxist-Leninist legal theory
Slovenia (22 May 1992)	EUR	F, 1/1	F, 19		MF, 2.75	6.1	H, .881	DEM, parliamentary democratic republic	CI	Based on civil-law system
Solomon Islands (19 Sep 1978)	EAP	PF, 3/3	F, 25				M, .632	DEM, parliamentary democracy tending toward anarchy	CO	English common law, which is widely disregarded

Table A1 (continued)

A Jurisdiction (date admitted to UN)	B Region	C FH rating: political/ civil (1–7)	D FH rating: media (1–100)	E FH rating: religion (1–7)	F HF rating: economic (1–5)	G FI rating: economic (10–1)	H UNDP HDI (1–0)	I Government type	J Type of legal system	K Description of legal system
Somalia (20 Sep 1960)	AF	NF, 6/7	NF, 80					AR, no permanent national government; transitional, parliamen- tary national government	CU	No national system; Sharia and secular courts are in some localities
South Africa (7 Nov 1945)	AF	F, 1/2	F, 25	F, 2	MF, 2.79	6.8	M, .684	DEM, republic	CU	Based on Roman-Dutch law and English com- mon law
South Georgia and the South Sandwich Islands (UK territory; also claimed by Argentina)	WH								CO	UK laws valid where applicable; the senior magistrate from the Falkland Islands presides over the Mag- istrates Court
Spain (14 Dec 1955)	EUR	F, 1/1	F, 16	F, 3	MF, 2.31	7.0	H, .918	DEM, par- liamentary monarchy	CI	Civil-law system, with regional applications
Spratly Islands (occupied and claimed by China, Taiwan, Vietnam, Ma- laysia, and the Philippines)	EAP								CI	

205

Table A1 (continued)

A Jurisdiction (date admitted to UN)	B Region	C FH rating: political/ civil (1–7)	D FH rating: media (1–100)	E FH rating: religion (1–7)	F HF rating: economic (1–5)	G FI rating: economic (10–1)	H UNDP HDI (1–0)	I Government type	J Type of legal system	K Description of legal system
Sri Lanka (14 Dec 1955)	SA	PF, 3/3	PF, 52	PF, 4	MU, 3.06	6.3	M, .730	DEM, republic	CO	Highly complex mixture of English common law, Roman-Dutch, Muslim, Sinhalese, and customary law
Sudan (12 Nov 1956)	AF	NF, 7/7	NF, 84	UF, 7	Not graded in 2003		M, .503	AR, authoritarian regime	CU	Based on English common law and Islamic law; as of 20 January 1991, the now defunct Revolutionary Command Council imposed Islamic law in the northern states; Islamic law applies to all residents of the northern states regardless of their religion; some separate religious courts
Suriname (4 Dec 1975)	WH	F, 1/2	F, 26		MU, 3.96		M, .762	DEM, constitutional democracy	CI	Based on Dutch legal system incorporating French penal theory
Svalbard (territory of Norway)	EUR								CI	
Swaziland (24 Sep 1968)	AF	NF, 7/5	NF, 74		MU, 3.18		M, .547	TM, monarchy; independent member of Commonwealth	CU	Based on South African Roman-Dutch law in statutory courts and Swazi traditional law and custom in traditional courts

206

Table A1 (continued)

A Jurisdiction (date admitted to UN)	B Region	C FH rating: political/ civil (1–7)	D FH rating: media (1–100)	E FH rating: religion (1–7)	F HF rating: economic (1–5)	G FI rating: economic (10–1)	H UNDP HDI (1–0)	I Government type	J Type of legal system	K Description of legal system
Sweden (19 Nov 1946)	EUR	F, 1/1	F, 8	F, 2	F, 1.90	7.1	H, .941	DEM, constitutional monarchy	CI	Civil-law system influenced by customary law
Switzerland (10 Sep 2002)	EUR	F, 1/1	F, 10		F, 1.84	8.0	H, .932	DEM, federal republic	CI	Civil-law system influenced by customary law; judicial review of legislative acts, except with respect to federal decrees of general obligatory character
Syrian Arab Republic (24 Oct 1945)	NE	NF, 7/7	NF, 80		MU, 3.88	5.2	M, .685	AR, republic under military regime since March 1963	CU	Based on Islamic law and civil-law system; special religious courts
Taiwan (multiparty democratic regime not recognized as an independent state)	EAP	F, 2/2	F, 24	F, 2	MF, 2.43	7.1		DEM, multiparty democratic regime headed by popularly elected president and unicameral legislature	CI	Based on civil-law system
Tajikistan (2 Mar 1992)	EUR	NF, 6/5	NF, 76		R, 4.15		M, .677	RDP, republic	CI	Based on civil-law system; no judicial review of legislative acts

Table A1 (continued)

A Jurisdiction (date admitted to UN)	B Region	C FH rating: political/ civil (1–7)	D FH rating: media (1–100)	E FH rating: religion (1–7)	F HF rating: economic (1–5)	G FI rating: economic (10–1)	H UNDP HDI (1–0)	I Government type	J Type of legal system	K Description of legal system
Tanzania, United Republic of (14 Dec 1961)	AF	PF, 4/3	PF, 47	PF, 4	MU, 3.29	6.2	L, .400	RDP, republic	CU	Based on English common law; judicial review of legislative acts limited to matters of interpretation
Thailand (16 Dec 1946)	EAP	F, 2/3	PF, 36		MF, 2.86	6.7	M, .768	DEM, constitutional monarchy	CI	Based on civil-law system, with influences of common law
Timor-Leste (East Timor) (27 Sep 2002)	EAP	PF, 3/3	F, 22	PF, 5				P, republic	CI	
Togo (20 Sep 1960)	AF	NF, 6/5	NF, 74		MU, 3.73	5.1	M, .501	DEM, republic under transition to multiparty democratic rule	CU	French-based court system
Tokelau (territory of New Zealand)	EAP								CO	New Zealand and local statutes
Tonga (14 Sep 1999)	EAP	PF, 5/3	PF, 32					RDP, hereditary constitutional monarchy	CO	Based on English law
Trinidad and Tobago (18 Sep 1962)	WH	PF, 3/3	F, 25		MF, 2.45	7.1	H, .802	DEM, parliamentary democracy	CO	Based on English common law; judicial review of legislative acts in the Supreme Court

208

Table A1 (continued)

A Jurisdiction (date admitted to UN)	B Region	C FH rating: political/ civil (1-7)	D FH rating: media (1-100)	E FH rating: religion (1-7)	F HF rating: economic (1-5)	G FI rating: economic (10-1)	H UNDP HDI (1-0)	I Government type	J Type of legal system	K Description of legal system
Tromelin Island (possession of France)	AF								CI	Laws of France valid where applicable
Tunisia (12 Nov 1956)	NE	NF, 6/5	NF, 78		MF, 2.94	6.4	M, .740	AR, republic	CU	Based on French civil-law system and Islamic law; some judicial review of legislative acts in the Supreme Court in joint session
Turkey (24 Oct 1945)	EUR	PF, 3/4	PF, 55	PF, 5	MU, 3.39	5.3	M, .734	DEM, republican parliamentary democracy	CI	Derived from various European continental legal systems
Turkmenistan (2 Mar 1992)	EUR	NF, 7/7	NF, 92	UF, 7	R, 4.31		M, .748	AR, republic	CI	Based on civil-law system
Turks & Caicos Islands (UK territory)	WH								CO	Based on laws of England and Wales, with a few adopted from Jamaica and the Bahamas
Tuvalu (5 Sep 2000)	EAP	F, 1/1	F, 16					DEM, constitutional monarchy with parliamentary democracy	CO	

209

Table A1 (continued)

A Jurisdiction (date admitted to UN)	B Region	C FH rating: political/ civil (1–7)	D FH rating: media (1–100)	E FH rating: religion (1–7)	F HF rating: economic (1–5)	G FI rating: economic (10–1)	H UNDP HDI (1–0)	I Government type	J Type of legal system	K Description of legal system
Uganda (25 Oct 1962)	AF	PF, 5/4	PF, 45		MF, 2.70	6.7	L, .489	AR, republic	CU	In 1995, the government restored the legal system to one based on English common law and customary law
Ukraine (24 Oct 1945)	EUR	PF, 4/4	NF, 67	F, 3	MU, 3.49	4.6	M, .766	DEM, republic	CI	Based on civil-law system; judicial review of legislative acts
United Arab Emirates (9 Dec 1971)	NE	NF, 6/6	NF, 74		MF, 2.60	7.5	H, .816	TM, federation	CU	Federal court system introduced in 1971; all emirates except Dubayy (Dubai) and Ra's al Khaymah are not fully integrated into the federal system; all emirates have secular and Islamic law for civil, criminal, and high courts
United Kingdom of Great Britain and Northern Ireland (24 Oct 1945)	EUR	F, 1/1	F, 18	F, 2	F, 1.79	8.2	H, .930	DEM, constitutional monarchy	CO	Common-law tradition with early Roman and modern continental influences; has judicial review of acts of Parliament under the Human Rights Act of 1998

Table A1 (continued)

A Jurisdiction (date admitted to UN)	B Region	C FH rating: political/ civil (1–7)	D FH rating: media (1–100)	E FH rating: religion (1–7)	F HF rating: economic (1–5)	G FI rating: economic (10–1)	H UNDP HDI (1–0)	I Government type	J Type of legal system	K Description of legal system
United States of America (24 Oct 1945)	WH	F, 1/1	F, 17	F, 1	F, 1.85	8.3	H, .937	DEM, constitution-based federal republic; strong democratic tradition	CO	Based on English common law; judicial review of legislative acts
Uruguay (18 Dec 1945)	WH	F, 1/1	F, 30		MF, 2.55	6.7	H, .834	DEM, constitutional republic	CI	Based on Spanish civil-law system
Uzbekistan (2 Mar 1992)	EUR	NF, 7/6	NF, 86	UF, 6	R, 4.29		M, .729	AR, republic; authoritarian presidential rule, with little power outside the executive branch	CI	Evolution of Soviet civil law; still lacks independent judicial system
Vanuatu (15 Sep 1981)	EAP	F, 2/2	F, 21				M, .568	DEM, parliamentary republic	CO	Unified system being created from former dual French and British systems
Venezuela (15 Nov 1945)	WH	PF, 3/4	NF, 68		R, 4.18	5.3	M, .775	DEM, federal republic	CI	Based on organic laws as of July 1999; open, adversarial court system
Vietnam (20 Sep 1977)	EAP	NF, 7/6	NF, 82	UF, 6	MU, 3.93		M, .688	TOT, Communist state	CI	Based on Communist legal theory and French civil-law system

Table A1 (continued)

A Jurisdiction (date admitted to UN)	*B* Region	*C* FH rating: political/ civil (1–7)	*D* FH rating: media (1–100)	*E* FH rating: religion (1–7)	*F* HF rating: economic (1–5)	*G* FI rating: economic (10–1)	*H* UNDP HDI (1–0)	*I* Government type	*J* Type of legal system	*K* Description of legal system
Virgin Islands (US territory)	WH								CO	Based on US laws
Wake Island (US territory)	EAP								CO	US laws valid where applicable
Wales (administrative division of the UK)	EUR								CO	
Wallis and Futuna (territory of France)	EAP								CI	French legal system
West Bank (governed by the Palestinian Authority)	NE		NF, 86				M, .731		CU	Treaty with Israel permits self-government of West Bank and Gaza Strip by Palestinian Authority
Western Sahara (disputed territory)	NE							Legal status of territory and issue of sovereignty unresolved (contested by Morocco and Polisario Front)	CU	

Table A1 (continued)

A Jurisdiction (date admitted to UN)	B Region	C FH rating: political/ civil (1–7)	D FH rating: media (1–100)	E FH rating: religion (1–7)	F HF rating: economic (1–5)	G FI rating: economic (10–1)	H UNDP HDI (1–0)	I Government type	J Type of legal system	K Description of legal system
Yemen (30 Sep 1947)	NE	PF, 5/5	NF, 69		MU, 3.70		L, .470	RDP, republic	CU	Based on Islamic law, Turkish law, English common law, and local tribal customary law
Yugoslavia, Socialist Federal Republic of[c]	EUR							AR	CI	
Zambia (1 Dec 1964)	AF	PF, 4/4	NF, 63		MU, 3.50	6.8	L, .386	AR, republic	CU	Based on English common law and customary law; judicial review of legislative acts in an ad hoc constitutional council
Zimbabwe (25 Aug 1980)	AF	NF, 6/6	NF, 88	F, 3	R, 4.54	4.0	L, .496	RDP, parliamentary democracy	CU	Mixture of Roman-Dutch and English common law

[c]Yugoslavia is no longer a state; it splintered into the five states of the Republic of Slovenia, the Republic of Croatia, the Former Yugoslav Republic of Macedonia, Bosnia and Herzegovina, and Serbia and Montenegro.

Table A2. Normalized freedom and human development ratings for 193 selected jurisdictions

A Jurisdiction	B Region	C Normalized FH rating: political/civil	D Normalized FH rating: media	E Normalized FH rating: religion	F Normalized HF rating: economic	G Normalized FI rating: economic	H Normalized UNDP HDI	I Government type[a]	J Type of legal system[b]	K D_a
Afghanistan	SA	NF, 1.6666/1.6666	NF, 2.2263					TOT	CU	1.99
Albania	EUR	PF, 6.6666/6.6666	PF, 5.0505		MU, 4.75	5.1111	M, 7.35	DEM	CI	5.93
Algeria	NE	NF, 1.6666/3.3333	NF, 3.8383		MU, 4.225	3.5555	M, 7.04	AR	CU	3.94
Andorra	EUR	F, 10/10	F, 9.2929					DEM	CI	9.76
Angola	AF	NF, 1.6666/3.3333	NF, 2.8282				L, 3.77	AR	CI	2.89
Antigua and Barbuda	WH	PF, 4.9999/8.3333	PF, 5.5555				M, 7.98	RDP	CO	6.72
Argentina	WH	F, 8.3333/8.3333	PF, 6.1616	F, 6.6666	MU, 3.8	6.1111	H, 8.49	DEM	CI	6.84
Armenia	EUR	PF, 4.9999/4.9999	NF, 3.5353	PF, 4.9999	MF, 5.925		M, 7.29	DEM	CI	5.29
Australia	EAP	F, 10/10	F, 8.6868		F, 7.8	7.7777	H, 9.39	DEM	CO	8.94
Austria	EUR	F, 10/10	F, 7.7777	F, 8.3333	MF, 7.3	7.3333	H, 9.29	DEM	CI	8.58
Azerbaijan	EUR	NF, 1.6666/3.3333	NF, 2.7272	PF, 3.3333	MU, 4.025		M, 7.44	AR	CI	3.75
Bahamas	WH	F, 10/10	F, 8.9898		MF, 6.875	6.2222	H, 8.12	DEM	CO	8.37
Bahrain	NE	PF, 3.3333/3.3333	NF, 3.2323		MF, 7.3	6.7777	H, 8.39	TM	CU	5.39
Bangladesh	SA	PF, 4.9999/4.9999	NF, 3.5353	UF, 1.6666	MU, 3.25	5.1111	M, 5.02	DEM	CO	4.08
Barbados	WH	F, 10/10	F, 8.6868		MF, 6.475	5.3333	H, 8.88	DEM	CO	8.23
Belarus (Bye-lorussia)	EUR	NF, 1.6666/1.6666	NF, 1.8181	PF, 3.3333	R, 2.275		H, 8.04	AR	CI	3.13
Belgium	EUR	F, 10/10	F, 9.1919	F, 6.6666	MF, 7.025	7.1111	H, 9.37	DEM	CI	8.48
Belize	WH	F, 10/8.3333	F, 7.7777		MF, 5.775	5.8888	M, 7.76	DEM	CO	7.59
Benin	AF	F, 8.3333/8.3333	F, 7.2727		MU, 3.9	5.1111	L, 4.11	DEM	CU	6.18

Table A2 (continued)

A Jurisdiction	B Region	C Normalized FH rating: political/civil	D Normalized FH rating: media	E Normalized FH rating: religion	F Normalized HF rating: economic	G Normalized FI rating: economic	H Normalized UNDP HDI	I Government type[a]	J Type of legal system[b]	K D_a
Bhutan	SA	NF, 1.6666/3.3333	NF, 3.0303	UF, 1.6666			M, 5.11	TM	CO	2.96
Bolivia	WH	PF, 6.6666/6.6666	F, 7.0707		MF, 6.025	6.1111	M, 6.72	DEM	CI	6.54
Bosnia and Herzegovina	EUR	PF, 4.9999/4.9999	PF, 5.1515		MU, 4.25		M, 7.77	P	CI	5.43
Botswana	AF	F, 8.3333/8.3333	F, 7.0707	F, 8.3333	MF, 6.125	6.7777	M, 6.14	DEM	CU	7.30
Brazil	WH	F, 8.3333/6.6666	PF, 6.2626	F, 8.3333	MU, 4.75	5.3333	M, 7.77	DEM	CI	6.78
Brunei Darussalam	EAP	NF, 1.6666/3.3333	NF, 2.4242				H, 8.72	TM	CO	4.04
Bulgaria	EUR	F, 10/8.3333	F, 7.0707	PF, 4.9999	MU, 4.8	4.7777	M, 7.95	DEM	CI	6.85
Burkina Faso	AF	PF, 4.9999/4.9999	PF, 6.1616		MU, 4.3		L, 3.30	AR	CU	4.75
Burundi	AF	PF, 3.3333/3.3333	NF, 2.4242		Not graded in 2003	4.5555	L, 3.37	AR	CU	3.40
Cambodia	EAP	NF, 1.6666/3.3333	NF, 3.6363		MF, 5.25		M, 5.56	RDP	CI	3.89
Cameroon	AF	NF, 1.6666/1.6666	NF, 3.5353		MU, 3.425	5.1111	L, 4.99	RDP	CU	3.40
Canada	WH	F, 10/10	F, 8.3838		F, 7.55	7.8888	H, 9.37	DEM	CO	8.87
Cape Verde	AF	F, 10/10	F, 7.0707		MF, 5.35		M, 7.27	DEM	CI	7.94
Central African Republic	AF	NF, 0/3.3333	NF, 3.3333		MU, 4.05	4.3333	L, 3.63	DEM	CU	3.11
Chad	AF	NF, 1.6666/3.3333	NF, 3.3333		MU, 3.65	5.1111	L, 3.76	RDP	CU	3.48
Chile	WH	F, 10/10	F, 7.8787	F, 6.6666	F, 7.725	6.9999	H, 8.31	DEM	CI	8.23

Table A2 (continued)

A Jurisdiction	B Region	C Normalized FH rating: political/civil	D Normalized FH rating: media	E Normalized FH rating: religion	F Normalized HF rating: economic	G Normalized FI rating: economic	H Normalized UNDP HDI	I Government type[a]	J Type of legal system[b]	K D_a
China, People's Republic of	EAP	NF, 0/1.6666	NF, 2.0202	UF, 1.6666	MU, 3.4	4.9999	M, 7.21	AR	CI	2.99
Colombia	WH	PF, 4.9999/4.9999	NF, 3.7373	PF, 4.9999	MU, 4.675	4.8888	M, 7.79	DEM	CI	5.16
Comoros	AF	PF, 3.3333/4.9999	PF, 5.7575				M, 5.28	RDP	CU	4.84
Congo, Democratic Republic of the (formerly Zaire)	AF	NF, 1.6666/1.6666	NF, 1.8181		Not graded in 2003	3.2222	L, 3.63	AR	CU	2.40
Congo, Republic of the	AF	PF, 3.3333/4.9999	PF, 4.5454		MU, 2.75	3.8888	M, 5.02	AR	CU	4.09
Costa Rica	WH	F, 10/8.3333	F, 8.6868		MF, 5.725	6.7777	H, 8.32	DEM	CI	7.97
Côte d'Ivoire (Ivory Coast)	AF	NF, 1.6666/3.3333	NF, 3.2323		MU, 4.55	5.4444	L, 3.96	AR	CU	3.69
Croatia	EUR	F, 8.3333/8.3333	PF, 6.7676		MU, 4.725	5.5555	H, 8.18	DEM	CI	6.98
Cuba	WH	NF, 0/0	NF, 0.6060	UF, 1.6666	R, 2.3		H, 8.06	TOT	CI	2.11
Cyprus	EUR	F, 10/10	F, 8.2828		F, 7.625	5.7777	H, 8.91	DEM	CI	8.43
Czech Republic	EUR	F, 10/8.3333	F, 7.7777		MF, 6.525	6.5555	H, 8.61	DEM	CI	7.97
Denmark	EUR	F, 10/10	F, 8.9898		F, 8.0	7.3333	H, 9.30	DEM	CI	8.94
Djibouti	AF	PF, 3.3333/3.3333	NF, 3.5353		MU, 4.425		L, 4.62	DEM	CU	3.85
Dominica	WH	F, 10/10	F, 8.6868				M, 7.76	DEM	CO	9.11

Table A2 (continued)

A Jurisdiction	B Region	C Normalized FH rating: political/civil	D Normalized FH rating: media	E Normalized FH rating: religion	F Normalized HF rating: economic	G Normalized FI rating: economic	H Normalized UNDP HDI	I Government type[a]	J Type of legal system[b]	K D_a
Dominican Republic	WH	F, 6.6666/8.3333	PF, 6.7676		MU, 3.725	6.2222	M, 7.37	DEM	CI	6.51
Ecuador	WH	PF, 6.6666/6.6666	PF, 5.9595		MU, 3.5	4.4444	M, 7.31	DEM	CI	5.76
Egypt	NE	NF, 1.6666/1.6666	NF, 2.1212	PF, 3.3333	MU, 4.3	6.1111	M, 6.48	RDP	CU	3.67
El Salvador	WH	F, 8.3333/6.6666	PF, 6.2626	F, 6.6666	MF, 6.9	6.8888	M, 7.19	DEM	CI	6.99
Equatorial Guinea	AF	NF, 0/1.6666	NF, 1.1919		MU, 3.275		M, 6.64	AR	CI	2.55
Eritrea	AF	NF, 0/1.6666	NF, 1.7171				L, 4.46	AR	CU	1.96
Estonia	EUR	F, 10/8.3333	F, 8.3838	F, 10	F, 8.1	7.2222	H, 8.33	DEM	CI	8.62
Ethiopia	AF	PF, 3.3333/3.3333	NF, 3.6363		MU, 4.175		L, 3.59	AR	CU	3.61
Fiji	EAP	PF, 4.9999/6.6666	F, 7.1717		MU, 4.85	5.6666	M, 7.54	DEM	CO	6.15
Finland	EUR	F, 10/10	F, 9.0909	F, 10	F, 7.625	7.4444	H, 9.30	DEM	CI	9.07
France	EUR	F, 10/10	F, 8.3838	F, 6.6666	MF, 5.925	6.3333	H, 9.25	DEM	CI	8.08
Gabon	AF	PF, 3.3333/4.9999	PF, 4.2424		MU, 3.925	4.6666	M, 6.53	AR	CU	4.62
Gambia	AF	PF, 4.9999/4.9999	NF, 3.5353		MU, 3.65		L, 4.63	AR	CU	4.36
Georgia	EUR	PF, 4.9999/4.9999	PF, 4.4646	PF, 4.9999	MU, 4.525		M, 7.46	DEM	CI	5.24
Germany	EUR	F, 10/10	F, 8.5858	F, 6.6666	MF, 7.425	6.9999	H, 9.21	DEM	CI	8.41
Ghana	AF	F, 8.3333/8.3333	F, 7.0707		MU, 4.0	5.3333	M, 5.67	DEM	CU	6.46
Greece	EUR	F, 10/8.3333	F, 7.2727	PF, 4.9999	MF, 5.5	6.3333	H, 8.92	DEM	CI	7.34
Grenada	WH	F, 10/8.3333	F, 8.6868				M, 7.38	DEM	CO	8.60
Guatemala	WH	PF, 4.9999/4.9999	PF, 4.2424	F, 6.6666	MU, 4.6	5.8888	M, 6.52	DEM	CI	5.42

Table A2 (continued)

A Jurisdiction	B Region	C Normalized FH rating: political/civil	D Normalized FH rating: media	E Normalized FH rating: religion	F Normalized HF rating: economic	G Normalized FI rating: economic	H Normalized UNDP HDI	I Government type[a]	J Type of legal system[b]	K D_a
Guinea	AF	NF, 1.6666/3.3333	NF, 2.6262		MU, 4.4		L, 4.25	AR	CU	3.26
Guinea-Bissau	AF	PF, 1.6666/4.9999	PF, 4.0404		MU, 2.75	3.7777	L, 3.73	DEM	CI	3.49
Guyana	WH	F, 8.3333/8.3333	F, 7.9797		MU, 4.675	5.8888	M, 7.40	DEM	CO	7.10
Haiti	WH	NF, 1.6666/1.6666	NF, 2.1212		MU, 3.05	5.5555	L, 4.67	DEM	CI	3.12
Honduras	WH	PF, 6.6666/6.6666	PF, 4.9494		MU, 3.675	5.6666	M, 6.67	DEM	CI	5.72
Hong Kong (SAR of China)	EAP	PF, 3.3333/6.6666			F, 9.15	8.4444	H, 8.89	DEM	CO	7.29
Hungary	EUR	F, 10/8.3333	F, 7.7777	F, 6.6666	MF, 6	6.6666	H, 8.37	DEM	CI	7.69
Iceland	EUR	F, 10/10	F, 9.2929		MF, 7.5	7.3333	H, 9.42	DEM	CI	8.92
India	SA	F, 8.3333/6.6666	PF, 5.5555	PF, 3.3333	MU, 3.675	5.6666	M, 5.90	DEM	CO	5.59
Indonesia	EAP	PF, 6.6666/4.9999	PF, 4.4444	PF, 3.3333	MU, 3.1	5.1111	M, 6.82	DEM	CI	4.93
Iran, Islamic Republic of	NE	NF, 1.6666/1.6666	NF, 2.4242	UF, 0	R, 1.85	5.2222	M, 7.19	AR	CU	2.86
Iraq	NE	NF, 0/3.3333	NF, 0.5050		Not graded in 2003			AR	CU	1.28
Ireland	EUR	F, 10/10	F, 8.4848	F, 10	F, 8.15	7.7777	H, 9.30	DEM	CO	9.10
Israel	NE	F, 10/6.6666	F, 7.3737	F, 6.6666	MF, 6.6	6.1111	H, 9.05	DEM	CU	7.49
Italy	EUR	F, 10/10	F, 7.2727		MF, 6.85	6.6666	H, 9.16	DEM	CI	8.32
Jamaica	WH	F, 8.3333/6.6666	F, 8.0808		MF, 5.475	6.6666	M, 7.57	DEM	CO	7.13
Japan	EAP	F, 10/8.3333	F, 8.3838	F, 8.3333	MF, 6.175	6.7777	H, 9.32	DEM	CI	8.19

218

Table A2 (continued)

A Jurisdiction	B Region	C Normalized FH rating: political/civil	D Normalized FH rating: media	E Normalized FH rating: religion	F Normalized HF rating: economic	G Normalized FI rating: economic	H Normalized UNDP HDI	I Government type[a]	J Type of legal system[b]	K D_a
Jordan	NE	PF, 3.3333/3.3333	NF, 3.5353		MF, 5.675	6.5555	M, 7.43	RDP	CU	4.98
Kazakhstan	EUR	NF, 1.6666/3.3333	NF, 2.7272	PF, 4.9999	MU, 3.25		M, 7.65	AR	CI	3.94
Kenya	AF	PF, 6.6666/6.6666	NF, 3.2323		MU, 4.35	6.2222	L, 4.89	AR	CU	5.34
Kiribati	EAP	F, 10/10	F, 7.4747					DEM	CO	9.16
Korea, Democratic People's Republic of	EAP	NF, 0/0	NF, 0.4040	UF, 0	R, 0			TOT	CI	0.08
Korea, Republic of	EAP	F, 8.3333/8.3333	F, 7.1717	F, 8.3333	MF, 5.775	6.7777	H, 8.79	DEM	CI	7.64
Kuwait	NE	PF, 4.9999/3.3333	PF, 4.6464		MF, 5.75	6.5555	H, 8.20	TM	CU	5.58
Kyrgyzstan	EUR	NF, 1.6666/3.3333	NF, 2.9292	PF, 4.9999	MU, 4.1		M, 7.27	DEM	CI	4.05
Lao People's Democratic Republic (formerly Laos)	EAP	NF, 0/1.6666	NF, 2.0202		R, 1.375		M, 5.25	TOT	CU	2.06
Latvia	EUR	F, 10/8.3333	F, 8.2828	F, 6.6666	MF, 6.6	6.2222	H, 8.11	DEM	CI	7.74
Lebanon	NE	NF, 1.6666/3.3333	NF, 2.9292	PF, 4.9999	MU, 4.675		M, 7.52	AR	CU	4.19
Lesotho	AF	F, 8.3333/6.6666	PF, 5.8585		MU, 3.75		M, 5.10	RDP	CU	5.94
Liberia	AF	NF, 1.6666/1.6666	NF, 2.1212					DEM	CU	1.82
Libyan Arab Jamahiriya	NE	NF, 0/0	NF, 1.1111		R, 1.125		M, 7.83	AR	CU	2.01
Liechtenstein	EUR	F, 10/10	F, 8.9899					DEM	CI	9.66

219

Table A2 (continued)

A Jurisdiction	B Region	C Normalized FH rating: political/civil	D Normalized FH rating: media	E Normalized FH rating: religion	F Normalized HF rating: economic	G Normalized FI rating: economic	H Normalized UNDP HDI	I Government type[a]	J Type of legal system[b]	K Dₐ
Lithuania	EUR	F, 10/8.3333	F, 8.2828	F, 8.3333	MF, 7.025	5.7777	H, 8.24	DEM	CI	7.99
Luxembourg	EUR	F, 10/10	F, 8.6868		F, 8.225	7.4444	H, 9.30	DEM	CI	8.94
Macedonia, the former Yugoslav Republic of	EUR	PF, 6.6666/6.6666	PF, 5.0505	PF, 4.9999	MU, 4.9		M, 7.84	DEM	CI	6.02
Madagascar	AF	PF, 6.6666/6.6666	PF, 6.2626		MU, 4.65	5.1111	L, 4.68	DEM	CI	5.67
Malawi	AF	PF, 6.6666/4.9999	PF, 4.3434		MU, 3.85	4.2222	L, 3.87	DEM	CU	4.66
Malaysia	EAP	PF, 3.3333/4.9999	NF, 2.9292	PF, 4.9999	MU, 4.6	5.9999	M, 7.90	RDP	CO	4.97
Maldives	SA	NF, 1.6666/3.3333	NF, 3.6363				M, 7.51	AR	CO	4.04
Mali	AF	F, 8.3333/8.3333	F, 7.6767		MU, 4.15	5.3333	L, 3.37	DEM	CU	6.19
Malta	EUR	F, 10/10	F, 8.7878		MF, 6.225	5.9999	H, 8.56	DEM	CO	8.26
Marshall Islands	EAP	F, 10/10	F, 9.0909					DEM	CO	9.69
Mauritania	AF	NF, 1.6666/3.3333	NF, 3.9393	UF, 1.6666	MF, 5.15		L, 4.54	AR	CU	3.38
Mauritius	AF	F, 10/8.3333	F, 7.6767		MF, 5.025	6.9999	M, 7.79	AR	CU	7.64
Mexico	WH	F, 8.3333/8.3333	PF, 6.2626	PF, 4.9999	MF, 5.25	5.7777	H, 8.00	RDP	CI	6.71
Micronesia, Federated States of	EAP	F, 10/10	F, 8.3838					DEM	CO	9.46
Moldova, Republic of	EUR	PF, 6.6666/4.9999	PF, 4.1414	PF, 4.9999	MU, 4.775		M, 7.00	DEM	CI	5.43
Monaco	EUR	F, 8.3333/10	F, 9.1919					DEM	CI	9.18

220

Table A2 (continued)

A Jurisdiction	B Region	C Normalized FH rating: political/civil	D Normalized FH rating: media	E Normalized FH rating: religion	F Normalized HF rating: economic	G Normalized FI rating: economic	H Normalized UNDP HDI	I Government type[a]	J Type of legal system[b]	K D_a
Mongolia	EAP	F, 8.3333/8.3333	PF, 6.4646	F, 6.6666	MF, 5.25		M, 6.61	DEM	CI	6.94
Morocco	NE	PF, 3.3333/3.3333	PF, 4.3434	PF, 4.9999	MF, 5.175	5.3333	M, 6.06	TM	CU	4.65
Mozambique	AF	PF, 6.6666/4.9999	PF, 5.3535		MU, 4.3		L, 3.56	DEM	CI	4.98
Myanmar (formerly Burma)	EAP	NF, 0/0	NF, 0.6060	UF, 0	R, 1.375	3.1111	M, 5.49	AR	CI	1.51
Namibia	AF	F, 8.3333/6.6666	PF, 6.3636	F, 8.3333	MF, 5.1	6.3333	M, 6.27	DEM	CI	6.77
Nauru	EAP	F, 10/10	F, 7.4747					DEM	CO	9.16
Nepal	SA	PF, 3.3333/4.9999	NF, 3.5353	PF, 3.3333	MU, 3.675	5.2222	L, 4.99	DEM	CO	4.16
Netherlands	EUR	F, 10/10	F, 8.5858	F, 10	MF, 7.4	7.5555	H, 9.38	DEM	CI	8.99
New Zealand	EAP	F, 10/10	F, 9.2929		F, 8.25	7.9999	H, 9.17	DEM	CO	9.12
Nicaragua	WH	PF, 6.6666/6.6666	PF, 6.0606		MF, 5.15	5.9999	M, 6.43	DEM	CI	6.16
Niger	AF	PF, 4.9999/4.9999	PF, 4.7474		MU, 3.925	5.1111	L, 2.92	DEM	CU	4.45
Nigeria	AF	PF, 4.9999/4.9999	PF, 4.7474	PF, 3.3333	MU, 2.625	5.1111	L, 4.63	DEM	CU	4.35
Norway	EUR	F, 10/10	F, 9.1919	F, 10	MF, 6.625	6.7777	H, 9.44	DEM	CI	8.86
Oman	NE	NF, 1.6666/3.3333	NF, 2.7272		MF, 5.5	7.1111	M, 7.55	TM	CU	4.65
Pakistan	SA	NF, 1.6666/3.3333	PF, 4.2424	UF, 1.6666	MU, 4.0	4.8888	L, 4.99	AR	CO	3.54
Palau	EAP	F, 10/10	F, 9.1919					DEM	CO	9.73
Panama	WH	F, 10/8.3333	PF, 6.6666		MF, 5.425	6.8888	M, 7.88	DEM	CI	7.53
Papua New Guinea	EAP	PF, 6.6666/6.6666	F, 7.5757			5.3333	M, 5.48	DEM	CO	6.34
Paraguay	WH	PF, 6.6666/6.6666	PF, 4.5454		MU, 4.025	5.8888	M, 7.51	DEM	CI	5.88

Table A2 (continued)

A Jurisdiction	B Region	C Normalized FH rating: political/civil	D Normalized FH rating: media	E Normalized FH rating: religion	F Normalized HF rating: economic	G Normalized FI rating: economic	H Normalized UNDP HDI	I Government type[a]	J Type of legal system[b]	K D_a
Peru	WH	F, 8.3333/6.6666	PF, 6.5656		MF, 5.425	6.3333	M, 7.52	AR	CI	6.81
Philippines	EAP	F, 8.3333/6.6666	F, 7.0707	F, 6.6666	MU, 4.875	6.2222	M, 7.54	DEM	CI	6.77
Poland	EUR	F, 10/8.3333	F, 8.2828	F, 8.3333	MF, 5.475	5.5555	H, 8.41	DEM	CI	7.78
Portugal	EUR	F, 10/10	F, 8.5858		MF, 6.55	6.8888	H, 8.96	DEM	CI	8.50
Qatar	NE	NF, 1.6666/1.6666	NF, 3.9393		MF, 5.35		H, 8.26	TM	CU	4.18
Romania	EUR	F, 8.3333/8.3333	PF, 6.2626	F, 6.6666	MU, 3.35	4.1111	M, 7.73	DEM	CI	6.40
Russian Federation	EUR	PF, 3.3333/3.3333	NF, 3.4343	PF, 4.9999	MU, 3.85	4.4444	M, 7.79	DEM	CI	4.45
Rwanda	AF	NF, 1.6666/3.3333	NF, 2.0202		MU, 4.1	4.6666	L, 4.22	AR	CU	3.33
Saint Kitts and Nevis	WH	F, 10/8.3333	F, 8.2828				H, 8.08	DEM	CO	8.67
Saint Lucia	WH	F, 8.3333/10	F, 9.2929				M, 7.75	DEM	CO	8.84
Saint Vincent and the Grenadines	WH	F, 10/8.3333	F, 8.3838				M, 7.55	DEM	CO	8.57
Samoa (formerly Western Samoa)	EAP	F, 8.3333/8.3333	F, 7.6767				M, 7.75	DEM	CO	8.02
San Marino	EUR	F, 10/10	F, 9.1919					DEM	CI	9.73
Sao Tome and Principe	AF	F, 8.3333/8.3333	F, 8.1818				M, 6.39	DEM	CI	7.81
Saudi Arabia	NE	NF, 0/0	NF, 2.0202	UF, 0	MU, 4.875		M, 7.69	TM	CU	2.43

Table A2 (continued)

A Jurisdiction	B Region	C Normalized FH rating: political/civil	D Normalized FH rating: media	E Normalized FH rating: religion	F Normalized HF rating: economic	G Normalized FI rating: economic	H Normalized UNDP HDI	I Government type[a]	J Type of legal system[b]	K D_a
Senegal	AF	F, 8.3333/6.6666	PF, 6.2626		MU, 5	5.3333	L, 4.30	RDP	CI	5.98
Serbia and Montenegro	EUR	F, 6.6666/8.3333	PF, 6.0606		Not graded in 2003			DEM	CI	7.02
Seychelles	AF	PF, 6.6666/6.6666	PF, 5.0505				H, 8.40	DEM	CU	6.69
Sierra Leone	AF	PF, 4.9999/6.6666	NF, 3.9393		MU, 3.175	4.6666	L, 2.75	DEM	CU	4.37
Singapore	EAP	PF, 3.3333/4.9999	NF, 3.4343	PF, 4.9999	F, 8.475	8.3333	H, 8.84	AR	CO	6.06
Slovakia	EUR	F, 10/8.3333	F, 7.9797		MF, 6.4	5.5555	H, 8.36	DEM	CI	7.77
Slovenia	EUR	F, 10/10	F, 8.1818		MF, 5.625	5.6666	H, 8.81	DEM	CI	8.05
Solomon Islands	EAP	PF, 6.6666/6.6666	F, 7.5757				M, 6.32	DEM	CO	6.81
Somalia	AF	NF, 1.6666/0	NF, 2.0202					AR	CU	1.23
South Africa	AF	F, 10/8.3333	F, 7.5757	F, 8.3333	MF, 5.525	6.4444	M, 6.84	DEM	CU	7.58
Spain	EUR	F, 10/10	F, 8.4848	F, 6.6666	MF, 6.725	6.6666	H, 9.18	DEM	CI	8.25
Sri Lanka	SA	PF, 6.6666/6.6666	PF, 4.8484	PF, 4.9999	MU, 4.85	5.8888	M, 7.30	DEM	CO	5.89
Sudan	AF	NF, 0/0	NF, 1.1616	UF, 0	Not graded in 2003		M, 5.03	AR	CU	1.24
Suriname	WH	F, 10/8.3333	F, 7.4747		MU, 2.6		M, 7.62	DEM	CI	7.21
Swaziland	AF	NF, 0/3.3333	NF, 2.6262		MU, 4.55		M, 5.47	TM	CU	3.19
Sweden	EUR	F, 10/10	F, 9.2929	F, 8.3333	F, 7.75	6.7777	H, 9.41	DEM	CI	8.79
Switzerland	EUR	F, 10/10	F, 9.0909		F, 7.9	7.7777	H, 9.32	DEM	CI	9.01
Syrian Arab Republic	NE	NF, 0/0	NF, 2.0202		MU, 2.8	4.6666	M, 6.85	AR	CU	2.72

Table A2 (continued)

A Jurisdiction	B Region	C Normalized FH rating: political/civil	D Normalized FH rating: media	E Normalized FH rating: religion	F Normalized HF rating: economic	G Normalized FI rating: economic	H Normalized UNDP HDI	I Government type[a]	J Type of legal system[b]	K Dα
Taiwan (multiparty democratic regime not recognized as an independent state)	EAP	F, 8.3333/8.3333	F, 7.6767	F, 8.3333	MF, 6.425	6.7777		DEM	CI	7.65
Tajikistan	EUR	NF, 1.6666/3.3333	NF, 2.4242		R, 2.125		M, 6.77	RDP	CI	3.26
Tanzania, United Republic of	AF	PF, 4.9999/6.6666	PF, 5.3535	PF, 4.9999	MU, 4.275	5.7777	L, 4.00	RDP	CU	5.15
Thailand	EAP	F, 8.3333/6.6666	PF, 6.4646		MF, 5.35	6.3333	M, 7.68	DEM	CI	6.80
Timor-Leste (East Timor)	EAP	PF, 6.6666/6.6666	F, 7.8787	PF, 3.3333				P	CI	6.14
Togo	AF	NF, 1.6666/3.3333	NF, 2.6262		MU, 3.175	4.5555	M, 5.01	DEM	CU	3.39
Tonga	EAP	PF, 3.3333/6.6666	PF, 6.8686					RDP	CO	5.62
Trinidad and Tobago	WH	PF, 6.6666/6.6666	F, 7.5757		MF, 6.375	6.7777	H, 8.02	DEM	CO	7.01
Tunisia	NE	NF, 1.6666/3.3333	NF, 2.2222		MF, 5.15	5.9999	M, 7.40	AR	CU	4.29
Turkey	EUR	PF, 6.6666/4.9999	PF, 4.5454	PF, 3.3333	MU, 4.025	4.7777	M, 7.34	DEM	CI	5.09
Turkmenistan	EUR	NF, 0/0	NF, 0.8080	UF, 0	R, 1.725		M, 7.48	AR	CI	1.67
Tuvalu	EAP	F, 10/10	F, 8.4848					DEM	CO	9.49
Uganda	AF	PF, 3.3333/4.9999	PF, 5.5555		MF, 5.75	6.3333	L, 4.89	AR	CU	5.14
Ukraine	EUR	PF, 4.9999/4.9999	NF, 3.3333	F, 6.6666	MU, 3.775	3.9999	M, 7.66	DEM	CI	5.06

Table A2 (continued)

A Jurisdiction	B Region	C Normalized FH rating: political/civil	D Normalized FH rating: media	E Normalized FH rating: religion	F Normalized HF rating: economic	G Normalized FI rating: economic	H Normalized UNDP HDI	I Government type[a]	J Type of legal system[b]	K D_a
United Arab Emirates	NE	NF, 1.6666/1.6666	NF, 2.6262		MF, 6.0	7.2222	H, 8.16	TM	CU	4.56
United Kingdom of Great Britain and Northern Ireland	EUR	F, 10/10	F, 8.2828	F, 8.3333	F, 8.025	7.9999	H, 9.30	DEM	CO	8.85
United States of America	WH	F, 10/10	F, 8.3838	F, 10	F, 7.875	8.1111	H, 9.37	DEM	CO	9.11
Uruguay	WH	F, 10/10	F, 7.0707		MF, 6.125	6.3333	H, 8.34	DEM	CI	7.98
Uzbekistan	EUR	NF, 0/1.6666	NF, 1.4141	UF, 1.6666	R, 1.775		M, 7.29	AR	CI	2.30
Vanuatu	EAP	F, 8.3333/8.3333	F, 7.9797				M, 5.68	DEM	CO	7.58
Venezuela	WH	PF, 6.6666/4.9999	NF, 3.2323	UF, 1.6666	R, 2.05	4.7777	M, 7.75	DEM	CI	4.91
Vietnam	EAP	NF, 0/1.6666	NF, 1.1818	UF, 1.6666	MU, 2.675		M, 6.88	TOT	CI	2.35
Yemen	NE	PF, 3.3333/3.3333	NF, 3.1313		MU, 3.25		L, 4.70	RDP	CU	3.55
Zambia	AF	PF, 4.9999/4.9999	NF, 3.7373		MU, 3.75	6.4444	L, 3.86	AR	CU	4.63
Zimbabwe	AF	NF, 1.6666/1.6666	NF, 1.2121	F, 6.6666	R, 1.15	3.3333	L, 4.96	RDP	CU	2.95

[a]For more information, see description of government in table A1.
[b]For more information, see description of legal system in table A1.

Table A3. 193 selected jurisdictions sorted by aggregated index value of democracy (D_a), from highest to lowest

A Jurisdiction (date of admission to UN)	B Region	C Government type	D Type of legal system	E D_a
Andorra (28 Jul 1993)	EUR	DEM, parliamentary democracy	CI	9.76
San Marino (2 Mar 1992)	EUR	DEM, independent republic	CI	9.73
Palau (15 Dec 1994)	EAP	DEM, constitutional government in free association with the United States	CO	9.73
Marshall Islands (17 Sep 1991)	EAP	DEM, constitutional government in free association with the United States	CO	9.69
Liechtenstein (18 Sep 1990)	EUR	DEM, hereditary constitutional monarchy on a democratic parliamentary basis	CI	9.66
Tuvalu (5 Sep 2000)	EAP	DEM, constitutional monarchy with parliamentary democracy	CO	9.49
Micronesia, Federated States of (17 Sep 1991)	EAP	DEM, constitutional government in free association with the United States	CO	9.46
Monaco (28 May 1993)	EUR	DEM, constitutional monarchy	CI	9.18
Nauru (14 Sep 1999)	EAP	DEM, republic	CO	9.16
Kiribati (14 Sep 1999)	EAP	DEM, republic	CO	9.16
New Zealand (24 Oct 1945)	EAP	DEM, parliamentary democracy	CO	9.12
Dominica (18 Dec 1978)	WH	DEM, parliamentary democracy; republic within the Commonwealth	CO	9.11
United States of America (24 Oct 1945)	WH	DEM, constitution-based federal republic; strong democratic tradition	CO	9.11
Ireland (14 Dec 1955)	EUR	DEM, republic	CO	9.10
Finland (14 Dec 1955)	EUR	DEM, republic	CI	9.07
Switzerland (10 Sep 2002)	EUR	DEM, federal republic	CI	9.01
Netherlands (10 Dec 1945)	EUR	DEM, constitutional monarchy	CI	8.99

226

Table A3 (continued)

A Jurisdiction (date of admission to UN)	B Region	C Government type	D Type of legal system	E D_a
Luxembourg (24 Oct 1945)	EUR	DEM, constitutional monarchy	CI	8.94
Australia (1 Nov 1945)	EAP	DEM, democratic federal-state system recognizing the British monarch as sovereign	CO	8.94
Denmark (24 Oct 1945)	EUR	DEM, constitutional monarchy	CI	8.94
Iceland (19 Nov 1946)	EUR	DEM, constitutional republic	CI	8.92
Canada (9 Nov 1945)	WH	DEM, confederation with parliamentary democracy	CO	8.87
Norway (27 Nov 1945)	EUR	DEM, constitutional monarchy	CI	8.86
United Kingdom of Great Britain and Northern Ireland (24 Oct 1945)	EUR	DEM, constitutional monarchy	CO	8.85
Saint Lucia (18 Sep 1979)	WH	DEM, Westminster-style parliamentary democracy	CO	8.84
Sweden (19 Nov 1946)	EUR	DEM, constitutional monarchy	CI	8.79
Saint Kitts and Nevis (23 Sep 1983)	WH	DEM, constitutional monarchy with Westminster-style parliament	CO	8.67
Estonia (17 Sep 1991)	EUR	DEM, parliamentary republic	CI	8.62
Grenada (17 Sep 1974)	WH	DEM, constitutional monarchy with Westminster-style parliament	CO	8.60
Austria (14 Dec 1955)	EUR	DEM, federal republic	CI	8.58
Saint Vincent and the Grenadines (16 Sep 1980)	WH	DEM, parliamentary democracy; independent sovereign state within the Commonwealth	CO	8.57
Portugal (14 Dec 1955)	EUR	DEM, parliamentary democracy	CI	8.50
Belgium (27 Dec 1945)	EUR	DEM, federal parliamentary democracy under a constitutional monarch	CI	8.48
Cyprus (20 Sep 1960)	EUR	DEM, republic	CI	8.43
Germany (18 Sep 1973)	EUR	DEM, federal republic	CI	8.41

Table A3 (continued)

A Jurisdiction (date of admission to UN)	B Region	C Government type	D Type of legal system	E D_a
Bahamas (18 Sep 1973)	WH	DEM, constitutional parliamentary democracy	CO	8.37
Italy (14 Dec 1955)	EUR	DEM, republic	CI	8.32
Malta (1 Dec 1964)	EUR	DEM, republic	CO	8.26
Spain (14 Dec 1955)	EUR	DEM, parliamentary monarchy	CI	8.25
Chile (24 Oct 1945)	WH	DEM, republic	CI	8.23
Barbados (9 Dec 1966)	WH	DEM, parliamentary democracy; independent sovereign state within the Commonwealth	CO	8.23
Japan (18 Dec 1956)	EAP	DEM, constitutional monarchy with a parliamentary government	CI	8.19
France (24 Oct 1945)	EUR	DEM, republic	CI	8.08
Slovenia (22 May 1992)	EUR	DEM, parliamentary democratic republic	CI	8.05
Samoa (formerly Western Samoa) (15 Dec 1976)	EAP	DEM, constitutional monarchy under native chief	CO	8.02
Lithuania (17 Sep 1991)	EUR	DEM, parliamentary democracy	CI	7.99
Uruguay (18 Dec 1945)	WH	DEM, constitutional republic	CI	7.98
Costa Rica (2 Nov 1945)	WH	DEM, democratic republic	CI	7.97
Czech Republic (19 Jan 1993)	EUR	DEM, parliamentary democracy	CI	7.97
Cape Verde (16 Sep 1975)	AF	DEM, republic	CI	7.94
Sao Tome and Principe (16 Sep 1975)	AF	DEM, republic	CI	7.81
Poland (24 Oct 1945)	EUR	DEM, republic	CI	7.78
Slovakia (19 Jan 1993)	EUR	DEM, parliamentary democracy	CI	7.77
Latvia (17 Sep 1991)	EUR	DEM, parliamentary democracy	CI	7.74

Table A3 (continued)

A Jurisdiction (date of admission to UN)	B Region	C Government type	D Type of legal system	E D_α
Hungary (14 Dec 1955)	EUR	DEM, parliamentary democracy	CI	7.69
Taiwan (multiparty democratic regime not recognized as an independent state)	EAP	DEM, multiparty democratic regime headed by popularly elected president and unicameral legislature	CI	7.65
Mauritius (24 Apr 1968)	AF	AR, parliamentary democracy	CU	7.64
Korea, Republic of (17 Sep 1991)	EAP	DEM, republic	CI	7.64
Belize (25 Sep 1981)	WH	DEM, parliamentary democracy	CO	7.59
South Africa (7 Nov 1945)	AF	DEM, republic	CU	7.58
Vanuatu (15 Sep 1981)	EAP	DEM, parliamentary republic	CO	7.58
Panama (13 Nov 1945)	WH	DEM, constitutional democracy	CI	7.53
Israel (11 May 1949)	NE	DEM, parliamentary democracy	CU	7.49
Greece (25 Oct 1945)	EUR	DEM, parliamentary republic	CI	7.34
Botswana (17 Oct 1966)	AF	DEM, parliamentary republic	CU	7.30
Hong Kong (SAR of China)	EAP	DEM, limited democracy	CO	7.29
Suriname (4 Dec 1975)	WH	DEM, constitutional democracy	CI	7.21
Jamaica (18 Sep 1962)	WH	DEM, constitutional parliamentary democracy	CO	7.13
Guyana (20 Sep 1966)	WH	DEM, republic within the Commonwealth	CO	7.10
Serbia and Montenegro (1 Nov 2000)	EUR	DEM, republic	CI	7.02
Trinidad and Tobago (18 Sep 1962)	WH	DEM, parliamentary democracy	CO	7.01
El Salvador (24 Oct 1945)	WH	DEM, republic	CI	6.99
Croatia (22 May 1992)	EUR	DEM, presidential parliamentary democracy	CI	6.98
Mongolia (27 Oct 1961)	EAP	DEM, parliamentary	CI	6.94

229

Table A3 (continued)

A Jurisdiction (date of admission to UN)	B Region	C Government type	D Type of legal system	E D_a
Bulgaria (14 Dec 1955)	EUR	DEM, parliamentary democracy	CI	6.85
Argentina (24 Oct 1945)	WH	DEM, republic	CI	6.84
Peru (31 Oct 1945)	WH	AR, constitutional republic	CI	6.81
Solomon Islands (19 Sep 1978)	EAP	DEM, parliamentary democracy tending toward anarchy	CO	6.81
Thailand (16 Dec 1946)	EAP	DEM, constitutional monarchy	CI	6.80
Brazil (24 Oct 1945)	WH	DEM, federative republic	CI	6.78
Namibia (23 Apr 1990)	AF	DEM, republic	CI	6.77
Philippines (24 Oct 1945)	EAP	DEM, republic	CI	6.77
Antigua and Barbuda (11 Nov 1981)	WH	RDP, constitutional monarchy with UK-style parliament	CO	6.72
Mexico (7 Nov 1945)	WH	RDP, federal republic	CI	6.71
Seychelles (21 Sep 1976)	AF	DEM, republic	CU	6.69
Bolivia (14 Nov 1945)	WH	DEM, republic	CI	6.54
Dominican Republic (24 Oct 1945)	WH	DEM, representative democracy	CI	6.51
Ghana (8 Mar 1957)	AF	DEM, constitutional democracy	CU	6.46
Romania (14 Dec 1955)	EUR	DEM, republic	CI	6.40
Papua New Guinea (10 Oct 1975)	EAP	DEM, constitutional monarchy with parliamentary democracy	CO	6.34
Mali (28 Sep 1960)	AF	DEM, republic	CU	6.19
Benin (20 Sep 1960)	AF	DEM, republic under multiparty democratic rule	CU	6.18
Nicaragua (24 Oct 1945)	WH	DEM, republic	CI	6.16
Fiji (13 Oct 1970)	EAP	DEM, republic	CO	6.15
Timor-Leste (East Timor) (27 Sep 2002)	EAP	P, republic	CI	6.14

230

Table A3 (continued)

A Jurisdiction (date of admission to UN)	B Region	C Government type	D Type of legal system	E D_α
Singapore (21 Sep 1965)	EAP	AR, parliamentary republic	CO	6.06
Macedonia, the former Yugoslav Republic of (8 Apr 1993)	EUR	DEM, parliamentary democracy	CI	6.02
Senegal (28 Sep 1960)	AF	RDP, republic under multiparty democratic rule	CI	5.98
Lesotho (17 Oct 1966)	AF	RDP, parliamentary constitutional monarchy	CU	5.94
Albania (14 Dec 1955)	EUR	DEM, emerging democracy	CI	5.93
Sri Lanka (14 Dec 1955)	SA	DEM, republic	CO	5.89
Paraguay (24 Oct 1945)	WH	DEM, constitutional republic	CI	5.88
Ecuador (21 Dec 1945)	WH	DEM, republic	CI	5.76
Honduras (17 Dec 1945)	WH	DEM, democratic constitutional republic	CI	5.72
Madagascar (20 Sep 1960)	AF	DEM, republic	CI	5.67
Tonga (14 Sep 1999)	EAP	RDP, hereditary constitutional monarchy	CO	5.62
India (30 Oct 1945)	SA	DEM, federal republic	CO	5.59
Kuwait (14 May 1963)	NE	TM, nominal constitutional monarchy	CU	5.58
Bosnia and Herzegovina (22 May 1992)	EUR	P, emerging federal democratic republic	CI	5.43
Moldova, Republic of (2 Mar 1992)	EUR	DEM, republic	CI	5.43
Guatemala (21 Nov 1945)	WH	DEM, constitutional democratic republic	CI	5.42
Bahrain (21 Sep 1971)	NE	TM, constitutional hereditary monarchy	CU	5.39
Kenya (16 Dec 1963)	AF	AR, republic	CU	5.34
Armenia (2 Mar 1992)	EUR	DEM, republic	CI	5.29
Georgia (31 Jul 1992)	EUR	DEM, republic	CI	5.24

Table A3 (continued)

A Jurisdiction (date of admission to UN)	B Region	C Government type	D Type of legal system	E D_a
Colombia (5 Nov 1945)	WH	DEM, republic; executive branch dominates government structure	CI	5.16
Tanzania, United Republic of (14 Dec 1961)	AF	RDP, republic	CU	5.15
Uganda (25 Oct 1962)	AF	AR, republic	CU	5.14
Turkey (24 Oct 1945)	EUR	DEM, republican parliamentary democracy	CI	5.09
Ukraine (24 Oct 1945)	EUR	DEM, republic	CI	5.06
Jordan (14 Dec 1955)	NE	RDP, constitutional monarchy	CU	4.98
Mozambique (16 Sep 1975)	AF	DEM, republic	CI	4.98
Malaysia (17 Sep 1957)	EAP	RDP, constitutional monarchy	CO	4.97
Indonesia (28 Sep 1950)	EAP	DEM, republic	CI	4.93
Venezuela (15 Nov 1945)	WH	DEM, federal republic	CI	4.91
Comoros (12 Nov 1975)	AF	RDP, independent republic	CU	4.84
Burkina Faso (20 Sep 1960)	AF	AR, parliamentary republic	CU	4.75
Malawi (1 Dec 1964)	AF	DEM, multiparty democracy	CU	4.66
Oman (7 Oct 1971)	NE	TM, monarchy	CU	4.65
Morocco (12 Nov 1956)	NE	TM, constitutional monarchy	CU	4.65
Zambia (1 Dec 1964)	AF	AR, republic	CU	4.63
Gabon (20 Sep 1960)	AF	AR, republic; multiparty presidential regime	CU	4.62
United Arab Emirates (9 Dec 1971)	NE	TM, federation	CU	4.56
Russian Federation (24 Oct 1945)	EUR	DEM, federation	CI	4.45
Niger (20 Sep 1960)	AF	DEM, republic	CU	4.45

Table A3 (continued)

A Jurisdiction (date of admission to UN)	B Region	C Government type	D Type of legal system	E D_a
Sierra Leone (27 Sep 1961)	AF	DEM, constitutional democracy	CU	4.37
Gambia (21 Sep 1965)	AF	AR, republic under multiparty democratic rule	CU	4.36
Nigeria (7 Oct 1960)	AF	DEM, republic transitioning from military to civilian rule	CU	4.35
Tunisia (12 Nov 1956)	NE	AR, republic	CU	4.29
Lebanon (24 Oct 1945)	NE	AR, republic	CU	4.19
Qatar (21 Sep 1971)	NE	TM, traditional monarchy	CU	4.18
Nepal (14 Dec 1955)	SA	DEM, parliamentary democracy and constitutional monarchy	CO	4.16
Congo, Republic of the (20 Sep 1960)	AF	AR, republic	CU	4.09
Bangladesh (17 Sep 1974)	SA	DEM, parliamentary democracy	CO	4.08
Kyrgyzstan (2 Mar 1992)	EUR	DEM, republic	CI	4.05
Brunei Darussalam (21 Sep 1984)	EAP	TM, constitutional sultanate	CO	4.04
Maldives (21 Sep 1965)	SA	AR, republic	CO	4.04
Kazakhstan (2 Mar 1992)	EUR	AR, republic	CI	3.94
Algeria (8 Oct 1962)	NE	AR, republic	CU	3.94
Cambodia (14 Dec 1955)	EAP	RDP, multiparty democracy under a constitutional monarchy established in September 1993	CI	3.89
Djibouti (20 Sep 1977)	AF	DEM, republic	CU	3.85
Azerbaijan (2 Mar 1992)	EUR	AR, republic	CI	3.75
Côte d'Ivoire (Ivory Coast) (20 Sep 1960)	AF	AR, republic; multiparty presidential regime established 1960	CU	3.69
Egypt (24 Oct 1945)	NE	RDP, republic	CU	3.67
Ethiopia (13 Nov 1945)	AF	AR, federal republic	CU	3.61

Table A3 (continued)

A *Jurisdiction* *(date of admission to UN)*	B *Region*	C *Government type*	D *Type of* *legal system*	E D_a
Yemen (30 Sep 1947)	NE	RDP, republic	CU	3.55
Pakistan (30 Sep 1947)	SA	AR, federal republic	CO	3.54
Guinea-Bissau (17 Sep 1974)	AF	DEM, republic, multiparty since mid 1991	CI	3.49
Chad (20 Sep 1960)	AF	RDP, republic	CU	3.48
Cameroon (20 Sep 1960)	AF	RDP, unitary republic; multiparty presidential regime	CU	3.40
Burundi (18 Sep 1962)	AF	AR, republic	CU	3.40
Togo (20 Sep 1960)	AF	DEM, republic under transition to multiparty democratic rule	CU	3.39
Mauritania (27 Oct 1961)	AF	AR, republic	CU	3.38
Rwanda (18 Sep 1962)	AF	AR, republic; presidential, multiparty system	CU	3.33
Tajikistan (2 Mar 1992)	EUR	RDP, republic	CI	3.26
Guinea (12 Dec 1958)	AF	AR, republic	CU	3.26
Swaziland (24 Sep 1968)	AF	TM, monarchy; independent member of Commonwealth	CU	3.19
Belarus (Byelorussia) (24 Oct 1945)	EUR	AR, republic	CI	3.13
Haiti (24 Oct 1945)	WH	DEM, elected government	CI	3.12
Central African Republic (20 Sep 1960)	AF	DEM, republic	CU	3.11
China, People's Republic of (24 Oct 1945)	EAP	AR, Communist state	CI	2.99
Bhutan (21 Sep 1971)	SA	TM, monarchy; special treaty relationship with India	CO	2.96
Zimbabwe (25 Aug 1980)	AF	RDP, parliamentary democracy	CU	2.95
Angola (1 Dec 1976)	AF	AR, republic; nominally a multiparty democracy with a strong presidential system	CI	2.89
Iran, Islamic Republic of (24 Oct 1945)	NE	AR, theocratic republic	CU	2.86

234

Table A3 (continued)

A Jurisdiction (date of admission to UN)	B Region	C Government type	D Type of legal system	E D_α
Syrian Arab Republic (24 Oct 1945)	NE	AR, republic under military regime since March 1963	CU	2.72
Equatorial Guinea (12 Nov 1968)	AF	AR, republic	CI	2.55
Saudi Arabia (24 Oct 1945)	NE	TM, monarchy	CU	2.43
Congo, Democratic Republic of the (formerly Zaire) (20 Sep 1960)	AF	AR, dictatorship	CU	2.40
Vietnam (20 Sep 1977)	EAP	TOT, Communist state	CI	2.35
Uzbekistan (2 Mar 1992)	EUR	AR, republic; authoritarian presidential rule, with little power outside the executive branch	CI	2.30
Cuba (24 Oct 1945)	WH	TOT, Communist state	CI	2.11
Lao People's Democratic Republic (formerly Laos) (14 Dec 1955)	EAP	TOT, Communist state	CU	2.06
Libyan Arab Jamahiriya (14 Dec 1955)	NE	AR, military dictatorship	CU	2.01
Afghanistan (19 Nov 1946)	SA	TOT, transitional	CU	1.99
Eritrea (28 May 1993)	AF	AR, transitional government	CU	1.96
Liberia (2 Nov 1945)	AF	DEM, republic	CU	1.82
Turkmenistan (2 Mar 1992)	EUR	AR, republic	CI	1.67
Myanmar (formerly Burma) (19 Apr 1948)	EAP	AR, military regime	CI	1.51
Iraq (21 Dec 1945)	NE	AR, transitional	CU	1.28
Sudan (12 Nov 1956)	AF	AR, authoritarian regime	CU	1.24
Somalia (20 Sep 1960)	AF	AR, no permanent national government; transitional, parliamentary national government	CU	1.23
Korea, Democratic People's Republic of (17 Sep 1991)	EAP	TOT, authoritarian socialist; one-man dictatorship	CI	0.08

Appendix B

A Brief History of US Foreign Policy Concerning the Spread of Democracy around the World

This study argues that free nations should actively encourage the spread of democracy to unfree nations. A brief overview of US foreign policy will show how the United States has evolved from an isolationist nation to one that actively supports the spread of democracy as an instrument of international peace and security. Pres. George Washington advocated in his farewell address of 17 September 1796 that the United States "steer clear of permanent alliances with any portion of the foreign world" to avoid being entangled in the wars and controversies of other nations.[1] Similarly, Pres. Thomas Jefferson, who also served as the first US secretary of state, advocated isolationism in his first inaugural address of 4 March 1801 by endorsing "honest friendship with all nations, [and] entangling alliances with none."[2] This early American isolationism was the most effective policy available at the time to protect a young republic from the conflicts that continued to plague the European powers.[3]

As the colonies of the European powers continued to surround the United States in the Western Hemisphere, Pres. James Monroe extended Washington and Jefferson's concept of isolationism on 2 December 1823 in his annual message to Congress.[4] He declared that the United States would consider it a hostile act for any European power to colonize any independent nation in the Western Hemisphere or to extend monarchy to the Americas and that the United States would respect existing European colonies.[5] This form of early-American isolationism—remaining active yet neutral in world affairs—continued into the twentieth century, when contemporary isolationists "urged that our role in world affairs be confined to commerce, which they thought made for peace; to preaching the universal recognition of human liberty; and to setting a good example for less noble people and states."[6] Isolationism was so rooted in the American ethos in the early twentieth century that few Americans perceived any national interest in the outcome of World War I when the war began.[7]

Pres. Woodrow Wilson, however, passionately believed that an active yet neutral, isolationist approach to international politics would have to be radically reformed to rid the world of war. He believed that a concert of power, not a balance of power, was the key to peace. He envisioned a collective-defense and dispute-settlement framework embodied in a well-organized and permanent international organization of states inspired by American idealism. Even more persuaded after the failure of US neutrality and peacemaking to bring an end to World War I, Wilson led the United States into the war in April 1917 for the principal reason of creating such an international organization as a part of the peace process. Wilson believed that an international system of order based on a concert of power managed by a collective of states in accordance with the rules necessary for peaceful cooperation was in the supreme national interest of the United States. He also believed that such a collective of states was the only possible goal worthy of US entry into the war. Wilson announced a League of Nations to Congress on 8 January 1918 as a part of his concept for peace, and it became an integral part of the peace negotiations with the Germans later that year.[8]

The Treaty of Versailles established the League of Nations, which met for the first time in 1920 with 42 nations present. The League of Nations failed, however, primarily because the United States refused to become a member, and it dissolved itself in 1946.[9] Domestically, the US government and the American people were unable to break away from their interpretation of Washington's isolationist warning to avoid permanent foreign alliances. However, this was a significant failure on their part to adapt to the changes in the world balance of power. The US attempt to "escape down the rabbit-hole" of isolationism after World War I precipitated the failure of the League of Nations and was the ultimate cause of World War II.[10]

Pres. Franklin D. Roosevelt was an internationalist in the Wilson tradition, and during the years before World War II, he followed his mentor's footsteps by kindling the foreign policy debate over isolationism versus internationalism. In his famous 1937 "quarantine" speech, Roosevelt announced that undeclared war and lawlessness were "creating a state of international anarchy" that America could not "escape through mere isolation or neutrality."[11] However, Roosevelt was not able to overcome America's strong sense of isolationism even after World War II began in 1939, and the United States did not enter the war until after Japan attacked Pearl Harbor in 1941.[12]

After Roosevelt died in office on 12 April 1945, Pres. Harry Truman succeeded in developing a national consensus that Wilson was right all along, and his isolationist opponents were disastrously wrong. Truman launched a diplomatic initiative before the end of the war to establish the UN, which was supported overwhelmingly by the US Senate and Congress.[13] The UN came into being on 24 October 1945 after its charter was ratified by a majority of the signatories.

The thin veneer of postwar support by the Soviet Union for the UN and the ideals of democratic principles quickly dissolved the alliance of the Allied powers.[14] As the USSR moved to forcibly establish control over much of Eastern Europe and to spread Communism worldwide, a period of intense political tension as well as economic and diplomatic struggle known as the Cold War began.[15] Western fears of Soviet advances in Europe gave rise to the Truman Doctrine of containment announced on 12 March 1947, which offered economic and military aid to countries threatened by external aggression or internal subversion by Communist forces.[16] During a Harvard commencement speech on 5 June 1947, Secretary of State George C. Marshall proposed a plan to help European countries recover from the war, build their economies, and stem the spread of Communism. To fund the Marshall Plan, Congress authorized over $12.5 billion over the next 40 months. Containment became the central concept defining US foreign policy throughout the Cold War.[17] In 1949, Truman also supported the creation of NATO, a regional collective defense alliance intended to enhance peace by preventing the spread of Communism in Europe.[18]

Every US president since Truman has continued to actively contain the spread of Communism and support the spread of democracy worldwide as an instrument of international peace and security. In 1954, Pres. Dwight Eisenhower supported the creation of and US entry into the Southeast Asia Treaty Organization (SEATO), a regional collective defense alliance similar to NATO intended to enhance peace by preventing the spread of Communism in Southeast Asia and the South Pacific area.[19] In 1955, Eisenhower also supported the creation of the Central Treaty Organization (CENTO), a mutual defense alliance signed by Turkey, Iraq, Pakistan, Iran, and Britain; the United States did not join CENTO but participated as an observer.[20] On 5 January 1957, Eisenhower expanded the Truman Doctrine strategies of economic and military aid by asserting the right of the United States to use armed force to help any Middle Eastern nation defend itself against armed aggression by a Communist state.[21] Eisenhower also imposed an economic blockade on Cuba and created a Cuban counterrevolutionary force when Fidel Castro came to power in January 1959, bringing Communism to the Americas.[22]

In 1961, Pres. John F. Kennedy told a joint session of Congress that Communism was seeking to capture the "minds and souls as well as lives and territories" of people in developing countries.[23] He created the Peace Corps to promote world peace by sending American volunteers to perform humanitarian work in developing countries, and he actively promoted democracy through the US Information Agency. Kennedy also announced to Congress that the United States would provide military support against guerrilla warfare "where the local population is too caught up in its own misery to be concerned about the advance of Communism."[24] In April 1961, Kennedy unsuccessfully attempted to rout Communism in the Western Hemisphere when he backed an invasion by about 1,300 Cuban exiles, who were quickly defeated by the Cuban army when they landed in the Bay of Pigs to overthrow Castro.[25] In 1962, Kennedy told the Soviets there could be no peace between the two superpowers until the USSR carried out its promise at the end of World War II to allow free elections in Eastern Europe.[26] On 22 October 1962, Kennedy ordered a naval and air quarantine on the shipment of military equipment to Cuba to successfully counter a Soviet buildup of offensive missiles on the island.[27]

Pres. Lyndon Johnson embraced a doctrine that declared the principles of Communism as incompatible with the principles of the inter-American system and approved of using American troops to prevent the establishment of a Communist government anywhere in the Western Hemisphere.[28] He continued the US postwar policy of containment and was moderately successful in his efforts to improve relations between the United States and the USSR. In 1964, Johnson significantly expanded the presence of the US military in Southeast Asia to fight the Communist-supported civil war in Vietnam. In 1965, he ordered the Marines to the Dominican Republic to reinstall its freely elected president after his ouster in 1963 by a Communist-inspired coup.[29]

Pres. Richard Nixon announced in July 1969 that after Vietnam US combat troops would not bear the main burden of defending other nations, but the United States would use nuclear deterrence to provide military security for Japan and other friendly Asian nations. This policy became known as the Nixon Doctrine.[30] However, Nixon later expanded the war in Vietnam by authorizing the 1970 invasion of Cambodia to pursue North Vietnamese troops and assisting a South Vietnamese invasion of Laos in 1971. In 1972, Nixon authorized deep-penetration bombing raids over North Vietnam, the mining of major North Vietnamese ports, and air strikes against North Vietnamese railroad lines. When secret peace negotiations broke down in December 1972, Nixon ordered massive bombing against Hanoi and Haiphong until the North Vietnamese returned to the negotiating table in early 1973.[31] Nixon and the premier of the People's Republic of China declared in their 1972 Shanghai communiqué that the United States and China were agreed in opposing "any hegemonic power in Asia."[32] When the USSR probed the United States in the early 1970s to determine what its position would be should the USSR attack Chinese nuclear plants, Nixon secretly warned the USSR not to do so. During the 1973 Yom Kippur War, when Communist-supported Egypt attacked Israel, Nixon supported Israel and put the American strategic nuclear forces on alert after the USSR moved nuclear weapons to Egypt.[33]

Pres. Gerald Ford's policies toward the USSR, especially those policies such as the Helsinki Accords, which recognized existing borders between states including those that separated West and East Germany, were strongly opposed by many in the United States. He also ordered the evacuation of American security and embassy personnel as the North Vietnamese began the last offensive of the Vietnam War and captured Saigon.[34] Ford did, however, order a major show of military force in May 1975 when he ordered the Marines to rescue the crew of the US merchant ship SS *Mayaguez*, who had been taken hostage by the Communist Khmer Rouge regime of Cambodia. He also ordered air strikes of the Cambodian mainland and naval assets to recover the SS Mayaguez. Although the crew had been moved and the rescue attempt was unsuccessful, Cambodia returned the crew.[35] In his last year of office, Ford declared that the United States would never permit any Soviet domination of Eastern Europe.[36]

When the USSR invaded Afghanistan in 1979, Pres. Jimmy Carter ordered a partial embargo of US grain sales to the USSR and suspended the ratification of the second Strategic Arms Limitation Treaty (SALT II) in protest. In his State of the Union address on 23 January 1980, Carter also declared that the Persian Gulf's oil reserves are a vital US national interest and claimed that the United States would be justified in preventing outside domination of the region by military intervention.[37]

Pres. Ronald Reagan expressed fervent anticommunism, such as when he denounced the USSR in his 1993 "Evil Empire" speech as "the focus of evil in the modern world."[38] His firm and resolute containment doctrine and foreign policy have been credited with contributing to the demise of Communism in the USSR.[39] Reagan committed the United States to provide meaningful political and material support to democratic liberation movements around the world that fought against the Communist oppression that destroys freedom and the human spirit. Under Reagan, the United States intervened in Nicaragua and Grenada to contain Communism and provided support to the Afghan resistance. Nevertheless, Reagan was also noted for improving relations with the USSR despite his hard-line doctrine against Communism. The containment policy started by Truman ended circa 1989–90 as most of Eastern Europe's Communist regimes collapsed.[40]

Pres. George H. W. Bush led the United States and the international community through an extraordinary transition period as Communism collapsed in Eastern Europe and the USSR, marking the end of the Cold War. He believed that since "the Cold War began with the division of Europe," it "can only end when Europe is whole."[41] He was the first Western leader to declare his determination for "a Europe whole and free."[42] Bush signed a mutual nonaggression pact (the *Joint Declaration of Twenty-Two States*) with the USSR that served as a symbolic conclusion to the Cold War, and he forged an economic and political partnership with the USSR as it reformed toward democracy and capitalism. He also provided foreign aid to former Soviet-bloc nations of Eastern Europe to support their economic and political transformation. President Bush was an internationalist who took the world beyond containment. He believed that the international community must be actively engaged in maintaining international peace and security and was willing to commit US military forces to fight aggression and conduct humanitarian missions.[43] For example, he led an alliance of nations against Iraq when it invaded Kuwait and an international coalition in Somalia to use military force for food-delivery missions.

Pres. Bill Clinton built upon the internationalist legacies of Wilson and Roosevelt and the engagement policies of Reagan and Bush in developing his policy of democratic enlargement. Clinton's strategy of engagement and leadership abroad had three core objectives: "enhancing American security, bolstering [US] economic prosperity, and promoting democracy and human rights abroad."[44] Clinton stated that US security "depends upon the protection and expansion of democracy worldwide, without which repression, corruption and instability could engulf a number of countries and threaten the stability of entire regions."[45] In 1994, he demonstrated his resolve to use military force in support of democracy when he deployed a large military force to Haiti to reinstate that country's first elected president. At the last minute, Haitian military leaders stepped down and a conflict was avoided. Clinton then orchestrated an international military presence to maintain peace. In November 1995, Clinton hosted successful peace talks between the warring parties in Bosnia and Herzegovina and then arranged for an international military presence there as well to preserve the peace.[46]

In his inaugural address on 20 January 2001, Pres. George W. Bush declared that "America's faith in freedom and democracy was a rock in a raging sea" during the twentieth century and affirmed that the United States will continue to "lead the cause of freedom."[47] He also announced that the United States will remain "engaged in the world . . . shaping a balance of power that favors freedom" and democracy and will "defend our allies and our interests" and "meet aggression and bad faith with resolve and strength."[48] In response to the catastrophic terrorism of 11 September 2001, Bush has demonstrated his resolve to actively work with the international community to maintain peace and security and to commit US military forces when necessary to defend vital American interests. Bush declared in his administration's first *National Security Strategy* that freedom, democracy, and free enterprise constitute "a single sustainable model for national success."[49] Bush also articulated a strong national strategy of internationalism and engagement by declaring the United States "will actively work to bring the hope of democracy, development, free markets, and free trade to every corner of the world" and by recognizing that "alliances and multilateral institutions can multiply the strength of freedom-loving nations."[50] Key elements of Bush's *National Security Strategy* include strengthening alliances; expanding free markets, free trade, and democratic infrastructures; and working with others to defuse regional conflicts. However, to meet the security threat posed by rogue states and terrorists that is "more complex and dangerous" than the threat of the USSR during the Cold War, Bush also unmistakably declared a guiding principle of preemption where necessary to meet that threat: "The United States has long maintained the option of preemptive actions to counter a sufficient threat to our national security . . . even if uncertainty remains as to the time and place of the enemy's attack. To forestall or prevent such hostile acts by our adversaries, the United States will, if necessary, act preemptively."[51]

This brief discussion of the evolution of US national policy from isolationism to internationalism, containment, and engagement highlights those key policies and events that demonstrate how the global support for democracy has permeated US foreign policy since 1945. Table B1 summarizes the key doctrines and their proponents.

Table B1. American foreign policies from isolationism to engagement

President (term of office)	Foreign policy doctrine
Isolationist doctrines	
George Washington (1789–97)	Isolationism: The United States will avoid permanent foreign alliances in order to escape involvement in other nations' wars.
Thomas Jefferson (1801–09)	Isolationism: The United States will seek honest friendship with all nations, and entangling alliances with none.
James Monroe (1817–25)	Monroe Doctrine: The United States will consider it a hostile act for any European power to colonize any independent nation in the Western Hemisphere or to extend monarchy to the Americas; the United States will respect existing European colonies.
Internationalist doctrines	
Woodrow Wilson (1913–21)	Internationalism: The United States considers an international system of order based on a concert of power managed by a collective of states in accordance with the rules necessary for peaceful cooperation to be in its supreme national interest.
Franklin D. Roosevelt (1933–45)	Internationalism: The United States cannot escape war through mere isolation or neutrality.
Containment doctrines	
Harry Truman (1945–53)	Truman Doctrine: The United States will contain Communism by providing economic and military aid to countries threatened by external aggression or internal subversion by Communist forces.
Dwight Eisenhower (1953–61)	Eisenhower Doctrine: The United States has the right to use armed force to assist any nation in the general region of the Middle East requesting assistance against armed aggression by a Communist state.
John F. Kennedy (1961–63)	Containment and Humanitarianism: The United States will use military force to prevent the spread of Communism in the Western Hemisphere, provide military support to developing countries against Communist-sponsored guerrilla warfare, and promote world peace through humanitarian service and the spread of democracy.
Lyndon Johnson (1963–69)	Johnson Doctrine: The United States will use military force to prevent the spread of Communism in the Western Hemisphere.
Richard Nixon (1969–74)	Nixon Doctrine: The United States will not permit American combat troops to bear the main burden of defending other nations, but it will continue to provide military security for Japan and other friendly Asian nations through its nuclear deterrent.
Gerald Ford (1974–77)	Containment: The United States will not permit any Soviet domination of Eastern Europe.

Table B1 (*continued*)

President (term of office)	Foreign policy doctrine
Jimmy Carter (1977–81)	Carter Doctrine: The United States considers the Persian Gulf's oil reserves a vital national interest and will use military intervention to prevent outside domination of the Persian Gulf region.
Ronald Reagan (1981–89)	Reagan Doctrine: The United States will provide meaningful political and material support to democratic liberation movements around the world that fight Communist oppression.
Engagement doctrines	
George H. W. Bush (1989–93)	Engagement: The United States will remain actively engaged in maintaining international peace and security and will commit military forces to fight aggression and accomplish humanitarian missions.
Bill Clinton (1993–2001)	Democratic Enlargement: The United States will use military force for the protection and expansion of democracy worldwide as an important element of US security.
George W. Bush (2001–present)	Active Engagement, Global Leadership, and Preemption: The United States will be engaged in the world to shape a balance of power that favors freedom and democracy, defend US allies and interests, and meet aggression and bad faith with resolve and strength. The United States will, if necessary, use military force in self-defense to act preemptively to forestall or prevent hostile acts by terrorists and other adversaries, even if uncertainty remains as to the time and place of the enemy's attack.

Note: *This table presents a synopsis of each administration's foreign policy as expressed in speeches and other public statements or texts. Quotation marks are omitted. The sources of these statements are identified throughout the discussion in this appendix.*

Notes

1. President Washington, farewell address.
2. President Jefferson, inaugural address.
3. Rostow, *Toward Managed Peace*, 120.
4. President Monroe, annual message to Congress.
5. Rostow, *Toward Managed Peace*, 17, 118–20.
6. Ibid., 53–54.
7. Ibid., 169.
8. Ibid., 195–218.
9. Ibid., 367.
10. Ibid., 45, 234, 273–78.
11. President Roosevelt, speech.

12. Rostow, *Toward Managed Peace*, 271–74.
13. Ibid., 278.
14. Ibid., 298.
15. *Encarta 98 Desk Encyclopedia*, s.v. "Cold War."
16. President Truman, message to Congress.
17. *American Reference Library*, s.v. "containment policy."
18. *Encarta 98 Desk Encyclopedia*, s.v. "North Atlantic Treaty Organization."
19. Ibid., s.v. "Southeast Asia Treaty Organization."
20. *American Reference Library*, s.v. "Central Treaty Organization."
21. President Eisenhower, special message to Congress.
22. *Encarta 98 Desk Encyclopedia*, s.v. "Dwight David Eisenhower."
23. President Kennedy, special message to Congress.
24. Ibid.
25. *Encarta 98 Desk Encyclopedia*, s.v. "Bay of Pigs invasion."
26. Rostow, *Toward Managed Peace*, 13.
27. *Encarta 98 Desk Encyclopedia*, s.v. "Cuban missile crisis."
28. *American Reference Library*, s.v. "Johnson Doctrine."
29. *Encarta 98 Desk Encyclopedia*, s.v. "Lyndon Baines Johnson."
30. President Nixon, informal remarks with reporters.
31. *Encarta 98 Desk Encyclopedia*, s.v. "Richard Milhouse Nixon."
32. Rostow, *Toward Managed Peace*, 13.
33. Ibid., 319.
34. *Encarta 98 Desk Encyclopedia*, s.v. "Gerald Rudolph Ford."
35. *American Reference Library*, s.v. "SS Mayaguez incident."
36. Second Carter-Ford presidential debate.
37. President Carter, State of the Union address.
38. President Reagan, speech, National Association of Evangelicals.
39. *Encyclopædia Britannica*, s.v. "Ronald Wilson Reagan."
40. *American Reference Library*, s.v. "Reagan Doctrine" and "Ronald Reagan."
41. Pres. George H. W. Bush, speech.
42. Ibid.
43. *Encarta 98 Desk Encyclopedia*, s.v. "George Herbert Walker Bush."
44. President Clinton, *A National Security Strategy*, 3.
45. Ibid., 25.
46. *Encarta 98 Desk Encyclopedia*, s.v. "William Clinton."
47. Pres. George W. Bush, first inaugural address.
48. Ibid.
49. Pres. George W. Bush, *National Security Strategy*, iv.
50. Ibid., v–vi.
51. Ibid., 13–15.

Acronyms and Abbreviations

AF	Africa
AM	absolute monarchy
AR	authoritarian regime
C	colonial and imperial dependency
CENTO	Central Treaty Organization
CI	civil law
CIA	Central Intelligence Agency
CIDCM	Center for International Development and Conflict Management
CM	constitutional monarchy
CO	common law
CPI	Corruption Perceptions Index
CSIA	Center for Science and International Affairs
CU	customary law
D_a	aggregated index value of democracy
DEM	democracy
DOD	Department of Defense
EAP	East Asia and the Pacific
EU	European Union
EUR	Europe and Eurasia
F	free
FAO	Food and Agriculture Organization
FH	Freedom House
FI	Fraser Institute
G-7	Group of Seven
G-8	Group of Eight
GDP	gross domestic product
HDI	Human Development Index
HF	Heritage Foundation
ILO	International Labour Organization
JP	Joint Publication
M	monarchy
MF	mostly free
MU	mostly unfree
NATO	North Atlantic Treaty Organization
NE	Near East
NF	not free

P	protectorate
PF	partly free
R	repressed
RDP	restricted democratic practices
SA	South Asia
SALT	Strategic Arms Limitation Treaty
SAR	special administrative region
SEATO	Southeast Asia Treaty Organization
SIPRI	Stockholm International Peace Research Institute
TM	traditional monarchy
TOT	totalitarian regime
UF	unfree
UK	United Kingdom
UN	United Nations
UNDP	United Nations Development Programme
UNESCO	United Nations Educational, Scientific, and Cultural Organization
US	United States
USIP	United States Institute of Peace
USSR	Union of Soviet Socialist Republics
WH	Western Hemisphere

Bibliography

Achen, Charles H., and Duncan Snidal. "Rational Deterrence Theory and Comparative Case Studies." *World Politics* 41, no. 2 (January 1989): 143–69.

Ahlmark, Per. Speech to the European Liberal Democrats. European Parliament, Krakow, Poland, 8 April 1999. http://www.unwatch.org/site/c.bdKKISNqEmG/b.1289203/apps/s/content.asp?ct=1748057.

Allott, Philip. "Law and the Re-Making of Humanity." In *Democracy and the Rule of Law*, edited by Norman Dorsen and Prosser Gifford, 19–30. Washington, DC: CQ Press, 2001.

Beck, Nathaniel, Jonathan N. Katz, and Richard Tucker. "Taking Time Seriously: Time-Series–Cross-Section Analysis with a Binary Dependent Variable." *American Journal of Political Science* 42, no. 4 (October 1998): 1260–88.

Bloomfield, Lincoln P., and Allen Moulton. *Managing International Conflict: From Theory to Policy.* New York: St. Martin's Press, 1997.

British Broadcasting Corporation News. "What the EU Constitution Says." 22 June 2004. http://news.bbc.co.uk/1/hi/world/europe/2950276.stm.

Brownlie, Ian. *International Law and the Use of Force by States.* Oxford: Clarendon Press, 1963.

Bush, George H. W. Speech. Mainz, Federal Republic of Germany, 31 May 1989. http://bushlibrary.tamu.edu/research/papers/1989/89053104.html.

Bush, George W. First inaugural address. Washington, DC, 20 January 2001. http://www.gpoaccess.gov/sou/index.html.

———. Second inaugural address. Washington, DC, 20 January 2005. http://www.whitehouse.gov/news/releases/2005/01/20050120-1.html.

———. *The National Security Strategy of the United States of America.* Washington, DC: White House, 2002. http://www.whitehouse.gov/nsc/nss.pdf.

Care, Jennifer Corrin. "Conflict between Customary Law and Human Rights in the South Pacific." Paper presented to the 12th Commonwealth Law Conference, Kuala Lumpur, September 1999.

Carter, Jimmy. State of the Union address to 96th Cong., Joint Session, 23 January 1980. http://www.jimmycarterlibrary .org/documents/speeches/su80jec.phtml.

Central Intelligence Agency (CIA). *The World Factbook 2003.* Washington, DC: CIA, 2003. https://www.cia.gov/library/ publications/download/.

Churchill, Winston S. *The Hinge of Fate.* Cambridge, MA: Houghton Mifflin Co., 1950.

Claude, Inis L., Jr. "Theoretical Approaches to National Security and World Order." In *National Security Law,* edited by John Norton Moore, Frederick S. Tipson, and Robert F. Turner, 31–45. Durham, NC: Carolina Academic Press, 1990.

Clausewitz, Carl von. *On War.* Edited by Anatol Rapoport. Baltimore: Penguin Books, 1968.

Clinton, Bill. *A National Security Strategy for a New Century.* Washington, DC: White House, 1999.

Dahl, Robert. *On Democracy.* New Haven, CT: Yale University Press, 1998.

Deutsche Welle. "Prodi Unveils Vision of EU Constitution." 16 April 2003. http://www.dw-world.de/dw/article/0,,707459,00 .html.

Diamond, Larry. *Promoting Democracy in the 1990s: Actors and Instruments, Issues and Imperatives.* A Report to the Carnegie Commission on Preventing Deadly Conflict. Washington, DC: The Carnegie Commission on Preventing Deadly Conflict, 1995.

Downs, George W. "The Rational Deterrence Debate." *World Politics* 41, no. 2 (January 1989): 225–337.

Doyle, Michael W. "Kant, Liberal Legacies, and Foreign Affairs." *Philosophy and Public Affairs* 12, no. 3 (Summer 1983): 205–35.

Eisenhower, Dwight. "The Chance for Peace." Speech. American Society of Newspaper Editors, 16 April 1953. http:// www.eisenhower.archives.gov/speeches/Chance_For _Peace.html.

———. Special message to Congress on the Middle East. 85th Cong., 1st sess., 5 January 1957. H. Doc. 46, in *Congressional Record,* vol. 103, p. 181. http://www.eisenhower .archives.gov/speeches/Middle_East_Situation.html.

Elman, Miriam Fendius. "Preface" and "Introduction." In *Paths to Peace: Is Democracy the Answer?* Center for Science and International Affairs (CSIA) Studies in International Security. Cambridge, MA: MIT Press, 1997.

———. "Testing the Democratic Peace Theory." In *Paths to Peace: Is Democracy the Answer?* CSIA Studies in International Security. Cambridge, MA: MIT Press, 1997.

Europa. "A Constitution for Europe." Europa: Portal Site for the European Union. http://europa.eu/scadplus/constitution/introduction_en.htm.

"Ex-Dictators Are Not Immune." *The Economist*, 28 November 1998, 16.

Executive Order 12872. Blocking Property of Persons Obstructing Democratization in Haiti, 18 October 1993. 3 CFR Parts 100–102 at 658–59.

The Fraser Institute. "The Economic Freedom of the World Project." http://www.freetheworld.com/index.html.

———. Web site. http://www.fraserinstitute.ca/.

Frederick II, King of Prussia. *Frederick the Great on the Art of War*. Edited and translated by Jay Luvaas. New York: Free Press, 1966.

Freedom House. *Countries at the Crossroads 2007*. http://www.freedomhouse.org/template.cfm?page=139&edition=8.

———. *Democracy's Century: A Survey of Political Change in the Twentieth Century*. 7 December 1999. http://www.freedomhouse.org (report now inaccessible on Web site).

———. "End of Century Survey Finds Dramatic Gains for Democracy." Press release. 7 December 1999. http://www.freedomhouse.org/template.cfm?page=70&release=74.

———. "Freedom House: A History." http://www.freedomhouse.org/template.cfm?page=249.

———. "Freedom in the World (About the Survey)." Web site. http://www.freedomhouse.org/template.cfm?page=15.

———. *Freedom in the World 2003*. http://www.freedomhouse.org/template.cfm?page=363&year=2003.

———. *Freedom in the World 2004*. http://www.freedomhouse.org/template.cfm?page=363&year=2004.

———. "Freedom of the Press." Web site. http://www.freedomhouse.org/template.cfm?page=16.

———. *Freedom of the Press 2003.* http://www.freedomhouse
.org/template.cfm?page=251&year=2003.

———. "Global Freedom Gains Amid Terror, Uncertainty." Press
release. 18 December 2003. http://www.freedomhouse
.org/template.cfm?page=70&release=62.

———. "Global Press Freedom Deteriorates." Press release.
28 April 2004. http://www.freedomhouse.org/template
.cfm?page=70&release=43.

———. *Nations in Transit Country Report: Russia.* 2004 ed. Buda-
pest: Freedom House Europe, 2004. http://www.freedom
house.org/template.cfm?page=47&nit=342&year=2004.

———. *The World's Most Repressive Regimes.* Washington, DC:
Freedom House, 2003.

Freud, Sigmund. To Albert Einstein. Letter, Vienna, September
1932. In *Einstein on Peace*, edited by Otto Nathan and
Heinz Nordon. New York: Schocken Books, 1960.

Gelb, Leslie H. "A Bush Green Light to Iraq?" *New York Times*,
22 October 1992.

George, Alexander L., and Richard Smoke. "Deterrence and Foreign Policy." *World Politics* 41, no. 2 (January 1989): 170–82.

Gwartney, James, and Robert Lawson. *Economic Freedom of the
World: 2003 Annual Report.* Vancouver, BC: The Fraser Institute, 2003. http://www.fraserinstitute.org/Commerce
.Web/product_files/Complete%20Publication-4EFW
2003all.pdf.

Hamilton, Alexander, James Madison, and John Jay. *The Federalist Papers.* Edited by Clinton Rossiter. New York: New
American Library, 1961.

Hanzhang, Tao. *Sun Tzu's "Art of War": The Modern Chinese
Interpretation.* Translated by Yuan Shibing. New York:
Sterling Publishers, 1987.

The Heritage Foundation. "About Us." http://www.heritage
.org/about/.

The Heritage Foundation and the *Wall Street Journal. 2007 Index of Economic Freedom.* Web site. http://www.heritage
.org/research/features/index/index.cfm.

Hewitt, J. Joseph, Jonathan Wilkenfeld, and Ted Robert Gurr.
Peace and Conflict 2008: Executive Summary. College Park,
MD: Center for International Development and Conflict
Management, University of Maryland, 2008.

Higgins, Rosalyn. "Institutional Modes of Conflict Management." In *National Security Law*, edited by John Norton Moore, Frederick S. Tipson, and Robert F. Turner, 193–305. Durham, NC: Carolina Academic Press, 1990.

Huth, Paul, and Bruce Russett. "What Makes Deterrence Work: Cases from 1900 to 1980." *World Politics* 36, no. 4 (July 1984): 496–526.

Immelman, Aubrey. "The Clinton Chronicle: Diary of a Political Psychologist." Unit for the Study of Personality in Politics Web site, 16 November 1998. http://www.csbsju.edu/uspp/Clinton-WJ/Clinton_Chronicle.html.

International Criminal Tribunal for the Former Yugoslavia. *Rules of Procedure and Evidence.* Adopted 11 February 1994 by the International Tribunal for the Prosecution of Persons Responsible for Serious Violations of International Humanitarian Law Committed in the Territory of the Former Yugoslavia since 1991. UN Doc. IT/32, March 1994. Reprinted in 33 ILM 493–545, 1994.

Iraq. Interim Constitution. Adopted 1990. Translated by Axel Tschentscher, International Constitutional Law Project. http://www.servat.unibe.ch/law/icl/iz01000_.html.

Jefferson, Thomas. First inaugural address. Washington, DC, 4 March 1801. In *American Reference Library: The Ultimate Reference to American History and Political Science.* World Book Encyclopedia and the Western Standard Publishing Company, 1998. CD-ROM.

Jervis, Robert. "Rational Deterrence: Theory and Evidence." *World Politics* 41, no. 2 (January 1989): 183–207.

Joint Chiefs of Staff. *National Military Strategy of the United States of America: Shape, Respond, Prepare Now—A Military Strategy for a New Era.* Washington, DC: Joint Chiefs of Staff, 1997.

Joint Declaration of Twenty-Two States. International agreement. Paris, France, 19 November 1990. http://bushlibrary.tamu.edu/research/papers/1990/90111903.html.

Joint Publication (JP) 1-02. *Department of Defense Dictionary of Military and Associated Terms*, 12 April 2001, as amended through 12 July 2007.

Kagan, Donald. *On the Origins of War and the Preservation of Peace.* New York: Doubleday, 1995.

Kacowicz, Arie M. "Peru vs. Colombia and Senegal vs. Maurita-
    nia: Mixed Dyads and 'Negative Peace.'" In *Paths to Peace:
    Is Democracy the Answer?* edited by Miriam Fendius El-
    man. CSIA Studies in International Security. Cambridge,
    MA: MIT Press, 1997.

Kant, Immanuel. *Perpetual Peace.* Edited and translated by
    Lewis White Beck. New York: Liberal Arts Press, 1957.

Karatnycky, Adrian. "Liberty's Expansion in a Turbulent World:
    Thirty Years of the Survey of Freedom." In *Freedom in the
    World 2003.* http://www.freedomhouse.org/template.cfm
    ?page=130&year=2003.

Kaufmann, William W. *The Requirements of Deterrence.* Memo-
    randum No. 7. Princeton, NJ: Center for International
    Studies, 1954.

Kaysen, Carl, Steven E. Miller, Martin B. Malin, William D.
    Nordhaus, and John D. Steinbruner. *War with Iraq: Costs,
    Consequences, and Alternatives.* Cambridge, MA: Ameri-
    can Academy of Arts and Sciences, 2002.

Keegan, John. *A History of Warfare.* New York: Vintage, 1994.

Kennedy, John F. Special message to Congress. 87th Cong., Joint
    Session, 25 May 1961. http://www.jfklibrary.org/Historical
    +Resources/Archives/Reference+Desk/Speeches/JFK/
    003POF03NationalNeeds05251961.htm.

Khalilzad, Zalmay, and David Shlapak, with Ann Flanagan.
    "Overview of the Future Security Environment." In *Sources
    of Conflict in the Twenty-First Century: Regional Futures
    and U.S. Strategy,* edited by Zalmay Khalilzad and Ian O.
    Lesser, 7–42. Santa Monica, CA: RAND, 1998.

Kotzsch, Lothar. *The Concept of War in Contemporary History
    and International Law.* Geneva, Switzerland: E. Droz, 1956.

Layne, Christopher. "Kant or Cant: The Myth of the Democratic
    Peace." *International Security* 19, no. 2 (Autumn 1994): 5–49.

———. "Lord Palmerston and the Triumph of Realism: Anglo-
    French Relations 1830–48." In *Paths to Peace: Is Democracy
    the Answer?* edited by Miriam Fendius Elman. CSIA Studies
    in International Security. Cambridge, MA: MIT Press, 1997.

Lebow, Richard Ned, and Janice Gross Stein. "Rational Deter-
    rence Theory: I Think, Therefore I Deter." *World Politics* 41,
    no. 2 (January 1989): 208–24.

Lesser, Ian O. "Introduction." In *Sources of Conflict in the Twenty-First Century: Regional Futures and U.S. Strategy,* edited by Zalmay Khalilzad and Ian O. Lesser, 1–5. Santa Monica, CA: RAND, 1998.

Levy, Jack S. "The Causes of War: A Review of Theories and Evidence." In *Behavior, Society, and Nuclear War,* edited by Philip E. Tetlock, Jo L. Husbands, Robert Jervis, Paul C. Stern, and Charles Tilly, 209–333. Vol. 1. New York: Oxford University Press, 1989.

Lipson, Charles. *Reliable Partners: How Democracies Have Made a Separate Peace.* Princeton, NJ: Princeton University Press, 2003.

Locke, John. *Two Treatises of Government.* 1698. A facsimile of the third edition. The Classics of Liberty Library. New York: Gryphon Editions, 1992.

Luttwak, Edward N. "Toward Post-Heroic Warfare." *Foreign Affairs* 74, no. 3 (May–June 1995): 109–22.

Mansfield, Edward D., and Jack Snyder. "Democratization and War." *Foreign Affairs* 74, no. 3 (May–June 1995): 79–97.

Maoz, Zeev, and Nasrin Abdolali. "Regime Types and International Conflict, 1816–1976." *Journal of Conflict Resolution* 33, no. 1 (March 1989): 3–35.

Marshall, Monty G., and Ted Robert Gurr. *Peace and Conflict 2003: A Global Survey of Armed Conflicts, Self-Determination Movements, and Democracy.* College Park, MD: Center for International Development and Conflict Management, University of Maryland, 2003.

Marshall, Paul. *Religious Freedom in the World: A Global Report on Freedom and Persecution.* Nashville, TN: B&H Publishing Group, 2000.

McDougal, Myres S., and Florentino P. Feliciano. *Law and Minimum World Public Order: The Legal Regulation of International Coercion.* New Haven: Yale University Press, 1961.

Miles, Marc A., Edwin J. Feulner, and Mary Anastasia O'Grady. *2004 Index of Economic Freedom: Establishing the Link between Economic Freedom and Prosperity.* Washington, DC: The Heritage Foundation and Dow Jones & Company, Inc., 2004.

Monroe, James. Annual message to Congress. Washington, DC, 2 December 1823. In *Presidential Messages of the 18th Congress, ca. 12/09/1823–ca. 03/03/1825.* Rec. Group 46,

Records of the United States Senate, 1789–1990, National Archives.

Montross, Lynn. *War through the Ages.* 3rd ed. New York: Harper, 1960.

Moore, John Norton. *Crisis in the Gulf: Enforcing the Rule of Law.* New York: Oceana, 1992.

———. "Development of the International Law of Conflict Management." In *National Security Law,* edited by John Norton Moore, Frederick S. Tipson, and Robert F. Turner, 47–83. Durham, NC: Carolina Academic Press, 1990.

———. Seminar. University of Virginia School of Law, Charlottesville, VA, 22 January 1997.

———. Seminar. University of Virginia School of Law, Charlottesville, VA, 26 February 1997.

———. *Solving the War Puzzle: Beyond the Democratic Peace.* Durham, NC: Carolina Academic Press, 2004.

———. "Toward a New Paradigm: Enhanced Effectiveness in United Nations Peacekeeping, Collective Security, and War Avoidance." *Virginia Journal of International Law* 37 (Summer 1997): 811–90.

———. "The Use of Force in International Relations: Norms Concerning the Initiation of Coercion." In *National Security Law,* edited by John Norton Moore, Frederick S. Tipson, and Robert F. Turner, 85–192. Durham, NC: Carolina Academic Press, 1990.

National Priorities Project. "Cost of War." http://www.national priorities.org/Cost-of-War/Cost-of-War-3.html.

Nixon, Richard. Informal remarks with reporters. Guam, 25 July 1969. Nixon Presidential Library Archives, Public Papers 279. http://www.nixonlibrary.org/clientuploads/directory/archive/1969_pdf_files/1969_0279.pdf.

Norberg, Johan. *In Defence of Global Capitalism.* Stockholm: Timbro, 2001.

O'Connor, Raymond G. *Diplomacy for Victory: FDR and Unconditional Surrender.* New York: W. W. Norton, 1971.

O'Connor, Sandra Day. "Vindicating the Rule of Law: Balancing Competing Demands for Justice." In *Democracy and the Rule of Law,* edited by Norman Dorsen and Prosser Gifford, 31–38. Washington, DC: CQ Press, 2001.

Omar, Kaleem. "Is the US State Department Still Keeping April Glaspie Under Wraps?" *News International*, Pakistan, 25 December 2005. http://www.informationclearinghouse .info/article11376.htm.

Paine, Thomas. *Rights of Man: Being an Answer to Mr. Burke's Attack on the French Revolution.* 1791. Reprinted in *Common Sense and the Rights of Man.* The Classics of Liberty Library. New York: Gryphon Editions, 1992.

Parks, W. Hays. "Memorandum of Law: Executive Order 12333 and Assassination." *Army Lawyer*, December 1989, 4–8.

Peters, Ralph. "The Culture of Future Conflict." *Parameters* 25 (Winter 1995–96): 18–27.

Post, Jerrold M. "Explaining Saddam Hussein: A Psychological Profile." Prepared testimony. *Hearing of the House Armed Services Committee on the Persian Gulf Crisis.* 4 December 1990. Available at http://www.au.af.mil/au/awc/awcgate/ iraq/saddam_post.htm.

Powell, Colin L., with Joseph E. Persico. *My American Journey.* New York: Random House, 1995.

Preston, Richard A., and Sydney F. Wise. *Men in Arms: A History of Warfare and Its Interrelationships with Western Society.* 4th ed. New York: Holt, Rinehart, and Winston, 1979.

Ravitch, Diane, and Abigail M. Thernstrom, eds. *The Democracy Reader: Classic and Modern Speeches, Essays, Poems, Declarations, and Documents on Freedom and Human Rights Worldwide.* New York: Harper Collins, 1992.

Ray, James Lee. "Does Democracy Cause Peace?" *Annual Review of Political Science* 1 (1998): 27–46.

———. "Wars between Democracies: Rare or Nonexistent?" *International Interactions* 18 (1993): 251–76.

Reagan, Ronald. Speech. Moscow State University, USSR, 31 May 1988. http://www.reagan.utexas.edu/archives/speeches/ 1988/053188b.htm.

———. Speech. National Association of Evangelicals, Orlando, FL, 8 March 1983. http://www.reagan.utexas.edu/archives/ speeches/1983/30883b.htm.

Roosevelt, Franklin D. "The Four Freedoms." Annual message to Congress. Washington, DC, 6 January 1941. http:// www.fdrlibrary.marist.edu/4free.html.

———. Speech. Chicago, IL, 5 October 1937.

———. To Amb. William E. Dodd. Letter, 2 December 1935. In *The Roosevelt Letters*, vol. 3, edited by Elliott Roosevelt, 163. London: George G. Harrup & Co., Ltd., 1952.

———. Undelivered speech, prepared for 13 April 1945. In *FDR Speaks: Authorized Edition of Speeches, 1933–1945*, side 12 (recorded by Franklin D. Roosevelt, Jr.), edited by Henry Steele Commager. New York: Washington Records, Inc., 1960.

Rostow, Eugene V. *Toward Managed Peace: The National Security Interests of the United States, 1759 to the Present.* New Haven, CT: Yale University Press, 1993.

Rummel, R. J. "Democracies ARE Less Warlike than Other Regimes." *European Journal of International Relations* 1 (December 1995): 457–79.

———. "Democratic Peace Clock." http://www.hawaii.edu/powerkills/DP.CLOCK.HTM.

———. *In the Minds of Men: Principles Toward Understanding and Waging Peace.* Seoul, South Korea: Sogang University Press, 1984.

———. *Power Kills: Democracy as a Method of Nonviolence.* New Brunswick, NJ: Transaction Publishers, 1997.

———. "What Is the Democratic Peace?" http://www.hawaii.edu/powerkills/DP.IS_WHAT.HTM

Russett, Bruce. *Grasping the Democratic Peace: Principles for a Post-Cold War World.* Princeton, NJ: Princeton University Press, 1993.

Schelling, Thomas C. *Arms and Influence.* New Haven, CT: Yale University Press, 1966.

The Second Carter-Ford Presidential Debate. 6 October 1976. Transcript available at the Commission on Presidential Debates. http://www.debates.org/pages/trans76b.html.

Sen, Amartya. "Freedom and Needs." *The New Republic*, 10–17 January 1994, 31–38.

Sharp, Walter Gary, Sr. *CyberSpace and the Use of Force.* Falls Church, VA: Aegis Research Corp, 1999.

———. "The Effective Deterrence of Environmental Damage during Armed Conflict: A Case Analysis of the Persian Gulf War." *Military Law Review* 137 (Summer 1992): 1–66.

———. "International Obligations to Search for and Arrest War Criminals: Government Failure in the Former Yugoslavia?"

Duke Journal of Comparative & International Law 7, no. 2 (Spring 1997): 411–60.

———. *Jus Paciarii: Emergent Legal Paradigms for U.N. Peace Operations in the 21st Century.* Stafford, VA: Paciarii International, 1999.

———. "Revoking an Aggressor's License to Kill Military Forces Serving the United Nations: Making Deterrence Personal." *Maryland Journal of International Law and Trade* 22 (1998): 3–78.

Siegle, Joseph T., Michael M. Weinstein, and Morton H. Halperin. "Why Democracies Excel." *Foreign Affairs* 83, no. 5 (September/October 2004): 57–71.

Simma, Bruno, ed. *The Charter of the United Nations: A Commentary.* New York: Oxford University Press, 1994.

Stockholm International Peace Research Institute (SIPRI). "Press Release for the *SIPRI Yearbook 2004*." 9 June 2004. http://editors.sipri.se/pubs/yb04/pr04.pdf.

———. *SIPRI Yearbook 2004: Armaments, Disarmament and International Security.* New York: Oxford University Press, 2004.

Thompson, William R., and Richard Tucker. "A Tale of Two Democratic Peace Critiques." *Journal of Conflict Resolution* 41, no. 3 (June 1997): 428–54.

Transparency International. *Corruptions Perception Index 2004.* Berlin: Transparency International, 2004. http://www.transparency.org/policy_research/surveys_indices/cpi/2004.

Truman, Harry S. Message to Congress. 80th Cong., 1st sess., 12 March 1947. H. Doc. 171, Rec. Group 233, National Archives. http://www.ourdocuments.gov/doc.php?flash=true&doc=81.

Turner, Robert F. "Deception and Deterrence: Political Warfare as a Threat to World Peace." In *Deception and Deterrence in "Wars of National Liberation," State-Sponsored Terrorism, and Other Forms of Secret Warfare*, edited by John Norton Moore, 23–38. Durham, NC: Carolina Academic Press, 1997.

———. "Killing Saddam: Would It Be a Crime?" *Washington Post*, 7 October 1990.

United Nations (UN). *Affirmation of the Principles of International Law Recognized by the Charter of the Nürnberg Tribunal.*

261

G.A. Res. 95(I), UN GAOR, 1st Sess., 2d part, at 188, UN Doc. A/236, 1946.

———. *Charter of the United Nations and Statute of the International Court of Justice.* Signed 26 June 1945. Washington, DC: US Government Printing Office, 1946.

———. "East Timor." http://www.un.org/av/photo/etimor.htm.

———. "United Nations Development Programme." http://www.undp.org/policy/.

———. "United Nations Member States." http://www.un.org/members/list.shtml.

UN Development Programme (UNDP). *Human Development Report 2003: Millennium Development Goals: A Compact among Nations to End Human Poverty.* New York: Oxford University Press, 2003. http://hdr.undp.org/reports/global/2003/.

———. "Human Development Reports." http://hdr.undp.org/reports/default.cfm.

UN Educational, Scientific, and Cultural Organization (UNESCO). *Constitution of the UNESCO.* 16 November 1945. In *Manual of the General Conference.* 2002 ed. Paris: UNESCO, 2002, 7–21. http://unesdoc.unesco.org/images/0012/001255/125590e.pdf.

UN Food and Agriculture Organization (FAO). *The State of Food Insecurity in the World 2004: Monitoring Progress towards the World Food Summit and Millennium Development Goals.* Rome: FAO of the United Nations, 2004. http://www.fao.org/docrep/007/y5650e/y5650e00.htm.

UN International Labour Organization. *World Employment Report 2004–05: Employment, Productivity and Poverty Reduction.* Geneva, Switzerland: International Labour Office, 2005. http://www.ilo.org/public/english/employment/strat/wer2004.htm.

UN Population Division. "The Twenty Most Populous Countries in 1950, 1999 and 2050." *World Population Prospects: The 1998 Revision.* http://www.un.org/esa/population/pubsarchive/india/20most.htm.

UN Security Council. Resolution calling for the Secretary-General to issue a report on Rwanda. S/RES/935. 1 July 1994.

US Department of Defense (DOD). *Conduct of the Persian Gulf War: Final Report to Congress Pursuant to Title V of the Persian Gulf Conflict Supplemental Authorization and Person-*

nel Benefits Act of 1991 (Public Law 102-25). Washington, DC: US DOD, April 1992.

US Department of State. "Countries." http://www.state.gov/countries/.

———. "The Group of Seven and the Group of Eight." http://usinfo.state.gov/topical/econ/group8/g8what.htm.

———. *Patterns of Global Terrorism 2003*. Washington, DC: US Department of State, 2003.

———. *Trafficking in Persons Report 2003*. Washington, DC: US Department of State, June 2003. http://www.state.gov/g/tip/rls/tiprpt/2003/.

US Department of the Treasury, Office of Foreign Assets Control. Haitian Transaction Regulations: Blocked Individuals of Haiti. 31 CFR Part 580, 59 *Federal Register*, No. 67. 7 April 1994: 16548–16549.

United States, France, United Kingdom, and the USSR. "Agreement for the Prosecution and Punishment of the Major War Criminals of the European Axis" (The London Charter). 8 August 1945. *United States Statutes at Large* 59:1544.

United States Institute of Peace. http://www.usip.org/aboutus/index.html.

Walt, Stephen M. "Never Say Never: Wishful Thinking on Democracy and War." *Foreign Affairs* 78, no. 1 (January–February 1999): 146–51.

Walzer, Michael. *Just and Unjust Wars: A Moral Argument with Historical Illustrations*. New York: Basic Books, 1977.

Washington, George. Farewell address to the people of the United States. 17 September 1796. Reprinted in 106th Cong., 2nd sess., 2000, S. Doc. 106-21. Washington, DC: Government Printing Office, 2000, 27. http://www.access.gpo.gov/congress/senate/farewell/sd106-21.pdf.

Weart, Spencer R. *Never at War: Why Democracies Will Not Fight One Another*. New Haven, CT: Yale University Press, 1998.

———. "Peace among Democratic and Oligarchic Republics." *Journal of Peace Research* 31, no. 3 (August 1994): 299–316.

White, Matthew. *Historical Atlas of the Twentieth Century*. http://users.erols.com/mwhite28/20centry.htm.

Wright, Quincy. *A Study of War*. 2nd ed. Chicago: University of Chicago Press, 1965.

Index

Democracy and Deterrence
Foundations for an Enduring World Peace

Air University Press Team

Chief Editor
Demorah Hayes

Copy Editor
Lula Barnes

Cover Art and Book Design
L. Susan Fair

*Composition and
Prepress Production*
Mary P. Ferguson

Quality Review
Mary J. Moore

Print Preparation
Joan Hickey

Distribution
Diane Clark

www.ingramcontent.com/pod-product-compliance
Lightning Source LLC
Chambersburg PA
CBHW080326270326
41927CB00014B/3115